J. McWallone

29th Aug 2004.

Read – Oct 31st (completed)

Romans

Romans

An Exposition of Chapter 9
God's Sovereign Purpose

D. M. Lloyd-Jones

THE BANNER OF TRUTH TRUST

THE BANNER OF TRUTH TRUST
3 Murrayfield Road, Edinburgh EH12 6EL

*

© Mrs D. M. Lloyd-Jones 1991
First published 1991
ISBN 0 85151 579 7

*

Typeset in 10 on 12 pt Trump Medieval
at The Spartan Press Ltd
Lymington, Hants
Printed in Great Britain
by St. Edmundsbury Press, Bury
St. Edmunds and bound by
Hunter & Foulis, Edinburgh

*The sermons in this volume were preached
at Westminster Chapel
from October 5th 1962 to April 26th 1963*

Contents

Contents

One

*

As we begin our consideration of this new chapter of Romans, we are also embarking upon a new section in this mighty Epistle, a section that includes chapters 9, 10 and 11. This is rightly regarded as a famous section of Scripture, but it is one that we must obviously approach with care, and the first question that we must ask is, What is its relationship to what has gone before? Whenever you come to any new section of Scripture it is always a wise procedure to put that question to yourself and to put it, too, to the writer. Why is there a new section, and what exactly is it?

Now there are those who would say that at the end of chapter 8 we came to the end of the doctrinal part of Romans. They say that Paul has really finished with the great doctrine of salvation at the end of that chapter and that now there is no more doctrine as such, but that he takes up certain problems and difficulties which he deals with right to the end of the Epistle. But we must reject that idea immediately, because there is a great deal of very high and important doctrine in this particular section.

What, then, is it that we find here? Well, at the end of chapter 8 the great Apostle certainly has finished with his treatment of the doctrine of salvation from the standpoint of the individual believer. He has dealt with the doctrine of justification by faith only and of sanctification and of glorification; in addition to that, he shows us the final certainty of our entire deliverance in the

[1]

whole matter of glorification. But all along he has been dealing with it mainly from the standpoint of the individual believer.

So, then, the difference between this section and that which has gone before is that Paul is now dealing with the doctrine of salvation, and of God's purpose in salvation, in a more general manner. He is not so much now concerned with it in terms of an individual believer; he is dealing with it from a world standpoint, and in particular from the standpoint of Jew and Gentile. So it is still a question of salvation, but no longer is he dealing with what we may call 'the order of salvation', or 'the steps and stages in individual salvation', but rather with God's overall purpose.

What is it, then, that brings Paul to deal with this? Why should he go on at all? Having dealt with the ultimate glorification of the believer, why not finish his Epistle? Why does he especially introduce this section in chapters 9, 10 and 11? Now at this point I am sorry to have to disagree, as on one or two occasions before, with both Charles Hodge and Robert Haldane. It is not a vitally important matter, but to me it is a very interesting one, because the straighter we can get our exposition the better.

According to Charles Hodge, the Apostle, having dealt with the doctrine of salvation, now takes up as his main object and purpose this question of the calling of the Gentiles and the rejection of the Jews. In other words, he takes up a fresh subject and proceeds to deal with it. I reject that view, because although, of course, Paul does do that, it is not his main object.

What about Robert Haldane? He puts it like this: 'The Apostle had discoursed largely on the justification and the sanctification of believers, and he now proceeds to treat particularly of the doctrine of predestination, and to exhibit the sovereignty of God in his dealings both towards the Jews and Gentiles.' So, according to Haldane, the main object of this section is to deal with the doctrine of predestination and to illustrate it in that way. I reject that view also.

But there is another idea that is often put forward, and it is quite a popular one among many evangelical people. The moment you mention Romans 9, 10 and 11 to them, they say, 'Ah, it is the whole question of the Jews and their salvation, and of their going back to the land.' And they tend to think of this section solely in terms of that. It is, they say, a matter of prophetic teaching, and they stop at that. I reject that also.

How, then, are we to understand these chapters? Well, I suggest that the Apostle takes up this matter at the beginning of chapter 9 and goes on dealing with it in the other two chapters also, because it was something that he had to do as a good and as a wise teacher. I suggest that the connection between this section and the previous one is a most intimate one. It is not that Paul has finished something and takes up something quite different. This section, to me, follows logically from the previous one, and especially from what he has been saying at the end of chapter 8. Indeed, this section is inevitable because what he has just been saying there has reference, you remember,[1] to the doctrine of the assurance of the believer and in particular to the doctrine of the final perseverance of the believer.

The Apostle's argument in those great verses was this: 'We know that all things work together for good to them that love God, to them who are the called according to his purpose' [*Romans* 8 : 28]. It is God's purpose that guarantees the final perseverance of the saints, the final glorification of His people. And then Paul went on to tell us that this great purpose had been worked out in this manner: 'Whom he did foreknow, he also did predestinate to be conformed to the image of his Son, that he might be the firstborn among many brethren' [*Romans* 8 : 29]. That is the purpose, that is the object. Then, 'Moreover whom he did predestinate [in that way], them he also called: and whom he called, them he also justified: and whom he justified, them he also glorified' [*Romans* 8 : 30]. God's purpose is carried out in that way. And he says that it is absolutely certain.

We saw also that he puts up four challenges and then he demolishes their arguments. It is absolutely certain, he says, because it is the love of God in Christ Jesus, because it is the purpose of God, and there is nothing and no one in heaven or hell or anywhere else that can 'make Him His purpose forgo, or sever my soul from His love'. It was a tremendous argument. Our security is based upon the immutability of God's counsel, the guarantee that anything God has purposed must of necessity be carried out.

[1] See *Romans: An Exposition of Chapter 8:17–39: The Final Perseverance of the Saints*, 1975.

Then the Apostle imagines someone coming to him and saying, 'Wait a minute, Paul, you are allowing your eloquence to carry you away. What about the whole case of the Jews? You say that when God starts a thing He always completes it; you say that when something is the purpose of God nothing can frustrate it. But if your preaching of the Christian gospel, as you call it, is right, then God's purpose has gone very seriously astray, because the fact is that the vast majority of the Jews are not Christians; they are not in what you call the kingdom of God, which consists chiefly of Gentile believers. So, then, where is the purpose of God? Where is the immutability of His counsel?' That was the objection.

Now that was not an imaginary objection. It is what the Jews were saying, and they were saying it very loudly. They were saying that Paul was a traitor. Not only that, they had a second charge against him which was that he was throwing the Old Testament overboard. 'The Old Testament', they said, 'is a book that concentrates on the Jews only and all the others are outside; here is a teaching that brings the others in while the Jews are out. Paul is denying the teaching concerning God and His purpose as it is outlined and worked out in the Old Testament, which is full of promises to the Jews.' So it seems to me that the Apostle takes up this matter because he has to deal with that difficulty and with that objection. It is not an entirely new section therefore; it follows from the previous one.

Paul, then, takes up the challenge; he deals with this argument and he refutes it in his own way. It is interesting to note that the Apostle is doing something here that he has already done several times in this one Epistle. He always uses the same method, which is a perfect method of teaching. He makes his statements and then he deals with objections and difficulties and answers them. Now we have already seen him doing this.[2] He began his great doctrine in the first chapter, where he lays it down in verses 16, 17 and 18. Then, you remember, he works it out in terms of Gentiles and Jews. That brings him to the end of chapter 2. Then at the beginning of chapter 3 he takes up an objection. If, said the Jews – and they said it very vociferously at that time – what you are saying is

[2]See the earlier volumes on *Romans*.

[4]

right, well then, 'What advantage hath the Jew? or what profit is there of circumcision?' Paul digresses to deal with that objection and he goes on dealing with it until the end of verse 20 in that third chapter. Then having done that he comes back to his main theme in verse 21 and again gives an amazing exposition of his doctrine.

But still, you see, Paul knows that people are not quite happy about this. He knows that this doctrine of justification by faith seems to cut across everything that everybody believed about the Jews – that they were God's people because they were circumcised and because they kept the law, while the Gentiles were not circumcised; they did not have the law, nor did they keep it. So he devotes chapter 4 to answering that objection once and for ever. He takes the case of Abraham, which is the key case. If he can prove that all he has been saying was true even in the case of Abraham, he has demolished their position. And that is what he does throughout the chapter. It is, again, one of these sections that comes in to deal with an objection to the doctrine he has been laying down.

Then having done that, he proceeds to draw out the main results of the doctrine of justification by faith. He starts in the first verse of chapter 5: 'Therefore being justified by faith, we have peace with God . . .' And he goes on working it out throughout that chapter. And then immediately again he is up against two difficulties. This teaching of his seems to be doing two things. It seems to be encouraging people to go on sinning and it also seems to be putting the law of God entirely on one side. So the Apostle cannot go on with his teaching until he has refuted and dealt with those two particular objections to it. In chapter 6, he takes the first one: 'What shall we say then? Shall we continue in sin, that grace may abound?' 'God forbid', he replies. But he does not leave it at that; he works it out in detail.

In chapter 7 he takes up the whole question of the law: 'Know ye not, brethren, (for I speak to them that know the law,) how that the law hath dominion over a man as long as he liveth?' [*Romans* 7 : 1]. The whole chapter is devoted to a treatment of the functions, the purpose and the limits of the law of God. Chapters 6 and 7 are, therefore, really digressions to deal with the difficulties.

[5]

Then in chapter 8 he comes back to the main line once more with this glorious doctrine of assurance, leading eventually to the wonderful doctrine of the final perseverance of the saints. But, once more there is a difficulty; there is this objection to which I have already referred. And so in chapters 9, 10 and 11 he turns aside in order to reconcile what he has been saying with the whole of the Old Testament. So, you see, he does not just say, 'Well I have finished that, now what else? Ah yes, here is this question of Jew and Gentile; I must deal with that.' That is not it at all. There is no break here; this section follows inevitably. He has got to deal with this because people were in trouble about it, the Jews particularly so, and the Apostle is concerned to win them to the truth and to the faith. So in these three chapters he takes up the challenge; he deals with the arguments and he completely and entirely demolishes them.

What then are chapters 9 to 11? They are what must be called a theodicy, a justification of the ways of God with respect to man. It is a bigger subject than predestination. It is a bigger subject, even, than the calling of the Gentiles and the rejection of the Jews. It is an attempt at harmonizing the ways of God and we must not allow it to be reduced to any smaller dimensions than that. This section is the Apostle's way of harmonizing the Old Testament with the New – all that God has ever said and revealed with what He is still doing and with what He is going to do.

It is, in other words, the Apostle's way of showing us that though things may seem to be contradicting God's purpose, they are not doing so. He is just continuing to establish that God's purpose is absolute and that nothing can frustrate it. In these three chapters he demonstrates the eternal and glorious consistency of God: the consistency of God with Himself, His own nature and His own great and glorious purpose.

Now I can prove that this is so by referring to the way in which he winds up the whole section in chapter 11 verses 33 to 36. 'O the depth of the riches both of the wisdom and knowledge of God! how unsearchable are his judgments, and his ways past finding out! For who hath known the mind of the Lord? or who hath been his counsellor? Or who hath first given to him, and it shall be recompensed unto him again? For of him, and through him, and to him, are all things: to whom be glory for ever.

Amen.' That is altogether bigger than predestination which is only a part of it. And for anyone to exalt predestination as the main theme in this section is almost to be guilty of blasphemy. It is God Himself in the glory of His person and character. Predestination is merely one of the ways in which God works out His great purpose.

But there are, of course, a number of subsidiary themes in these chapters. I have often compared Paul's method to that of a musical composer and here it is, once more. There is the great central theme; then the subsidiary themes – the leitmotifs – are all worked in; then he ends with the great theme itself. What, then, are the subsidiary themes? Well, the first is the particularly tragic case of the Jews as rejectors of Christ their own Messiah. This was especially a tragedy to Paul himself, who was a Jew, and he does not forget to tell us that and to repeat it. So we shall see how he gives us the causes of that and puts them very plainly before us.

Secondly, there is the theme of God's freedom in His absolute sovereignty in the matter of election, and His right to call whom He will, whether Jew or Gentile. I put it like that because that is what Paul is dealing with here, not simply with election. We have already considered that in chapter 8, which is where he really deals with predestination. All he does here is to show God's *freedom* in election, which is a different thing.

The third subsidiary theme is the vindication of this Christian teaching concerning salvation for any individual, for Gentile as well as Jew, in the light of the teaching of the Old Testament. Now this is most important, and we shall find that the Apostle keeps on doing that. He was very sensitive on this point, and rightly so. He was a Jew and a Pharisee and an expert in the Old Testament, and one charge always touched him on the quick, as it were. People claimed that he was denying the Old Testament teaching. 'But I am not,' says Paul in effect, 'I can prove to you that everything I am teaching is there in the Old Testament.' So he justifies his teaching, his presentation of the Christian doctrine of salvation, in terms of the Old Testament teaching, and shows that the New, far from being a contradiction of the Old, is the fulfilling of the Old. He could use language used later by St Augustine: 'The New Testament is latent in the Old Testament, and the Old Testament is patent in the New Testament.'

[7]

The fourth subsidiary theme is the terrible danger of misunderstanding and misusing doctrine, and of drawing false
conclusions from doctrine. That was the whole trouble with the
Jews. They were drawing false deductions from the plain
teaching of the Old Testament concerning the purpose of God
for His people. And that is why they came to reject Christ. This
is a terrible danger. So, having shown how the Jews were guilty
of drawing false deductions from God's glorious doctrine, Paul
then turns to the Gentiles and says, 'You be careful also. If the
natural branches made that mistake, then you are not immune
from it.'

You see, these doctrines are glorious but at the same time
they are very dangerous. Here is this great doctrine of assurance
and the final perseverance of the saints; how many people have
argued as follows from it? 'I am a child of God, therefore it does
not matter what I do; because I am a child of God my
glorification is certain, so I can do as I like, because I am bound
to get there.' Antinomianism! It was rampant in the early
church. It has to be dealt with repeatedly, for people have been
guilty of it ever since then. It is a head knowledge, which makes
you ignore your heart and everything else. Antinomianism –
one of the greatest curses conceivable! And in this section we
shall find the Apostle warning us against this; the abuse of
doctrine, drawing false deductions from God's glorious truth
even to the damnation of the soul! That is what he is dealing
with. He shows it in the case both of the Jew and of the Gentile.

In the fifth subsidiary theme, Paul gives a very full explanation of the particular case of the Jews in the purpose of God. That
is mainly in chapter 11 of course. He explains what is happening
to them now and also what is going to happen to them.

Lastly, the sixth subsidiary theme is God's eternal purpose in
Christ, and salvation with respect to the whole universe: its
inscrutable and glorious character. That is a theme that keeps
on running right through the entire section. 'O the depth of the
riches both of the wisdom and knowledge of God! how
unsearchable are his judgments, and his ways past finding out!'
And if we have ever thought that we understand God's mind and
purpose, then I hope that this section will make us think again.
It is not quite as easy and as neat and as simple as we sometimes
tend to think! If all this doctrine does not lead us to wonder in

amazement and astonishment, and to worship, there is something wrong with our understanding of it. True understanding of doctrine should always lead to adoration, to praise, and to an utter humbling of ourselves in wonder before Him.

Those, then, are the themes which serve to bring out this great central theodicy, which is the theme that governs all, so let me now give you an analysis of the whole section in order that we shall be able to keep it in mind as we are working out its different parts and details. Here, again, one cannot but be fascinated by the Apostle's mind and method. It is a most interesting section from the standpoint of structure, and I shall divide my analysis into two sections – general and detailed. The general point is a brief one. Paul, let me remind you, did not divide his letters into chapters. That did not come in until about the thirteenth century. But whoever did it, did it very well, because they saw that the Apostle does the same thing in the three chapters of this section. Let us see what this is.

The first thing he does is this: in each chapter he identifies himself with the Jews, and he is very careful and courteous and loving in his treatment of their position. In chapter 9, he begins like this: 'I say the truth in Christ, I lie not, my conscience also bearing me witness in the Holy Ghost, that I have great heaviness and continual sorrow in my heart. For I could wish that myself were accursed from Christ for my brethren, my kinsmen according to the flesh.' Then the first two verses of chapter 10 read: 'Brethren, my heart's desire and prayer to God for Israel is, that they might be saved. For I bear them record that they have a zeal of God, but not according to knowledge.' Then chapter 11 verse 1: 'I say then, Hath God cast away his people? God forbid. For I also am an Israelite, of the seed of Abraham, of the tribe of Benjamin.' So in all three chapters, he identifies himself with the Jews. They are his fellow-countrymen, and he treats them in a gentle manner.

The second thing that is common to the three is an elaboration of doctrine. The main doctrine in chapter 9 is the doctrine of predestination and election, in chapter 10 it is the doctrine of justification by faith only, while the main doctrine in chapter 11 is the temporary rejection of the Jews. So, you see, he starts with the Jews, with whom he involves himself, and then he gives a statement of doctrine.

[9]

The third theme of the three chapters is Paul's confirmation of his doctrine from the Scriptures. At the end of each one, he quotes the Scriptures of the Old Testament to prove what he has just been saying in his doctrine, and the fact that he does so three times underlines the excellence of his method.

But now we must look at the details, so let me indicate the division to you.

Chapter 9 verses 1 to 3: Introduction of the subject in personal terms – as I have just said.

Verses 4 and 5: A description of the peculiar position and case of the Jews.

Verse 6: This is the key verse of chapter 9: 'Not as though the word of God hath taken none effect. For they are not all Israel, which are of Israel.'

Verses 7 to 13: Explanation and exposition of the key verse and of the true meaning of the term 'Israel'. God's Word, he proves there, has had effect, and it has done what God meant it to do. He only meant it to do a certain thing and it has done that. But we shall only understand that if we understand the true meaning of the term 'Israel.'

Verses 14 to 24: Objection to this as unfair. 'What shall we say then? Is there unrighteousness with God? God forbid.' That is a problem which arises out of what he has been saying in verses 7 to 13, and in answer the Apostle shows God's right to call whomsoever He wills, even the Gentiles – which he brings out in verse 24.

Verses 25 to 29: All this has been foretold in the Old Testament by the prophets. It is not a new and a strange doctrine; it had been prophesied and predicted.

Verses 30 to 33: A summing up of the position so far – the position, as it then was, of the Gentiles being in and the Jews remaining outside.

Chapter 10 verses 1 to 3: Introduction again of this whole case of the Jews. Here he gives a further statement concerning their tragic blindness. Chapter 10 is, in a sense, a minor digression in which Paul establishes and elaborates upon what he said in the summing up in verses 30 to 33 at the end of chapter 9. He works it out in detail.

Verses 4 to 11: An outline of the true way of salvation. The Apostle shows how the Jews have gone astray, and how they had a wrong view of salvation. Paul has said in verse 3, 'For they being ignorant of God's righteousness, and going about to establish their own righteousness, have not submitted themselves unto the righteousness of God.' But they have not understood this. And from verse 4 to verse 11 Paul tells us what it is that they have not understood: 'Christ is the end of the law for righteousness to every one that believeth.' It is a statement of the doctrine of justification by faith only.

Then he goes on to say in verses 12 to 17 that as salvation is the result of justification by faith, this is obviously for all, because God is the God of all. He is not only the God of the Jews; He is the God of the Gentiles also. He is the Creator of the whole universe. And therefore as it is a salvation which comes by faith as the result of hearing, it is as open to the Gentiles as to the Jews. That is what he works out in these verses. It is a matter of hearing and listening to and believing the gospel. Some, he says, refuse it – that is the trouble with the Jews; others believe it – that is mainly the Gentiles. And again in verses 18 to 21 he shows how that also had been predicted and prophesied by the Old Testament prophets.

That brings us to chapter 11. Again he starts in verse 1 with his statement concerning God's people, and again brings in himself as one of them. Then he makes this categorical statement: 'God hath not cast away his people'. In verses 2 to 6 he gives us the real doctrinal key to the understanding of this whole matter. And the key is again something he has already hinted at – that there is a difference between one person and another, and this comes under the general heading of 'Israel'. In other words, he introduces us to this wonderful biblical doctrine of 'the remnant', showing how it applied even in the Old Testament times and how it still applies – that Israel as a nation is outside, but the true Israel, the remnant, is inside, and how this division is always a matter of grace. That is the vital doctrine of verses 2 to 6.

Then in verse 7 he gives us another key verse: 'What then?' – in the light of this – 'Israel hath not obtained that which he seeketh for; but the election hath obtained it, and the rest were blinded.' You see, Israel is divided into two groups – the elect in Israel, and the rest. The rest were blinded, while the elect obtained it.

In verses 8 to 24 Paul works out what he has just said. He shows the difference between the elect and the rest, and he deals particularly with the rest, and what he shows is that all that is true of them now had long since been foretold in the Old Testament Scriptures. He therefore goes on to explain why it has happened; he says that it is only temporary, and he ends by giving a warning to the Gentiles, pointing out that if that could happen to the Jews, how much more can it happen to them? They must not presume therefore. So it is a mixture of doctrine and practical exhortation and application.

Then in verses 25 to 32 Paul sums up the position as it then was in his day and generation, and proceeds to give an outline of the carrying out of God's original and grand purpose which includes both Gentiles and Jews, and he shows how it is all going to end exactly and precisely as God purposed and planned it even before the foundation of the world.

And then, as we have seen, in verses 33 to 36 we have that grand final apostrophe, that burst of worship and of adoration and of praise: the marvel and the wonder of it all, and the ascription to God, and to Him alone, of all the honour and all the glory.

This has been, then, a general consideration of the point and purport of this great section of Scripture, and it is a good way to approach it. So often people get lost because they have not got an overall picture. We miss the wood because of the trees. And those who are interested in particular doctrines are particularly liable to this; the people who jump at predestination, the people who jump at the Jews and their destiny, and all the rest of the prophetic teaching. How sad it is that they miss the bigger thing, the greater thing, the more glorious thing – this wonderful theodicy, this justification of God's ways with respect to man, and the harmonization of what God permits with what God purposes, what God allows with what He has planned, and the showing of how all things do indeed work together for good and to the ultimate carrying out of God's eternal purpose.

Two

*

I say the truth in Christ, I lie not, my conscience also bearing me witness in the Holy Ghost, that I have great heaviness and continual sorrow in my heart. For I could wish that myself were accursed from Christ for my brethren, my kinsmen according to the flesh.

Romans 9 : 1–3

Having made a general analysis of this new section of Romans in our last study, and, having shown what the Apostle does in it, and up to a point why he does it, we can now start upon a detailed exposition of the passage. The first subdivision in chapter 9, you remember, consists of the first three verses, in which Paul introduces the subject and puts before us this whole question of the position of the Jews; and he does so particularly in terms of his own relationship to them and to the problem which they constituted.

Now this is one of the most remarkable statements which is to be found anywhere in Paul's own writings and in those of the other apostles, and, furthermore, it is a vital statement. So it seems to me that our best way of approaching it is to look first of all at what he actually says; then we can go on to consider why he made such a statement and why he put it in this form. And then, thirdly, we can draw certain lessons and conclusions from it.

So we begin with the terms themselves. Paul starts off by bursting suddenly into the whole problem: 'I say the truth in Christ . . .' Now the question that arises at once is whether he was taking an oath here. Was he, as it were, swearing by the name of Christ with respect to the truthfulness of the statement that he was about to make? This need not detain us, because the teaching of the New Testament, quite plainly, is that Christians do not habitually take oaths like this. We have the teaching of our Lord Himself in which He says, 'Swear not at all'; do not take an oath. There was, you remember, a discussion amongst the Pharisees on one of those legal niceties, in which they so much delighted: whether you swear by heaven, or by earth, or by the altar or the gift on the altar, and so on. And our Lord's teaching is, 'Swear not at all; but let your Yea be yea; and your Nay be nay'. The Pharisees were always so fond of emphasizing what they were saying by taking an oath, but our Lord discourages that. And that is the emphasis of the whole of the New Testament teaching, and it is an emphasis that is needed at the present time. People are always ready to take this kind of oath in order to assure us of the veracity of what they are saying. But it cuts right across our Lord's teaching and we do not find that Paul does it either in the records that we have of his life in Acts, or in his Epistles.

What, then, does Paul mean here? He is anxious, of course, that they should realize that he is making a very serious and a very solemn statement. So what he says, in effect, is this: 'I speak these words realizing that I am in the presence of Christ. Not only that; I am speaking as one who is in Christ, as a Christian, one who is a member of the body of Christ.' He is referring partly, of course, to what he has already said in chapter 5 – he who was in Adam is now in Christ. 'And', he says, 'I am speaking as a man who has been crucified with Christ, who died with Christ and who has risen with Christ to newness of life. I speak as such a man, not carelessly, or casually. I speak as one who realizes his position in the Lord Jesus Christ.'

Furthermore, I think he means that he is speaking as one who knows that Christ is looking down upon him as he does so. He says something similar in 1 Timothy 6 : 13. 'I give thee charge', he says to Timothy, 'in the sight of God, who quickeneth all things, and before Christ Jesus, who before Pontius Pilate witnessed a good confession.' He himself realizes, and he wants Timothy to realize too, that they are both in the presence of God, that He sees them, and that the Lord Jesus Christ is looking down upon them at the same time. So, too, here in Romans, he is saying, I cannot make a stronger statement than this – 'speaking the truth in Christ'.

And then, in order to make it stronger still, he introduces his negative, 'I lie not'. He is very anxious that everybody who reads this, or who hears it, should know that he is speaking this in the most serious and solemn manner conceivable. A negative often reinforces the positive assertion and it does so here.

But Paul goes even beyond that and says, 'my conscience also bearing me witness in the Holy Ghost'. This is a very interesting point. Why does he add this and bring in this question of conscience? Now, what you really have in the original is, 'my conscience also bearing witness with me', so what Paul is saying here in effect is, 'I am saying this but my conscience is bearing witness with me, or attesting to the truth of what I am saying.'

In other words, the Apostle is saying, 'It is not merely that I make this statement with all the honesty that I can command, it is not merely that there is no lie nor any thought of lying anywhere near me. I am saying this with all the sincerity that I can command; but I will tell you something further: my conscience bears witness to this.'

But why is this stronger? you ask. The answer is, of course, that our conscience is something that is independent of us. We all know that, do we not? We may say something, but that does not mean that our conscience is going to agree. That is what makes the conscience so important. Conscience is something, in a sense, apart from man. It has been put in him by God; it is a reminder of the voice of God within him, an inward monitor, and a man cannot really manipulate his conscience. He can go against it, but that is not manipulating it. It is possible, as this Apostle says again in writing to Timothy, for the conscience to be seared 'with a hot iron'. But nevertheless it is true to say that the conscience is an independent witness. So the Apostle very rightly says that his conscience is bearing witness to the truth of what he is saying. So we must always be very careful to listen to our conscience, because of its independence. Whatever we may think or say, the conscience is there and it will register its opinion. And it is equally important that we should never do anything against the conscience. We must always listen to what it has to say, because of this independent position, and because it is placed there in us by God. Paul was always concerned about this; he even refers to his own past life and makes that self-same point. In Acts 23 : 1 we read, 'And Paul, earnestly beholding the council, said, Men and brethren, I have lived in all good conscience before God until this day.' He was always careful about that, and we should be equally so. Though we are Christians, we must pay attention to the conscience; we must never act contrary to its dictates and its verdict.

But then Paul adds, 'my conscience also bearing me witness *in the Holy Ghost*'. This is another very important point about the conscience. Though it is an independent witness and we must always pay heed to it, the conscience is fallible and it needs to be enlightened. This again is something which is quite clear in the Scriptures and with which we all ought to be familiar in our own lives and experiences. The value of the conscience is almost entirely negative. It does not speak positively; it generally condemns. That is why we must always listen to it. But it does not mean that the conscience itself is perfect. It needs to be trained and educated. Let me give a simple illustration. There are many people in the world who, because of their upbringing and their ignorance, in perhaps the darkness of heathenism or paganism, regard certain things as wrong. Their consciences tell them that they are wrong, so they do not do those things. But if those people become Christians, they will find that many things which their conscience has condemned are not wrong, and their consciences will no longer condemn them concerning those particular things. In other words the conscience will have been enlightened and trained.

Let me illustrate this from Paul's letter to the church at Corinth. There was a problem there about eating meats that had been offered to idols, and the trouble arose because there were some Christians in Corinth who were more enlightened than others. There were the so-called 'stronger' brethren, and there were the less enlightened or 'weaker' brethren. The weaker brethren, because of their lack of enlightenment and understanding, were still in a kind of bondage on this matter whereas the stronger brethren had seen it quite clearly. They had come to see that you could eat any meat you liked, that there was no such thing as an idol, there was no other god, and that therefore there was nothing wrong with that meat. But the others had not seen this, so that while the stronger brethren were eating this meat, the consciences of the weaker brethren were offended. Why? Because their consciences were not fully enlightened.

[16]

There, then, is a proof of the fact that the conscience can be trained and can be enlightened. And what the Apostle is saying here in Romans 9 is that not only does his conscience bear witness to what he is saying, but that his conscience is a conscience that is now enlightened, by the teaching of the Christian message and by the direct teaching of the Holy Spirit Himself. He has an enlightened conscience in the Holy Ghost, which is the highest condition that the conscience can ever be in.

So let us sum up this matter in the following way: at any particular stage always listen to your conscience. Never do anything that your conscience condemns. But if your conscience becomes enlightened by the Holy Spirit and by Christian teaching it will then no longer condemn some of these things and you are entitled to do them. But do not argue with your conscience. It is the Holy Spirit and the teaching of the Scriptures that must enlighten it. And that is what the Apostle is saying here to us: not only is he making this statement and not lying, but his conscience also, enlightened by the Spirit, is saying Amen to this; it is agreeing, there is no condemnation in him. Now that is a wonderful position to be in.

So, this is a very solemn asseveration that Paul is making. He says, 'I tell you in this way that I have great heaviness and continual sorrow in my heart . . .' For whom? 'For . . . my kinsmen according to the flesh.' And as we look at the terms which Paul uses, we see that this, too, is a very strong statement. The words 'great heaviness' can be translated as 'bitter grief'. Paul grieved concerning his brethren, and it was a heaviness upon his spirit. Then 'continual sorrow' can be translated as 'incessant anguish'. He knew an anguish of mind and of heart because of the state and the condition of his countrymen. Now there is no depth of feeling that is greater than that and the Apostle tells us that this is how he feels with regard to the whole position of the Jews.

But, of course, all that we have been saying almost pales into insignificance in the light of the next thing he says: 'For I could wish that myself were accursed from Christ for my brethren, my kinsmen according to the flesh.' The word for 'accursed' in the original is *anathema* – 'I could wish that I myself were anathema from Christ.' Now we must give the full value to this statement. There are some people who find an obvious difficulty with it and they try to say here that it is merely as if the Apostle were saying, 'If it is my presence in the Christian church that is causing this offence to the Jews, then I am prepared to be excommunicated from the visible church in order that they may come in.' But of course that view cannot be accepted. He used the word *anathema*, 'accursed', and it does mean 'cursed by God'. And, you notice, he says 'from Christ'. Not from the church, but from Christ! He is speaking of being a reprobate, an outcast from Christ and His kingdom and the whole of Christian salvation. That is what he is saying.

But what does he mean? It is, of course, a great problem, and it is a problem that has engaged the minds of commentators at all times and in all places, so there are certain things about which we must be clear. The first exposition of this which we must reject is that of John Calvin. You see, we have no popes in Protestantism! We do not believe in the infallibility of John Calvin any more than we believe in the infallibility of the Pope. And any man who makes John Calvin a pope is denying Scripture and is really not doing a service even to John Calvin. He made mistakes; there are many of them in his commentaries and I believe he was very wrong at this point. Calvin's view is that Paul the Apostle, in a state of ecstasy, actually wished himself to be condemned in place of his countrymen, an outcast from the kingdom of God and excluded from salvation, in order that they might be saved and become Christians.

I reject this interpretation, because, obviously, that is something that no Christian can or would ever say. A person who is ignorant might talk loosely like this, but a Christian, who knows what to be accursed from Christ means, could never possibly or conceivably say it. Indeed, it would be very wrong for anyone to say so.

And the last man in the world who would ever say that is this Apostle Paul, because he has been telling us in the previous chapter that a man's salvation is not something that he determines, he cannot wish to be in or out. It is all in the purpose of God, and what God purposes, He predestinates, and He puts into operation all the steps and stages, until you eventually arrive at glorification. So a man who has spent the time that this Apostle has spent in saying all that would be just flatly contradicting himself if he now began to talk about contracting out of it. Salvation is certain and guaranteed, and those who are Christians and who have seen what this means thank God for it; and there is nothing more terrible to them than the thought of being outside it.

We also have to reject, unfortunately, the exposition of Robert Haldane. Haldane can see the fallacy of Calvin and he denounces it. But then he thinks that he has discovered a way out of the difficulty. He points out that the Apostle uses the past tense – 'I was wishing' or 'I did wish' – which means, according to Haldane, that the Apostle is referring now to his state and condition before his conversion. Then Haldane goes on to say that the word translated 'wish' could equally well be translated 'boast'. 'I myself boasted, or made it my boast, to be separated from Christ.' (He is, incidentally, quite wrong there and that, of course, vitiates his whole exposition.) In other words he says that the Apostle is here showing his sympathy with the Jews. He is speaking as a man who once upon a time boasted of the fact that he was accursed from Christ, and so he is very sorry for those fellow-countrymen of his who are now in exactly the same position.

We reject Haldane's exposition, because if the Apostle had meant that, he would have used the aorist tense of which he is so fond – the tense which describes a condition that obtained once but has now been finished. But that is not the tense he uses; he uses the imperfect tense instead. So the very tense of the verb should have been sufficient to save Haldane from that mistaken exposition.

Secondly, an unbeliever never wishes to be accursed from Christ or to boast that he is so accursed, because if he put it like that, it would imply that he believed in Christ somehow. It would imply that he recognized a condition of being accursed from Christ, which, of course, is a condition that no unbeliever can ever recognize. Indeed, Paul had never been in a position in which he said that he was proud of being 'accursed from Christ', because at one time he used to say that Christ was accursed. So he would never have talked of being accursed himself from one whom he regarded as being accursed; it is an utter impossibility.

Then, thirdly, there is no point in saying that here. The Apostle is not telling them what he once felt; he is telling them what he now feels, he is telling them about his present condition and his present attitude towards these unbelieving Jews who have rejected Christ and who are outside His salvation. So we must reject this attempt also to get us out of the difficulty. It is not that.

What, then, is the answer? It is to be found in the verb tense which the Apostle uses, this imperfect tense. Now the exposition which I shall give you has great authorities behind it; men like Charles Hodge, Henry Alford of the last century, and Marvin R. Vincent; it has A. T. Robertson behind it, perhaps the greatest Greek grammarian of this present century and, also, the well-known commentators Sanday and Headlam.

Henry Alford puts it like this. He says that the imperfect tense here should be translated like this: 'I was wishing, had it been possible', or 'I could wish if it were possible'. He does not say 'I do wish' but 'I could wish'. You see the difference? He says that the act is unfinished; he starts a process but an obstacle intervenes and he cannot complete it. Marvin R. Vincent says something quite similar; he says that literally it is 'I was wishing', but the imperfect here has a tentative force implying the wish begun but stopped at the outset by some antecedent consideration which renders it impossible, so that practically it was not entertained at all. It is, in other words, a man beginning to think and then he realizes something, and so it has to stop. 'I was on the point of wishing or of thinking' – but he did not get any further. That is, according to these grammarians, the force of the word.

Marvin R. Vincent also refers us to Philemon verse 13, (where Paul is talking about the slave Onesimus whom he is sending back to Philemon) which in the Authorized Version reads like this: 'Whom I would have retained with me, that in thy stead he might have ministered unto me in the bonds of the gospel: but without thy mind would I do nothing.' Paul began to think to himself, 'Now it would be rather wonderful to keep this fellow Onesimus, he could be a great . . .' Ah, he stops it at once. 'But that is impossible. I have no right to keep him; he belongs to my friend Philemon.' In other words, 'I could have wished to keep him with me if it had not been too much to ask.'

A. T. Robertson tells us that the right translation here is not 'I do wish' but 'I was on the point of wishing that myself were accursed from Christ for my kinsmen according to the flesh', while Sanday and Headlam translate it as, 'The wish was in my mind', or, 'The prayer was in my heart'. 'The wish was in my mind' – yes, but that does not mean to say that he wished it.

Then finally Charles Hodge puts it like this: 'I could wish, were the thing allowable and possible or proper . . .' He says, 'It implies the presence of a condition which is known to be impossible.' And that, I think, is the key to the understanding of this most extraordinary statement.

Now there are other parallels to this which throw some light upon it. Take, for instance, the account of Festus and Agrippa talking together about Paul in Acts 25 verse 22. In the Authorized Version we read, 'Then Agrippa said unto Festus, I would also hear the man myself. To morrow, said he, thou shalt hear him.' But it is the first phrase that matters; it is exactly the same tense, it should be translated, 'I was minded also myself to hear the man.' You see the difference? 'I was minded also myself to hear the man.' That is how really it should be translated.

There is another example in Galatians 4 verse 20, where Paul says, 'I desire to be present with you now, and to change my voice; for I stand in doubt of you', but the better translation of that first clause would be, 'I wish to be present with you just now'. It was the thought that entered Paul's mind, 'If only I could be with them now.' But he could not, of course; there was a long distance and there were circumstances which made it quite impossible.

In other words, what we have here in Romans is a very strong expression of Paul's feelings. He does not actually wish to be accursed from Christ, but he does say in effect, 'You know, I am so concerned about this that if somehow or other by being sacrificed myself it would help them . . .', then he leaves it. You cannot go on with that. 'The wish, the thought entered my mind; I was on the point of saying . . .', but then he stops.

There is a wonderful parallel to all this – indeed it is the only one in the whole of Scripture – in Exodus, chapter 32 verses 30–32. This is the incident when Moses had been up on the mount with God and he came down and found that the children of Israel had made a golden calf and they had sinned a grievous sin. 'And it came to pass on the morrow, that Moses said unto the people, Ye have sinned a great sin: and now I will go up unto the Lord; peradventure I shall make atonement for your sin. And

Moses returned unto the Lord, and said, Oh, this people have sinned a great sin, and have made them gods of gold. Yet now, if thou wilt forgive their sin –; and if not, blot me, I pray thee, out of thy book which thou hast written.'

What does this mean? Well, what we have here in these two great and mighty men of God, Moses and the Apostle Paul, is such an intense concern for the glory of God and for the souls of men that they feel it to this extent, that they come nearest of all to that mind which was in Christ Jesus when He gave Himself as an offering for sin, that others might be saved. It is difficult for us to understand this, is it not? The famous old commentator Bengel said, 'It is not easy to estimate the measure of love in a Moses and a Paul, for our limited reason does not grasp it, as a child cannot comprehend the courage of warriors.' These men so knew something about the burden of souls, that they were capable of using these expressions that fill us with a sense of amazement and astonishment – expressions which have often led lesser minds to criticize them and to misunderstand them. No, this is just a very intense expression by the great Apostle of his anguish of heart and of mind at the state and the condition of his fellow-countrymen, the Jews.

This brings us, then, to the second question: Why does the Apostle make this statement? We found a general answer to this in our last study. It is this great theodicy, this justification of the ways of God to men, Paul's harmonization of what is actually happening with what he has clearly been teaching. But there is undoubtedly a further reason. The Apostle was anxious to clear himself from the charges that were frequently brought against him. His fellow-countrymen regarded him as nothing but a renegade and a traitor who had sold himself.

You see, we must remember the times in which Paul lived; the Romans had conquered Palestine, as they had conquered so many other countries, and the worst type of individual in any country was one who became a servant of the Roman Empire. The publicans did that; they became tax-gatherers for the Romans, gathering from their own people and oppressing them; they were quislings and so they were despised. And these people were bringing that kind of charge against the Apostle Paul. They said that he had cashed in, as it were; that he could see that this new religion, because it seemed to be cutting across Judaism, was going to be popular with the masters and with the Gentiles, and that as a real traitor he had turned his coat and was just going into it.

Indeed, people not only said that at that time; I met a man once who said that to me. I was coming back from America on one of the Atlantic liners and was persuaded to give an address one Sunday evening. And as I was walking along the deck later that night, I was stopped by a Jewish doctor who told me that he had been in the meeting. He said, 'I tell you quite frankly, I came out of sheer curiosity because of your medical past.' 'But', he said, 'I listened to you and you were talking about Paul.' And we then proceeded to have a discussion about the Apostle. 'Oh', he said, 'there is no difficulty about Paul! I am not criticizing myself or my own nation when I say that', he went on, 'but Paul was a typical Jew and a first-rate businessman; he could see that the old religion was played out and was finishing, and he wanted to get in to the new one as quickly as he could. That is the explanation of the Apostle Paul. No conversion, none of this that you tell us,' he said, 'the thing is quite simple; of course he had to put up some sort of a case, but, to me, it is obvious. He was an astute man, he had an eye to business; he saw what was happening, got in on the ground floor and he was going to do well out of it.' They were saying it then, they are still saying it about him.

But not only that; Paul's critics were saying that he was indifferent to the Jews and to their fate. They were even saying that he had become hostile to them, that he was an enemy of his own nation, and the great Apostle felt this to the very depth of his intense nature and being. And so he says, 'I say the truth in Christ, I am not lying, and my conscience enlightened by the Spirit is bearing me witness. I am not only not against my fellow-countrymen; the thought has even entered my mind that if somehow or another my being accursed could save them – well, I would almost be prepared to put up with that.' He wants these people in Rome to know this – most of them were Gentiles but there were some Jewish converts amongst them and he knew that they could spread the news to others – he wanted to nail this lie. He is not an anti-Jew. Quite the reverse!

But he is also doing something more than that. He wants to unfold the tragedy of the position of the Jews, and he knows what he is talking about. He is a Jew, and not only a Jew but a Pharisee, 'a Pharisee of the Pharisees', a man who has been steeped in the law, and in the history of this nation. Remember what he says in Philippians 3 about it all. He is an Israelite, of the tribe of Benjamin, and so on. If ever a man had a right to speak, he is the one, and he wants to try to show the tragedy of the position of the Jews, the tragedy that only a Jew like himself could possibly understand and appreciate. That is why he speaks like this and makes this particularly strong statement. But in verses 4 and 5, as we shall see, he expounds in detail the particular character of this amazing tragedy, the greatest tragedy the world has ever known – that 'he came unto his own, and his own received him not'. That they, of all people, should have betrayed Him and crucified Him and got rid of Him and rejected Him, that is the tragedy of tragedies!

Now Paul is concerned to show how this hurts him in his heart, his mind and his spirit; it leads to a constant bitterness and incessant anguish. He is anxious to show how he himself as a Jew views all this, because his ultimate intention is that perhaps, even through such an exposition, the eyes of the Jews may be partially opened, or some at any rate amongst them may see the error and the fallacy of it all and may turn to and believe the gospel.

Three

*

I say the truth in Christ, I lie not, my conscience also bearing me witness in the Holy Ghost, that I have great heaviness and continual sorrow in my heart. For I could wish that myself were accursed from Christ for my brethren, my kinsmen according to the flesh.

Romans 9 : 1–3

We have already considered what it was that the Apostle Paul was saying in these verses and why he made such a statement; but before we go on to consider what he says in the next two verses I feel that it is essential that we should draw certain deductions and conclusions, and gather to ourselves certain lessons from this most extraordinary statement.

It is a unique statement in many ways, a very personal statement, and, as I have pointed out, one of the most remarkable which the Apostle ever made concerning himself. He repeats it, though not so fully, at the beginning of the next chapter, and, indeed, of the eleventh chapter, but here it is in its most striking and remarkable form. And to me it is so important that I cannot just leave it with an exposition of the exact meaning of the terms.

We must always be careful that our study of the Scriptures is not merely mechanical. Our object in going through this great Epistle is not simply that we may understand it intellectually. Of course that is what we must always put first. But we must never stop at that, because the Scripture is always to be applied. That is why I never draw a distinction between what some people call 'lecturing' on the Bible, and preaching. The Bible is always to be preached. We must never approach the Bible in a theoretical or in an academic manner.

That is why I personally have never believed in having examinations in connection with biblical knowledge. I believe it is a false thing to do in and of itself. We tend to lose this idea that the Bible is given to us in order that it may build us up in our faith, in order that it may do something to us spiritually. There is nothing more dangerous than to have our heads packed with knowledge concerning the contents of the Bible, if that stops in the head and does not move our hearts and does not influence our wills. It is the high road to Antinomianism in its various forms. So it is important that we should remember that the main object of our being given the Scriptures is that they might be food for our souls. It is designed to bring us to a deeper and a greater experimental knowledge of God the Father, God the Son and God the Holy Spirit, and the riches of God's grace as they are given to us in this Christian salvation.

Now that is why I cannot move on from these first three verses immediately. I know that there are probably many who are most anxious to get on, because we have this great statement coming, about predestination and election, and that is the only thing they find in Romans 9. I have already indicated that that is tragic. No, we must learn from the Scriptures in every part and portion. We must not become devotees of favourite passages. Everything in the Bible is of great value to us, and it seems to me that there is very rich teaching in these first three verses of which we all probably stand in great need. Therefore let me try to show you some of the comments and lessons which should strike us immediately as we read these verses.

First of all, can you read these three verses without being struck and, indeed, deeply impressed, by the fact that the gospel is something which divides and separates? Here is the Apostle having to write like this about his own fellow-countrymen, the Jews. Something has happened. The gospel has come in, and it has acted as a great dividing force. There are many people who do not seem to understand this as they should and they therefore find themselves in considerable trouble. Does it not strike you as being curious that the Apostle Paul of all men should ever have found himself in this position? Because, as we see in Philippians 3, if ever there was a man in this world who attached great significance to nationality and background and natural advantages it is this man. He was by nature an ardent

Jew, a man who was unusually proud of the fact that he was a Jew and that he belonged to this favoured race and nation. And yet here we find him in this position in which his fellow-countrymen are antagonistic to him and he has to write in this particular way and manner.

What is it that has produced this? It is the gospel. There is a loose, foolish notion about Christianity that it is something which abolishes all divisions and distinctions and brings everybody together in a nice, happy, cheerful feeling of fellowship, of brotherhood and of friendship, so that we are all nice to one another and everything is smoothed over. It is entirely wrong! Our blessed Lord Himself, of course, warned us about this. He said, 'Think not that I am come to send peace on earth: I came not to send peace, but a sword', and then he goes on to say, 'For I am come to set a man at variance against his father, and the daughter against her mother, and the daughter in law against her mother in law. And a man's foes shall be they of his own household' [*Matthew* 10 : 34–36]. He warned us that He has come to do that. The gospel of Jesus Christ comes as a sword. It divides people even in the most tender relationships: husband and wife, father and mother, parents and children; it causes this extraordinary separation. And the Apostle is reminding us of that very thing here in these first three verses of this great chapter.

Then secondly we should notice the profound character of the division. It is not merely that those of us who become Christian take up a new idea, a new hope, or something like that, which others are not interested in. It is not that. There are many things which divide people in that way, but it is a superficial division. Here, however, we have a very deep and profound division, something that puts people into two different compartments, something indeed that so divides and separates them, that they can no longer understand one another. That is what had happened to Paul and the Jews. Here was this typical Jew, this Pharisee; he understood them, they understood him, they were all one. Then he became a Christian and there was a great gulf between them; they did not understand him at all. That is why they treated him as they did.

Now again, Paul was very concerned about this, because in writing to the Corinthians he says, 'He that is spiritual judgeth [or understandeth] all things, yet he himself is judged of no man'

[*1 Corinthians* 2 : 15]. That is the depth of the division. The moment people become Christians they are in a position that nobody else can understand. Their nearest and dearest cannot understand them. Something has come down between them, a kind of shutter, and there they are looking at one another. And those who are still not Christians are bewildered and upset by this. They can see now that the other has got hold of something that means everything to him or her, and they do not understand it, they know nothing about it. And that is why they so hate Christianity, because when it takes hold of us and brings us into this new position and puts the life of God in us, it makes us feel that this is the biggest and the most important thing of all.

Indeed, our Lord again in Matthew chapter 10 goes on to say that, and this has often perplexed people and caused them to stumble. He says, 'He that loveth father or mother more than me is not worthy of me: and he that loveth son or daughter more than me is not worthy of me' [*Matthew* 10 : 37]. And you have that same statement in Luke 14, put in a still more striking manner: 'If any man come to me', He says, 'and hate not his father, and mother, and wife, and children, and brethren, and sisters, yea, and his own life also, he cannot be my disciple' [*Luke* 14 : 26]. People are often troubled by that, but they should not be. He is saying that when people become Christians it becomes the supreme thing in their lives. It must come first, it must transcend every other relationship, even the most delicate, the most sensitive and the most wonderful of human relationships. In other words, the division that is caused by the gospel is a very deep and profound division, and all that is implicit in these three verses.

Then we find next that the gospel not only divides us from our old relationships, but it also brings us into new relationships and into a new company. Paul says here, 'I could wish that myself were accursed from Christ for my brethren, my kinsmen according to the flesh.' In other words, because he has become a Christian, he now has two sorts of brethren. There was a time, when he was not a Christian, when he only had one kind. They were the race and the nation to which he belonged and the people of whom he was part. But that is no longer true of him. Now, as a Christian, he has new brethren, brethren 'in Christ Jesus', and it does not matter whether these are Jews or Gentiles.

He writes to them as his 'beloved brethren', as, for example, when writing to a Gentile church like that at Philippi, he says, 'Therefore, my brethren dearly beloved and longed for, my joy and crown . . .'. He writes like that because he is now thinking of himself as a member of the family of God. No longer is he thinking of himself as a member of an earthly, human family or race or nation. He is addressing the Philippians as 'dearly beloved and longed for' because they are all together brethren in Christ Jesus. So, here in Romans 9 verse 3 he has to bring in a qualifying phrase. It is not enough to say 'my brethren'; he says, 'I mean my kinsmen according to the flesh'.

Now this is something that is true of every one of us who is a Christian. The gospel does this for us quite inevitably. We still belong to certain natural orders; we still belong to the families and to the nation into which we were born. Yes, but, as Christians, we are also in this new nation, this people of God. We are all related there, we are all brothers and sisters, we all belong together, so that we are aware of a kind of dualism in us: that which was there always by nature, and this which has come into being as the result of the operation of the Holy Spirit of God upon us. So that, like the Apostle, we now recognize these different allegiances. We have not ceased to be natural, but we are very aware of this new relationship. I emphasize these points because they help to bring home to us the profound character of the change which takes place when we become Christians. We are aware that we are now members of the household of God, that we are citizens of this eternal kingdom, and that we belong to heaven.

And so, to Paul, these people who belong there with him are the people who are now nearest and dearest to him. These are his real brethren. The others have become 'kinsmen according to the flesh'. That is what he is telling us. And in doing so, of course, he is opening our eyes and giving us a glimpse into this amazing thing which is the result of the rebirth, of regeneration; that we are literally 'partakers of the divine nature', that we are related to one another, brethren together in Christ, and that this is the firmest and the closest association of anything.

There are many ways in which we can look at these things. Indeed it is a very good way of testing ourselves. Men and women who have an intellectual interest in these things do not feel that, neither do they know it, or understand it. But those who are truly regenerate know this immediately, they recognize their own; they recognize God's children always. They feel that they belong to them; these are their people now and they want to be with them, while the others have become their 'kinsmen according to the flesh'. So, if anybody is in doubt as to whether he or she is a Christian, I suggest to you that this is a very valuable test. Are you aware of this division and this new relationship? Are you aware of a new alignment, of belonging to a new people? Are you aware of the fact that your real brethren now are those who are 'in Christ Jesus' even as you are yourself?

So we go on from that; there is the basis and the foundation on which the Apostle's whole argument will rest.

The next point is that, though all that is perfectly true of us, it does not mean that we have ceased to be interested in the old relationship. We must not say that. All I am saying is that the new relationship is the one that becomes supreme. But it does not cancel the other. Now this is a point which some people seem to find difficult to grasp. The Christian is never meant to be unnatural. He is spiritual, but that does not mean that he becomes unnatural, he does not sever completely the old relationship. He is in a new one, there is this essential difference, but it does not mean that he has ceased altogether to belong to the 'order of nature', so-called.

This is true, of course, in all our relationships. There are some people who have tried to argue that because the Apostle says, 'There is neither Greek nor Jew, circumcision nor uncircumcision, Barbarian, Scythian, bond nor free' [*Colossians* 3 : 11], that the Christian is some sort of supernationalist, but that does not follow at all. Paul does not mean that a man ceases to belong to his nation. What he does mean is that those things do not matter at all as far as salvation is concerned. The Jew must no longer think that he alone is the man who belongs to the chosen people, because God is taking His people out of all nations. Salvation is not determined, Paul says, in a national manner. But it does not mean that there is no sense or meaning in these national divisions and distinctions. It means that we are not governed by them but it does not abolish them.

Now that comes out very clearly here. The Apostle, though he is in this entirely new condition, is still very concerned about his fellow Jews, and that is what he is emphasizing here. These three verses above everything else show the Apostle's deep concern for his 'kinsmen according to the flesh', for he would not write like this at all were that not the case. And the point is that he has not finished with them; rather, he has this great and deep concern for them.

So the question I ask is this: Do we know something of the same concern? We have no right to rush over these three verses and go on to the great theological point that is coming, without stopping for a moment and asking ourselves, Have I this 'grief' that Paul talks about for those members of my own family or of my own nation that are not Christians? Do we know this? The Apostle does, and he testifies to it in this bold language. What is the value of all knowledge unless it leads to this? If we do not have it then we have failed somehow or other to realize the truth about salvation itself; and, still more, we have failed to realize the condition and the fate of the lost. It was because he had such a depth of spiritual experience, because he was enjoying the glory of salvation, and because he knew the fate of the unredeemed, that the Apostle had this great heaviness and continual sorrow in his heart for his 'kinsmen according to the flesh'.

Let me put it as a principle: There is no better test of our spiritual state and condition than our missionary zeal, our concern for lost souls. That is always the thing that divides people who are just theoretical and intellectual Christians from those who have a living and a vital spiritual life. This is something that I can prove abundantly from history. Look at the case of the Apostle himself. Here is a man who had the knowledge more than anybody, and yet you notice his concern, his heart-break for his fellow Jews who were rejecting Christ.

And this has been true of all the great men and women of God, the ones God has used most signally throughout the centuries. Few men, for instance, understood these truths in the way that Jonathan Edwards did, with his brilliant intellect and his genius – and yet look at his missionary zeal. It is inevitable. You find the same thing with Whitefield. He could not keep still, he was indefatigable. Travelling and preaching when he ought to be resting, half killing himself, dying at an early age; simply because of this passion for souls, his concern about people. He was grieved, for instance, at his own townspeople in Gloucester being in the state and condition they were in and he felt he could not keep quiet, he must preach. It was the same with William Carey and Charles Haddon Spurgeon and it is characteristic of all such people always. So we cannot ride over these three verses and say, 'Of course, that is just a personal statement, I want to get on to the doctrine.' Do you? Let me hold you there for a moment, my friend. Are you burdened about the lost; the lost in your own family? Does it grieve you? Does it pain you? Is it a continual sorrow in your heart?

If it is not, then there is something wrong with your knowledge and with your understanding; there is something defective in your enjoyment of this great salvation. For it is human nature after all, if there is something that you really enjoy and which is giving you great benefits, to want to share it. You want people to have it, and with whom do you start? Obviously with those who are nearest and dearest to you, the people of your own family, the people of your own nation. And here that is displayed before us in all this fulness by the great Apostle. 'If ye know these things, happy are ye if ye do them.' If ye know these things, happy are ye if ye feel them. If ye know these things, happy are ye if they bring forth fruit in your lives. And this is the first fruit, surely, a concern about those who are outside. Do we really believe that those who are not saved are going to eternal damnation? If we do, is it not inevitable that we should have a concern about them and especially those who are nearest to us? So, let us examine ourselves, let us test ourselves in the light of this. I am not engaging in these studies of Romans merely to give an intellectual entertainment. I am not doing this even simply to divide up the Scriptures. It is my task to divide them in order that we may apply them, in order that they may bring forth fruit in our lives and make of us men and women who shall approximate more and more to the pattern and the example which we have before us in the case of the great Apostle. There is no value in any knowledge unless it leads to this kind of result.

But then let us go on to something very practical. Consider the way in which the Apostle handles these kinsmen of his according to the flesh. The gospel has come, it has divided him from them and it has put him into a new relationship. There they are, rejecting Christ, blaspheming Him. Yet how does the Apostle react to that? Now I do trust that we all see the practical import of all this. How do we react to members of our family and friends and fellow-countrymen, who are not Christians? Well, notice this Apostle; he displays no trace of annoyance with them. There is not a suspicion of any contemptuous attitude towards them. He does not dismiss them, denounce them, attack them; he is not even irritated by them.

Now I make this point because if any man ever had cause to be annoyed or hurt by his fellow-countrymen it was the Apostle Paul; if any man had a right to regard them with contempt also for their blindness, it was this man. But there is no trace of it. You remember how they treated him? He tells us in 2 Corinthians 11 verse 24: 'Of the Jews five times received I forty stripes save one' – a most cruel treatment. They were, as he tells us elsewhere, constantly thwarting him, doing everything they could to hinder him, plotting against him, circulating lies concerning him, vilifying him. Never was a man treated more badly by his kinsmen according to the flesh than was this mighty Apostle Paul, yet how does he react to them? There is not a trace of bitterness. He does not attack them, he does not denounce them. Rather, we find that he is full of compassion and pity, he is full of sorrow. Moreover, he tells them that he is ready to do anything he can in order to bring them to this knowledge and to deliver them out of their bondage and their blindness.

Now the question for us is this: How can he behave like this with respect to them? It is not easy, is it? Do not we all know what it is to be annoyed by people because they do not believe the gospel? We have seen the truth so plainly, but there they are, still rejecting it; how easy it is to dismiss them as hopeless, to turn our backs upon them and to have nothing more to do with them. And there are many Christians who do that. Of course, it is much easier to cut off relationships than it is to handle them in the way that the Apostle does. This is very difficult; nevertheless the Apostle does it. And I suggest to you that what enables him to do this is that, in his mind, he puts himself in their position! So, that is what we too should always do; it is absolutely essential.

In other words, you do not react against these people or look at them objectively and denounce them. You stop and you say to yourself, 'Why are they rejecting Christ, why are they refusing the gospel?' I have often put it like this: we have all known the temptation – have we not? – when we have been putting the thing so plainly to somebody and they cannot see it; we feel like taking hold of them and shaking them; we feel like boxing their ears because of their dullness and their stupidity! And the moment we get like that we cannot help them.

Now the way to avoid all that is to put yourself into their position. The Apostle does that, and what he realizes is that they are blinded. He will tell us that at great length in the eleventh chapter; he is already feeling this and he is governed by it. So when we find ourselves asking how he could feel like that about these people who had so maltreated him, then we see that the way in which he does it is to say to himself – Why are they doing this? And the answer is: they are blinded by the devil. In 2 Corinthians 3 : 15 he tells us that, 'Even unto this day, when Moses is read, the vail is upon their heart'. They are looking at the words but they have missed the meaning; they are blinded by the god of this world. So then, realize that, says the Apostle, look at them properly and you will see their state and condition.

And then he goes on to do something else. He reminds himself that not long ago he, too, was exactly like that. I have known Christians make havoc in people's lives through forgetting that. I have seen them impatient and annoyed, and it is all due to the fact that they do not remind themselves that very recently they were like that themselves, and they forget that God was very patient with them. The moment you realize that, you will be patient with others. Paul says, in writing to Timothy, that he was once a blasphemer, an injurious person and a persecutor. I acted in ignorance and unbelief, he says [*1 Timothy* 1 : 13], I did not know what I was doing. And these other people do not either. So the moment you put yourself into the other person's position, you will come to understand that your irritation is simply due to the fact that you are not clear in your thinking. If you are clear in your theology and in your doctrine you will know that no natural man can believe the gospel. 'The natural man receiveth not the things of the Spirit of God: for they are foolishness unto him: neither can he know them, because they are spiritually discerned' [*1 Corinthians* 2 : 14]. So if you expect a natural man to believe the gospel simply because you are putting it to him, you are denying the gospel; you have not understood it yourself. He cannot do it. It is no use your getting excited or bringing pressure to bear upon him; it is all of no value. The man cannot help himself! He needs the enlightenment that the Holy Spirit alone can give. You needed it; he still needs it. The Apostle realizes all this, and so he is able to write in this way and manner concerning his kinsmen according to the flesh.

Are we as patient as we should be with these others? Do we bear with them, do we understand them, do we take this trouble to get it clearly in our minds that they are what they are because they are still spiritually dead? It is a tragic thing that so often we hinder our own preaching because of our failure at this point to remind ourselves of the state and the condition of our 'kinsmen according to the flesh' who are still outside. So this important lesson is here on the surface of these verses.

Then, the last lesson is that the Apostle's position, as he describes it here, teaches us the importance of always keeping ourselves open to the leading and the guidance and the call of God. In many ways, the most amazing thing that has ever happened in history, is that this man, the Apostle Paul, of all men in the world, should have become the Apostle to the Gentiles. In Galatians 2 he says that God had given him this commission to the Gentiles, as He had given Peter the commission to the circumcision. It is a most astonishing thing, that this intense Jew, this essential Jewish nationalist, should have had to spend the greater part of his life as the Apostle to the Gentiles.

I have found a very great lesson here, one of the most salutary lessons I think I have ever learned in my life. I am quite certain I am right in saying that the last thing in the world that the Apostle would ever have chosen for himself was to be the Apostle to the Gentiles. All his natural likes and dislikes, all his natural prejudices, all his background, upbringing, training, everything, seemed to fit him to be the Apostle to the Jews. He was such an expert Pharisee; he knew the law and excelled everybody in it. You would have thought that this man above all men should have been appointed to the Jews, but he was actually appointed to the Gentiles!

Why was this? Now, this is something to which Paul refers here and there. Take, for instance, how he puts it in writing to the Galatians, in chapter 1 verses 13 and following: 'For ye have heard of my conversation in time past in the Jews' religion, how that beyond measure I persecuted the church of God, and wasted it: and profited in the Jews' religion above many my equals in mine own nation, being more exceedingly zealous of the traditions of my fathers.' Of all men he was the most zealous. 'But when it pleased God, who separated me from my mother's womb, and called me by his grace, to reveal his Son in me, that I might preach him among the heathen . . .' There it is, this most astounding fact that he is sent to the heathen; and here is his secret: 'immediately I conferred not with flesh and blood' – not his own flesh and blood, nor anybody else's – 'neither went I up to Jerusalem to them which were apostles before me; but I went into Arabia, and returned again unto Damascus.' Then he says, 'Then after three years I went up to Jerusalem to see Peter . . . But other of the apostles saw I none, save James the Lord's brother. Now the things which I write unto you, behold, before God, I lie not. Afterwards I came into the regions of Syria and Cilicia; and was unknown by face unto the churches of Judæa which were in Christ: but they had heard only, That he which persecuted us in times past now preacheth the faith which once he destroyed. And they glorified God in me.'

And before Agrippa and Festus he makes exactly the same statement: 'My manner of life from my youth, which was at the first among mine own nation at Jerusalem, know all the Jews; which knew me from the beginning, if they would testify, that after the most straitest sect of our religion I lived a Pharisee [*Acts* 26 : 4–5]. There it is again. One of the greatest and most intense Jewish nationalists that the world has ever known, and yet here he is, Apostle to the Gentiles. And you remember the account he gives us in other places in Acts as to how this happened to him. Take, for example, Acts 13, beginning at verse 44: 'The next sabbath day came almost the whole city together to hear the word of God. But when the Jews saw the multitudes, they were filled with envy, and spake against those things which were spoken by Paul, contradicting and blaspheming.' Now here is a crucial point, you see: 'Then Paul and Barnabas waxed bold, and said, It was necessary that the word of God should first have been spoken to you: but seeing ye put it from you, and judge yourselves unworthy of everlasting life, lo, we turn to the Gentiles. For so hath the Lord commanded us, saying, I have set thee to be a light to the Gentiles, that thou shouldest be for salvation unto the ends of the earth.' You find a similar account in Acts 18 verse 6.

And so, you see, it comes to pass that Paul, the great Jew, is able to say, as he does in Romans chapter 11 verse 13, 'For I speak to you Gentiles, inasmuch as I am the apostle of the Gentiles, I magnify mine office.' How staggering this is – that such a man should glory in the fact and magnify his office, that he has been made the apostle to the Gentiles.

What, then, is his secret? We have seen the answer in all those passages. This man has become a true Christian, he is regenerate. And, therefore, he is no longer governed by prejudices or opinions. But so many of us are. We want to do certain things, we feel we are cut out for them and they are the things that we really like. But as true Christians, we must no longer go on like that; we must no longer be controlled by likes or dislikes. There are some people who would dearly like to be foreign missionaries and it is very difficult for such people to stay at home. But sometimes that is God's will for them. We do not decide these things. The Apostle did not. He did not consult with flesh and blood, he did not work it out himself and reason it and come to his own decision and conclusion. He did not do what he wanted to do. There is no question but that as a natural man, he would have wanted to be the Apostle to his own nation. But he no longer thought like that. All he wanted to know now was, 'What is God's will?' All he was concerned about was to do that will, and, of course, he was living a life in the Spirit, and had become sensitive to the leading and the guidance of the Holy Spirit.

There is a perfect illustration of all this in Acts 16 verses 6 and 7. 'Now', says Luke, 'when they had gone throughout Phrygia and the region of Galatia, and were forbidden of the Holy Ghost to preach the word in Asia, after they were come to Mysia, they assayed to go into Bithynia: but the Spirit suffered them not.' Now that is the secret. The Apostle Paul quite clearly had decided he wanted to go and preach the Word in Asia, but we are told that he is forbidden of the Holy Ghost to do that, and he is quite content. And afterwards 'they assayed' – they attempted, they tried – 'to go into Bithynia'.

Obviously Paul's thinking had led him to go there; he wanted to go there and proposed to do so, but again we read, 'the Spirit suffered them not'. And when he was conscious of the fact either that the Spirit was not giving him liberty or that the Spirit was raising a doubt inside his heart, he did not do it; he did not go, because he knew that that was wrong.

Where, then, was he to go? He did not know, but eventually he arrived down at Troas, and he came up against the sea there. There was nothing in front of him but the sea, and he must have wondered what was happening to him. But then he was given that vision in the night; the man of Macedonia appeared to him and he became quite clear in his understanding, as well as in every other respect, that he had been hindered from going into Asia and into Bithynia because God's plan was that he should go to Europe. And so Paul's secret was that he did not act apart from the clear indication of the Spirit.

And this is the only way in which we can be certain that we are always doing what God wants us to do. I have always laid this down as a principle in the matter of guidance. I have not hesitated to say to people, 'When you have worked it all out; if you have decided on a certain course and if you consult other people and they agree with you and everybody seems to be on that side, unless you have got absolute freedom in your spirit do not do it – wait.' The final signal before we should ever move is that the Spirit authenticates within us what reason and understanding, exposition of the Scripture, and consultation with Christian people, seem to suggest. It is only when the Spirit has given His assent and confirmation, that the signal has dropped and you are allowed to go. The Apostle was so sensitive to the leading of the Spirit that whatever he may have felt as a natural man, he was no longer governed by it, so this intense and brilliant and most Jewish Jew became the Apostle to the Gentiles, and magnified his office. And now, through the letter to the Romans, he will explain to his fellow-countrymen, the Jews, why this is the case. He will explain to them the tragedy of the Jews, why he feels as he does about them, and why he is able to say, 'I could wish that myself were accursed from Christ for my brethren, my kinsmen according to the flesh.'

May God give us grace to examine ourselves in the light of these things, both in our relationship to others and with respect to what we are doing in this world, our vocation, our service for the living God. It does not matter what we are doing; the one thing that matters is this: Is this God's will for me? Is this what God has called me to? Is this the thing the Spirit has led me to? It does not matter what it is, whether I am in one place or another, whether it is with my own nation or another nation, whatever it involves it does not matter. The only thing that matters is, that I should know that I am in the centre of God's will, and that I should be doing, to the utmost of my ability by the power of His Spirit, the thing for which He has called me.

Four

*

Who are Israelites; to whom pertaineth the adoption, and the
glory, and the covenants, and the giving of the law, and the service
of God, and the promises; whose are the fathers, and of whom as
concerning the flesh Christ came, who is over all, God blessed for
ever. Amen.

Romans 9 : 4–5

We have been considering in the past three studies the great
opening statement of the Apostle in which he expresses his grief
over his fellow Jews. Now here, in these two verses, he proceeds
to give us his detailed reasons for feeling this continual sorrow
in his heart, and his great heaviness for his 'kinsmen according
to the flesh'. We have seen that it is God who has appointed the
bounds of all nations and has ordained that we should come into
this world into families, so we have emphasized that there is
nothing wrong in feeling and experiencing such sentiments as
the Apostle gives expression to here. But we must not stop at
that, because it is made abundantly plain and clear that the
Apostle's chief concern for his kinsmen was not a national or
even a natural one, but was indeed particularly a religious one.
And what makes him grieve as he does is his realization, as he
points out to us, of their unique relationship to God.

The Apostle, after all, was now primarily and essentially a
Christian and an Apostle – a man with a profound understanding of God's ways with respect to men, and the whole great
purpose and scheme and plan of salvation. And it is as he
contemplates the condition of the Jews in the light of that, and
particularly in the light of God's purpose of salvation as it was
worked out under the Old Testament dispensation, that he finds

himself thus in a state of perpetual great heaviness and continual sorrow of heart. So we must now look at these two verses in which he shows us the unique position of the Jews, the children of Israel, the people to whom he belonged by nature. Here he puts before us the unique privileges that they had always enjoyed because they were the people that they were.

These two verses are important for many reasons. One is that an understanding of them and their meaning is absolutely essential to following the Apostle's argument both in this chapter and in the following chapters. That is why he puts it here at the beginning. If we are not clear about these people and what was true of them, we shall obviously be in difficulties when we come to try to follow his detailed argument as he works it out in chapter 11.

But this statement is also important in another way, and this, too, is a very practical one. These two verses, I suggest to you before we look at them any further, are a very good test of us, a very good test of our method of Bible-study and Bible-reading. We have probably read these two verses many times, but what have they really conveyed to us? How easy it is to skip over them and to read them without stopping to consider what exactly they are saying to us, and what exactly they mean. I wonder what the result would be if I turned this study into a kind of examination and just said, What has been the significance to you of these two verses, and what effect have they had upon you?

I say that because while I am, of course, in entire agreement with all systems of Bible-reading, it does seem to me that we must always remember that the mere reading of the Bible in and of itself is not sufficient; indeed it can be quite useless. How do we read? Are we merely content with saying, I have done my daily portion, and then go on to something else? Or do we stop and allow the Scriptures to speak to us and to give us their own message and to lead us into the truth? So what have these two verses said to us in the past? Have we found that they are verses that make us stop and explore them, or have we just regarded them as a kind of catalogue of things that are true about the children of Israel, without realizing the great argument that comes later? 'Let a man examine himself.' It is very valuable, therefore, from that purely practical standpoint.

Then another value of these two verses is that they really do give us a most masterly and extraordinary summary of the whole of the Old Testament. So that they are of extreme importance in that respect. They are a summary not only of the teaching of the Old Testament, but also of the history of the Old Testament. I emphasize that because there are certain superficial foolish people in the church at the present time who call themselves Christians but who think that it is clever to attack the Old Testament, and particularly its history. Such people not only think they are being clever; they think they are being very spiritual. They are not interested in the history, they maintain; they are interested in the Jesus of the New Testament and what He has to say. So they are not interested in the giving of the law, and Mount Sinai, and things like that, and they are very doubtful about Abraham and so on. Now these two verses alone show us the utter vacuity of such a position. You cannot divide the two Testaments in that way.

But still more important – and this is the last general point – is this. Here we are shown very plainly how essential the Old Testament is to a true understanding of the New. Indeed there are terms which are used in the New Testament which are quite meaningless unless we know something about the Old. That is, undoubtedly, why the Christian church at the beginning, when she came to form this book which we call the Bible, was led of the Holy Spirit not to throw overboard the Old Testament but to incorporate it with her new documents. So it is one book, one volume, because the two are so intermingled; the Old points to the New, and the New is constantly pointing back to the Old.

So having established that let us proceed to an examination of the very statements which are made by the Apostle. 'Who are Israelites': that is how he introduces it. 'I could wish that myself were accursed from Christ for my brethren, my kinsmen according to the flesh: who are Israelites.' Now the word translated here 'who' is very interesting, and it is really not enough by itself. The Apostle here used a double word, a double relative, in order to bring out the element of character and of quality in these people about whom he is writing. It is a very strong word: 'my kinsmen according to the flesh: *who are such that* . . .' would be a better translation, or 'the very ones who inasmuch as they are Israelites . . .'. Or again you might put it like this: 'who are of such a character or quality to be Israelites'. That is perhaps the best of them all. And then come the various items in the list that he puts before us.

So you see that this in itself is a matter of interest and of importance. The Apostle is out to show us this almost inconceivable tragedy, that Christ 'came unto his own, and his own received him not' [*John* 1 : 11]. John is amazed at it in his Prologue, and the Apostle Paul here is expressing the same thing but with much greater fulness, in order to bring out his utter astonishment at the fact. So the little word translated 'who' in and of itself opens up a kind of vista – they are of such a character and such a quality as to be . . .

And the next word we come to is the word 'Israelites'. Now why did the Apostle use this particular word? Why did he not say, 'who are Jews' or 'who are Hebrews', because both things are true of them. But he says 'who are Israelites' and this, of course, has very real significance. Let me put it like this. Take these three terms – 'Jew', 'Hebrew', 'Israelite'. You will generally find that the one or the other is used in particular places with a very definite and specific object. Now we must not press this too far. There are friends who do that, and they form movements as a result. There are those who would say that we in this kingdom are Israelites. We are not Jews, but we are British Israelites, and they say that because they over-press the distinction between these various terms. So we must not do that, but we must on the other hand recognize that there is a difference.

Let us start, therefore, with the commonest which is 'Jew'. Now this word is generally used in order to draw the contrast and the distinction between the Jew and the Gentile. The Jew is generally the opposite, the antithesis of the Gentile. There is an example of that in the twenty-fourth verse of this very chapter which we are studying: 'Even us,' he says, 'whom he hath called, not of the Jews only, but also of the Gentiles.' Then we find it again in the twelfth verse of the next chapter, where we read: 'For there is no difference between the Jew and the Greek: for the same Lord over all is rich unto all that call upon him', and, too, we have already met it in chapter 3 verse 29: 'Is he the God of the Jews only? is he not also of the Gentiles?' It is exactly the same distinction.

Then let us look at the second term, 'Hebrew'. I am 'an Hebrew of the Hebrews,' says the Apostle [*Philippians* 3 : 5]. Now this is used in order to bring out the fact that these people spoke Hebrew. There were certain Jews at the time of our Lord and during the first century, the Jews of the Dispersion, who no longer spoke Hebrew. They had long since left the land of Palestine, and they had mixed with other races and nations and people and were no longer Hebrew-speaking people. They had adopted the Greek language, or other languages, and therefore they could not be called Hebrews, though they were still Jews. They still had their Old Testament, but they used the Septuagint, the Greek translation, instead of the Hebrew Old Testament. You will find that in the New Testament they are sometimes referred to as 'Hellenists', which simply tells us that they were Greek-speaking Jews. You find this in Acts 6 verse 1: 'And in those days, when the number of the disciples was multiplied, there arose a murmuring of the Grecians against the Hebrews, because their widows were neglected in the daily ministration.' The point is that both groups were Jews, but the distinction is between the Greek-speaking and the Hebrew-speaking Jews, and it was between them that this dispute arose. So that when you get the term 'Hebrew' it generally brings out the idea that they were those who still spoke that language.

So, then, why does Paul say here, 'who are Israelites' and not 'who are Jews' or 'who are Hebrews'? This is the significant point, of course, and in order to understand it we must go back to Genesis 32 to that incident in the life of Jacob when, alone at Peniel one fateful night, a Man came to him and they struggled until the breaking of the day. 'And he said, Let me go, for the day breaketh. And he said, I will not let thee go, except thou bless me. And he said unto him, What is thy name? And he said, Jacob. And he said, Thy name shall be called no more Jacob, but Israel: for as a prince hast thou power with God and with men, and hast prevailed' [*Genesis* 32 : 26–28]. From that point he is known as 'Israel', and 'Israelites' are the descendants of Jacob.

What, then, is the significance of this? It is, as is pointed out in that passage, in the giving of the name to Jacob. He is one who had prevailed with God and with men; he therefore became a prince, and an object of special attention on God's part. His descendants become God's chosen people in this particular

[44]

manner, and are given this name to show that they are God's covenant people. God is now in a new and a unique relationship to them; they become a kind of theocracy, a people governed by God directly and immediately.

Now that was true of no other nation. You find this term constantly in the Old Testament and the New. We read that we as Christians now have become 'a chosen generation, a royal priesthood, an holy nation, a peculiar people' – a people for God's own peculiar possession. That is what it means, and that is the essence of this term 'Israelite'. It is through these people now that God is going to do His great work in this world and carry out His great purpose of salvation. So you see the Apostle uses the term 'Israelite' very deliberately indeed. And this word in itself really sums up all the terms that are to follow, apart from the reference to our Lord Himself. But all these other things that are true of these people – the adoption and the glory and the covenants and the giving of the law and the service of God and the promises – are all the result of the fact that they have become 'Israelites'.

Now you notice that the Apostle uses the term here of the people as a whole. That is something that is done very commonly in the Bible. There are statements made about the whole nation. Later on we shall find him saying, 'They are not all Israel, which are of Israel'. But here he is using it of them all. Then he narrows it down later when he wants to talk in particular about the saved; they are the 'true Israel'. But here he is using the term in as wide and as broad a manner as is possible to cover all who are the physical, lineal descendants of Jacob who shall first of all be called Israel – Israelites! There is, therefore, a real significance in the choice of this word; it is an advance upon the word 'Jew'. The Israelites are still Jews; yes, but this term emphasizes their unique relationship to God as His people: 'I will be their God; they shall be my people.' It is said of them, and of them alone. As Amos puts it, 'You only have I known of all the nations of the earth.' And all that is in this word 'Israelite'.

Let me ask a question at this point. Did you always stop when you read this verse and ask yourself, 'Why Israelite and not Jew; is there any significance?' In other words, when we come to the Scripture let us remember that it is the Word of God. We need the Holy Spirit, we need to be enlightened, we need to watch everything because there is hidden treasure everywhere if we take the trouble to look for it. Let us make sure that we understand it. Let us grapple with it, let us ask questions, let us see exactly what it is saying and why it is saying it: 'Israelite', not 'Jew'.

The next term is the term 'adoption.' 'Who are Israelites; to whom pertaineth the adoption.' You may feel that there is no difficulty about that because we have already met that word in the previous chapter where we read in verses 14 and 15: 'For as many as are led by the Spirit of God, they are the sons of God. For ye have not received the spirit of bondage again to fear; but ye have received the Spirit of adoption, whereby we cry, Abba, Father.' We have met it also in verse 23: 'Not only they, but ourselves also, which have the firstfruits of the Spirit, even we ourselves groan within ourselves, waiting for the adoption, to wit, the redemption of our body.'[1] Does 'adoption' here therefore not just mean precisely what is meant in Romans chapter 8 verses 15 and 23?

And the answer is, of course, most certainly not! Why not? For this reason: in the fifteenth verse of that eighth chapter he is talking in particular about those who are truly the sons of God, spiritually so. They are led by the Spirit. He is including those who have become Christians from amongst the Jews, and, also, the Gentiles who have become Christians. He is talking about the true Christian, the one who is born again, and he says we have the Spirit of adoption because God has adopted us into His family. In verse 23 he is obviously using it in a different sense; it is something yet to come. We are 'waiting' for the adoption.

But here, in chapter 9 : 4 we are told that these Israelites had the adoption, that it 'pertained' unto them. So that here, we see again that we must not merely look at words. This is another snare in Bible-study, is it not? You just become a student of words, and you turn up your lexicon, and that is valuable because it is essential to know the meaning of a word. But you must pay attention to the context also. Let the context speak to you as well as the particular meaning, otherwise you can be easily side-tracked, and you can become a heretic without

[1] See *Romans: An Exposition of Chapter 8:5–17: The Sons of God*, 1974.

realizing it. So then, the term is clearly not used here in the same way as it is in chapter 8. And indeed the whole of the following argument also makes this abundantly clear. In other words, the Apostle here is using this term as he used the term 'Israelite', in a very general and broad sense. He is saying that this is something that was true of the whole nation, of these descendants of Abraham, Isaac and of Jacob.

Let me illustrate to you exactly what he means. In Exodus 4 : 22 in the instructions given to Moses, we read, 'And thou shalt say unto Pharaoh, Thus saith the Lord, Israel is my son, even my firstborn.' Now that is a statement about the whole nation. Then go on to Deuteronomy 14 : 1: 'Ye are the children of the Lord your God', and because of that, 'ye shall not cut yourselves, nor make any baldness between your eyes for the dead' – because you are the children of God. Then in Jeremiah, chapter 31 verse 9, there is again a statement which will help us to illustrate this matter: 'They shall come with weeping, and with supplications will I lead them: I will cause them to walk by the rivers of water in a straight way, wherein they shall not stumble: for I am a father to Israel, and Ephraim is my firstborn.'

You see, it is the same idea in all these instances. Let me give you one more from the book of the prophet Hosea, chapter 11 verse 1: 'When Israel was a child, then I loved him, and called my son out of Egypt.' It was the entire company that went out of Egypt and you remember that most of them died in the wilderness. But it does not matter; the reference to them as 'child' covers the whole nation, and it is in that sense that the Apostle is using it here in Romans 9.

Then compare that with Matthew chapter 8 verses 11 and 12: 'I say unto you, That many shall come from the east and west, and shall sit down with Abraham, and Isaac, and Jacob, in the kingdom of heaven. But the children of the kingdom shall be cast out into outer darkness: there shall be weeping and gnashing of teeth.' Clearly it is a general use there again. Though they are described as 'children', they are cast out. The true spiritual children will never be cast out, as Romans 8 has proved to us, but in this general use of the terms 'adoption', 'son', and 'children', there is the possibility, in this way, of being cast out.

[47]

The Apostle here is preparing us for what he is going to say. His argument will be that though they are all in a sense Israelites, and though they are all in the adoption, they nevertheless are 'not all Israel, which are of Israel'. They are not all truly adopted who appear to be adopted, they are not all truly sons who have the general designation of sons and of children. God placed this nation into the position of His son – 'Israel is my son', and that is one of the other privileges, says the Apostle, that was true of these 'kinsmen according to the flesh' who are denying and rejecting the Lord Jesus Christ. God has not only given them this name, establishing them as His own especial people, He has dealt with them as children, throughout the whole of the story that we read in the Old Testament. So that is the meaning of the expression, 'to whom pertaineth the adoption'.

Then we go on to the next term, which is 'and the glory'. Now there are those who would say that it just means the privilege and the dignity of their position. We use this term sometimes in conversation when we say that glory attaches to certain positions. There are some, indeed, who would connect it with the previous word 'adoption'. They say, 'the glory of the adoption', or 'the glorious adoption'. But that interpretation is to be rejected on many grounds, one of which is that the Apostle here is giving us a series of statements about the Israelites and this is obviously a separate statement. So that purely on grounds of grammar and syntax, we say that it does not just qualify the adoption or anything else, and it is not just a general statement.

But there are stronger reasons for saying that. Here is one of these remarkable things about these people, and I detect that there is a kind of gradation here, that the Apostle is leading from one thing to the other. They are Israelites, they have been put into the position of a son. Not just a people that God governs, not merely a theocracy, but much more. He narrows it down, you see, from the state idea to a family idea. It goes from 'Israelite' to 'adoption'. And then this next term, 'the glory'. What does this mean exactly? Well, this, to me, is one of those astounding truths. It means that God has shown to these people something of Himself and of His own glorious nature. 'The glory'! The glory of God Himself!

There are many records of that in the Old Testament. Take,

for instance, what happened to Moses when he was on the side
of the mountain with the sheep. You remember how he
suddenly saw a burning bush – a bush aflame and burning and
yet it was not consumed. Now, that is a manifestation of the
glory of God. It was given to him, of course, for a special purpose.
It was really the call of Moses at that point and something very
special was needed. So God gave him some glimpse of the
everlasting glory which is God.

There are further instances of this. We read in Exodus 14 : 19–
20 of the way in which the children of Israel were taken through
the Red Sea, and we are told, 'And the angel of God, which went
before the camp of Israel, removed and went behind them; and
the pillar of the cloud went from before their face, and stood
behind them: and it came between the camp of the Egyptians
and the camp of Israel; and it was a cloud and darkness to them,
but it gave light by night to these: so that the one came not near
the other all the night.' The fiery, cloudy pillar! That is a
manifestation of the glory.

Or look at it again in Exodus 16 : 10: 'And it came to pass, as
Aaron spake unto the whole congregation of the children of
Israel, that they looked toward the wilderness, and, behold, the
glory of the Lord appeared in the cloud.' No other nation ever
had this. But God gave these glimpses, these manifestations of
Himself and His own eternal being, to these people. But look,
says Paul, look at this tragedy! These are the people who are
rejecting the Son of God and yet they have had glimpses of the
glory given to them; 'to whom pertaineth the adoption, and the
glory'. The Apostle is not just talking about the glory of their
position, but of their having had glimpses of the glory itself.

Again, in Exodus 29 : 43 – I am giving these in detail because
the whole subject is such an important one for us to grasp – God
says, 'And there I will meet with the children of Israel, and the
tabernacle shall be sanctified by my glory.' And then there is
that great story of Moses in conversation with God after the
incident of the golden calf, where Moses rises to the height of his
daring and says, 'I beseech thee, shew me thy glory' [*Exodus
33* : 18]. And God's answer to him was, 'There is a place by me,
and thou shalt stand upon a rock: and it shall come to pass,
while my glory passeth by, that I will put thee in a clift of the
rock, and will cover thee with my hand while I pass by: and I

will take away mine hand, and thou shalt see my back parts: but my face shall not be seen.' A glimpse again of the glory of God! A most amazing and astonishing thing.

Another illustration of this is found in Exodus 40 : 34: 'Then a cloud covered the tent of the congregation, and the glory of the Lord filled the tabernacle.' But, of course, we must remember, too, that in the innermost sanctuary in the tabernacle which the children of Israel had in the wilderness, and again later when they had their temple in Jerusalem, that in that Holiest of All, there was a mercy seat, and the glory of the Lord appeared there. It was to signify God's presence amongst His people, so that they might know that He was always with them. 'I will be to you a God, and you shall be to me a people.' And there through their high priest, who went in once a year only with an offering of blood, they were able to meet with God and to speak with Him.

We find the account of that in the case of the temple in I Kings 8 : 10–11. 'And it came to pass, when the priests were come out of the holy place, that the cloud filled the house of the Lord, so that the priests could not stand to minister because of the cloud: for the glory of the Lord had filled the house of the Lord.' The children of Israel later came to refer to this glory of the Lord in the most holy place as the Shekinah, which means 'the presence of God', the fact that God dwelt among the people. That luminous cloud that led them out of Egypt through the Red Sea on their journey, that same sign that rested upon the mercy seat, this is a manifestation, some conception of the glory of the everlasting and eternal God. And that is the most wonderful thing that can ever happen to a nation or to a people or to an individual.

Now we have gone into all this detail with these great terms because they are all of supreme importance. The teaching of the New Testament is that we, who are Gentiles by nature, have been brought into a share of all this. We are told this in Ephesians 2: You, says the Apostle to people in Ephesus, were at that time outside the commonwealth of Israel, you were not sharers in these things. 'Remember,' he says, 'that ye being in time past Gentiles in the flesh, who are called Uncircumcision by that which is called the Circumcision in the flesh made by hands; that at that time ye were without Christ, being aliens

from the commonwealth of Israel, and strangers from the covenants of promise, having no hope, and without God in the world.
But', he continues, 'now in Christ Jesus, ye who sometimes were
far off are made nigh by the blood of Christ.' Then notice, 'Now
therefore ye are no more strangers and foreigners, but fellow-
citizens with the saints, and of the household of God' [*Ephesians*
2 : 11–13, 19]. That is what happens to us when we become
Christians; we are brought into the realm of these great and
glorious privileges that had been given to these people of God in
the past. And there were their descendants not recognizing all
this, and denying Christ; that was what broke the Apostle's
heart.

Yes, but let us remember the other side – that we now become a
part of the Israel of God, a part of the people of God. That is how
Peter puts it: 'But ye are a chosen generation, a royal priesthood,
an holy nation, a peculiar people; that ye should shew forth the
praises' – His glory, if you like, His excellencies –'of him who
hath called you out of darkness into his marvellous light' [*1 Peter*
2 : 9]. What was true of them becomes true of us. That is why
these things are so important for us. And, furthermore, 'Israelites'! We have entered into this. We are in the commonwealth, we
become God's children. 'Adoption'! 'And the glory'! We get to
know God. We are no longer 'without God in the world'. We get to
know Him, and if we take advantage of what is offered to us we
will know something about this 'glory' – manifestations of God
to the soul! We ask God in our hymns, 'Manifest Thyself to me',
and there are manifestations promised. Our Lord, you remember,
in John chapter 14 says that He is going to give them 'another
Comforter' and He says of those who love Him, 'I will manifest
myself to him.' He says, 'My Father will love him and we' – the
Father and the Son – 'will come unto him and make our abode
with him' [*John* 14 : 16, 21, 23].

'The glory'! Not the glory of our position only, but a knowledge
of the glory, some glimpse into it, some understanding of it, some
experience of it, some realization of it. Very well, says the
Apostle, the glory had been manifested to these people and yet in
spite of all these great and high privileges which had been theirs,
here they are rejecting their Saviour, their Messiah, and in their
blindness turning their backs upon so great and so glorious a
salvation.

Five

*

Who are Israelites; to whom pertaineth the adoption, and the glory, and the covenants, and the giving of the law, and the service of God, and the promises; whose are the fathers, and of whom as concerning the flesh Christ came, who is over all, God blessed for ever. Amen.

Romans 9 : 4–5

In our consideration of these two important verses we come now to the word 'covenants'.

This is one of the terms which I had in mind when I said in an earlier study that unless we are familiar with their meaning, and understand something of them there must indeed be whole sections of the Old Testament and the New Testament which convey nothing at all to us, because this word 'covenant' is a word that is used in both the Old and the New. In Ephesians 2 Paul says in verses 11 and 12, 'Wherefore remember, that ye being in time past Gentiles in the flesh, who are called Uncircumcision by that which is called the Circumcision in the flesh made by hands; that at that time ye were without Christ, being aliens from the commonwealth of Israel, and strangers from the *covenants of promise'*. Now that is the very term that we are considering. The Apostle is making the same point there as he is here, because he wants the Ephesians to realize the greatness of the privilege of being Christians.

So what is it? Well, the thing that Paul puts first is that when those of us who are born Gentiles become Christians we begin to share in the blessings of the 'covenants' that God made with His ancient people. So we cannot understand much of the New Testament unless we understand this term. There is a great benediction in Hebrews 13 which runs, 'Now the God of peace, that brought again from the dead our Lord Jesus, that great shepherd of the sheep, through the blood of the everlasting covenant, make you perfect in every good work to do his will . . .' What does the writer mean by 'covenant' there? You will find also the term used in Hebrews 9, and again in Galatians 3 verses 15 and 17, and I give you these verses in order to show you the importance of going into the meaning of these terms in detail. It is not merely that we are interested in Romans chapter 9 verses 4 and 5. If you study any one part of Scripture thoroughly it will help you with every other part; but here is one of these key words which is really quite essential to a true understanding of the biblical doctrine of salvation.

So the question is, What exactly does the term mean? Let me first answer that negatively in the form of a quotation from Professor William Barclay of Glasgow, who is a popular writer, even sometimes, I am amazed to find, amongst people who call themselves evangelical. This is how, in his commentary on the Epistle to the Romans, Professor William Barclay defines a covenant here in this verse. He says, 'A covenant is a relationship entered into between two people. It is a bargain for mutual profit, an engagement for mutual friendship' – and that is all he tells us about it here. And therefore, of course, he obviously suggests that that is true of the covenants that we are reading about here; they were a bargain or an engagement, which constituted a relationship that was entered into between God and the children of Israel. He is not alone, of course, in that kind of idea. But that is the exact opposite of the true meaning of covenant! It is not a contract between two people who meet together and strike a bargain, one putting up his side, the other putting up his side, and eventually they arrive at an agreement with each side stipulating its conditions. It is not something that must be thought of in terms of a bilateral agreement.

Of course, what Professor William Barclay says about covenants as made between men is perfectly acceptable. But we are dealing here with covenants between God and man, and he does not draw any distinction; he makes no difference. When you talk about 'covenant' as it is used in the Bible, to say that it is the same as two people arriving at an agreement is not only an inadequate conception, it is an utterly false conception and entirely wrong.

What, then, is a covenant? Well, a covenant in the Bible is a sovereign act of God's grace in which He pledges Himself to do something. There is not a single instance or illustration in the Bible of God meeting with the people and, as the result of a kind of bargaining discussion, God and the people agreeing for their mutual benefit to do certain things. Covenant in the Bible is always something that is entirely and solely and only from God's side. God, moved by nothing in us at all, but entirely by His own grace and His own eternal love comes to the people and He says, 'I am going to do so and so and I pledge Myself that I will do it.' In the famous instance of the covenant with Abraham He confirmed it, as we are reminded in Hebrews 6 : 13–20, 'by an oath: that by two immutable things, in which it was impossible for God to lie, we might have a strong consolation, who have fled for refuge to lay hold upon the hope set before us'.

That is the biblical notion of a covenant. We must get rid of this idea of a bargain; it is quite false. It is entirely God's sovereign act; it is altogether from Him, and it is in no sense dependent upon us. We put in no terms or conditions. It is true and right to say that a part of God's covenant is that it imposes certain obligations on us. But that is a very different matter. God comes and He makes His statement to the children of Israel. He says, 'I am going to choose you and do this, that and the other to you. Therefore because I am going to do this, this is what I expect from you.' That is not a bargain; it is God imposing the terms! And that is the whole biblical notion of a covenant.

When Paul says here that the covenants pertained to these Israelites, these kinsmen of his according to the flesh, he is saying that God chose Israel and pledged Himself to her in this sense, that she was to be the nation which He was going to use as a channel to bring His great salvation to the human race. That is the essence of the covenant that God made with the children of Israel. Notice also that Paul puts it in the plural – 'the covenants' – and he does that because the covenant that God made with this nation was repeated several times, as we shall see.

Now we must be clear about this. It is not that God made a covenant and then for some reason or another put it on one side, or revoked it and then made another one. There are notes in certain Bibles which tend to teach that, but they are quite wrong. We must not think that each covenant or each renewal of the covenant was something fresh which had not existed before. There is only one real covenant, but God repeats it and in each repetition He puts emphasis upon a particular aspect. It is all in the original one. So it is the one great covenant reiterated and repeated and emphasized for the sake of clarity and particularly for the sake of calling forth a certain response from the people.

So, then, that being our definition, let us look at some of the main statements of this covenant that we have in the Old Testament. The Apostle regards this as something which was of the greatest importance and significance. It is a part of the whole tragedy of the Jews, because it was with them that God had made this great covenant. Now we shall not go back to the third chapter of Genesis as we might do if we were dealing with covenants in a more general form. We shall deal, instead, with the specific part which the Apostle has in his mind here. The first quotation is in Genesis 6 verse 18; this is Noah and the covenant made with him before the Flood, when the whole world is going to be destroyed: 'With thee will I establish my covenant; and thou shalt come into the ark, thou, and thy sons, and thy wife, and thy sons' wives with thee.'

But then let us look at the covenant after the Flood: 'And God spake unto Noah, and to his sons with him, saying, And I, behold, I establish my covenant with you, and with your seed after you; and with every living creature that is with you, of the fowl, of the cattle, and of every beast of the earth with you . . .' [*Genesis* 9 : 8–11]. Then in verses 12–15: 'And God said, This is the token of the covenant which I make between me and you and every living creature that is with you, for perpetual generations: I do set my bow in the cloud, and it shall be for a token of a covenant between me and the earth. And it shall come to pass, when I bring a cloud over the earth, that the bow shall be seen in the cloud: and I will remember my covenant, which is between me and you and every living creature of all flesh; and the waters shall no more become a flood to destroy all flesh . . .' Then God says in verse 16: 'And I will look upon it, that I may remember the everlasting covenant between God and every living creature of all flesh that is upon the earth. And God said unto Noah, This is the token of the covenant, which I have established between me and all flesh that is upon the earth.' That is a most important illustration of this idea of covenant.

[55]

But it is the covenant made with Abraham that is the significant one and the one that is so constantly repeated. It was more or less general in Noah's case, of course. His son Shem, in particular, was selected as the one through whom the covenant should be carried out. But you really come to what may be called the true history of Israel in the matter of the covenant that was made with Abraham, and my first quotation here is in Genesis 15 : 18: 'In the same day the Lord made a covenant with Abram, saying, Unto thy seed have I given this land, from the river of Egypt unto the great river, the river Euphrates: the Kenites, and the Kenizzites, and the Kadmonites, and the Hittites, and the Perizzites, and the Rephaims, and the Amorites, and the Canaanites, and the Girgashites, and the Jebusites.'

Now that is the first part of the covenant made with Abraham, and it refers, you notice, to the land. But in Genesis 17 there is a further and most important statement beginning at the first verse: 'And when Abram was ninety years old and nine, the Lord appeared to Abram, and said unto him, I am the Almighty God; walk before me, and be thou perfect. And I will make my covenant between me and thee, and will multiply thee exceedingly. And Abram fell on his face: and God talked with him, saying, As for me, behold, my covenant is with thee, and thou shalt be a father of many nations. Neither shall thy name any more be called Abram, but thy name shall be Abraham; for a father of many nations have I made thee. And I will make thee exceeding fruitful, and I will make nations of thee, and kings shall come out of thee. And I will establish my covenant between me and thee and thy seed after thee in their generations for an everlasting covenant, to be a God unto thee, and to thy seed after thee. And I will give unto thee, and to thy seed after thee, the land wherein thou art a stranger, all the land of Canaan, for an everlasting possession; and I will be their God . . .'

You see there the characteristics of the covenant: 'When Abram was ninety years old and nine, the Lord appeared to Abram, and said unto him . . .' This whole notion of a bargain and negotiation is entirely wrong; the movement is entirely from God's side. Abraham stumbles; he cannot understand it, but God just tells him. It is altogether of grace; it is the sovereign act of God. And the other indication of the covenant with

Abraham is in Genesis 22 : 15–18: 'And the angel of the Lord called unto Abraham out of heaven the second time. And said, By myself have I sworn, saith the Lord, for because thou hast done this thing, and hast not withheld thy son, thine only son' – this is after the incident of the offering of Isaac on Mount Moriah – 'that in blessing I will bless thee, and in multiplying I will multiply thy seed as the stars of the heaven, and as the sand which is upon the sea shore; and thy seed shall possess the gate of his enemies; and in thy seed shall all the nations of the earth be blessed; because thou hast obeyed my voice.' Now that is absolutely crucial, and we have already seen how the Apostle makes use of it in Romans chapter 4 verses 16–17.[1]

Then this covenant with Abraham was repeated to Isaac and to Jacob, and the essence of it is that it is out of the loins of Abraham, from the seed of Abraham, that a Saviour is to appear. Here is the great promise of salvation. Abraham is to be turned into a nation, kings will come out of him, and through this one nation that comes from him all the nations of the earth are going to be blessed. This is crucial and it has all the characteristics of the covenant as I have described it to you. It was confirmed to Isaac and to Jacob and you find that stated in Exodus 2 : 24–25. There were the children of Israel down in the bondage, the captivity of Egypt, 'And God heard their groaning, and God remembered his covenant with Abraham, with Isaac, and with Jacob. And God looked upon the children of Israel, and God had respect unto them.'

We come next to the covenant as given and as renewed and elaborated to Moses, the so-called Mosaic covenant, though, as we shall see, it is the same fundamental covenant. We have already read it in Exodus 2 : 24–25 but then we need to go on to Exodus 3 : 16–17. It is clear why it was renewed at this point. The children of Israel were now about to begin a new chapter in their whole history; they were to be taken out of Egypt and its bondage, and they were to be taken to their promised land, the land of Canaan, the land flowing with milk and honey. And God, to reassure them, to remind them of His purpose in bringing them out, repeated His covenant. He emphasized certain particular aspects; so, in Exodus 3 : 16–17, we read, 'Go,

---

[1]See *Romans: An Exposition of Chapters 3:20–4:25: Atonement and Justification*, 1970.

and gather the elders of Israel together, and say unto them, The Lord God of your fathers, the God of Abraham, of Isaac, and of Jacob, appeared unto me, saying, I have surely visited you, and seen that which is done to you in Egypt: and I have said, I will bring you up out of the affliction of Egypt unto the land of the Canaanites . . . unto a land flowing with milk and honey.' It was because of His covenant He did that, and then He told them what He was going to do with them. He opened their eyes to this new chapter and at the same time He reminded them, of course, of their obligations in the light of that.

But, finally, consider Exodus 6 : 2–7: 'And God spake unto Moses, and said unto him, I am the LORD: and I appeared unto Abraham, unto Isaac, and unto Jacob, by the name of God Almighty, but by my name JEHOVAH was I not known to them. And I have also established my covenant with them, to give them the land of Canaan, the land of their pilgrimage, wherein they were strangers. And I have also heard the groaning of the children of Israel, whom the Egyptians keep in bondage; and I have remembered my covenant. Wherefore say unto the children of Israel, I am the LORD, and I will bring you out from under the burdens of the Egyptians, and I will rid you out of their bondage, and I will redeem you with a stretched out arm, and with great judgments: and I will take you to me for a people, and I will be to you a God: and ye shall know that I am the LORD your God, which bringeth you out from under the burdens of the Egyptians.'

It is still the same covenant, you see. God keeps on saying it: 'This is the covenant I made with your fathers' – it is the same covenant, but now I am renewing it and taking you into this new phase, and you have got to realize that. And so He gave them the Ten Commandments and said, Now realize that you are My people, I am holy; therefore be ye holy. And that is a phrase that is constantly repeated in the whole of the Scriptures. But it is the same fundamental covenant as He had already made with Abraham.

It is just here, however, that some people and some of these notes on the Bible tend to go a little astray; they seem to think that this was something absolutely new, that God is, as it were, putting on one side His covenant with Abraham and is making a new covenant, a covenant of works, a covenant of law. That, of course, was the whole misunderstanding of the children of Israel, that was why they were rejecting Christ. And it is tragic, therefore, that certain people should still be making the same mistake and repeating the old error.

We must be quite clear about this. Read the Apostle's argument in Galatians 3 : 16: 'Now to Abraham and his seed were the promises made. He saith not, And to seeds, as of many; but as of one, And to thy seed, which is Christ. And this I say, that the covenant, that was confirmed before of God in Christ, the law, which was four hundred and thirty years after' – given, you remember, through Moses – 'cannot disannul, that it should make the promise of none effect. For if the inheritance be of the law, it is no more of promise: but God gave it to Abraham by promise. Wherefore then serveth the law? It was added because of transgressions, till the seed should come to whom the promise was made; and it was ordained by angels in the hand of a mediator.'

Now the whole point of that passage is just this. Paul is arguing that the fundamental covenant is that which God had made with Abraham, and that the covenant repeated through Moses was not doing away with the first one, it was bringing out this aspect of law because the people needed it. They had forgotten, and they were going into the new land, so the legal emphasis was brought in, not that they might have a new covenant of law and save themselves by law, but that they might be reminded of who they were in terms of the original promise which was made through Abraham. So, as Paul says, this addition of the law did not abrogate the promise; it simply shut them in, as it were, to understanding it in a still better way than they did before. The same covenant repeated but with a fresh emphasis to meet fresh conditions and circumstances!

And that brings us to the last great covenant of the Old Testament, and the one undoubtedly in the mind of the Apostle also at this point, which is the covenant made with David, and you will find this in 2 Samuel 7 : 8–17, where this covenant, repeated and emphasized in a new way again to David, is laid out before us. God is here giving instructions to the prophet Nathan as to what he is to say to David: 'Now therefore so shalt thou say unto my servant David, Thus saith the Lord of hosts, I took thee from the sheepcote, from following the sheep, to be ruler over

my people, over Israel: and I was with thee whithersoever thou
wentest, and have cut off all thine enemies out of thy sight, and
have made thee a great name, like unto the name of the great
men that are in the earth. Moreover I will appoint a place for my
people Israel, and will plant them, that they may dwell in a place
of their own, and move no more; neither shall the children of
wickedness afflict them any more, as beforetime, and as since
the time that I commanded judges to be over my people Israel,
and have caused thee to rest from all thine enemies. Also the
Lord telleth thee that he will make thee an house.' It is the same
great covenant, remember, but now something special is to
happen through the house of David – only one house in this
great family of Abraham: 'And when thy days be fulfilled, and
thou shalt sleep with thy fathers, I will set up thy seed after thee,
which shall proceed out of thy bowels, and I will establish his
kingdom. He shall build an house for my name, and I will
stablish the throne of his kingdom for ever. I will be his father,
and he shall be my son. If he commit iniquity, I will chasten him
with the rod of men, and with the stripes of the children of men:
but my mercy shall not depart away from him, as I took it from
Saul, whom I put away before thee. And thine house and thy
kingdom shall be established for ever before thee: thy throne
shall be established for ever. According to all these words, and
according to all this vision, so did Nathan speak unto David.'

Now this passage again is most significant. It tells us
something that we have not been told as clearly before, which is
that out of this seed of Abraham, now through the seed of David
in particular, the Messiah is to come, the One who is going to be
a king and who is going to rule over all. He is going to be this
great ruler. You see it is the same covenant but with the
emphasis put on this aspect.

That is the whole secret of understanding this matter of
the covenants and I do trust that as we have looked at all this
in such detail you can see the importance of going into these
matters. You see how the Old Testament history is involved. A
Christian who does not know his Old Testament is – forgive
the expression – just a fool. You need your Old Testament;
you cannot understand the New without it. We have just
been reading from one of the historical books in the Old Testament and we must know these things, because how can we

understand what we are going to read at the beginning of the Gospel according to Luke, unless we know something about 2 Samuel 7?

So then, turn to Luke 1 : 30. Here is the great angel Gabriel addressing Mary: 'And the angel said unto her, Fear not, Mary: for thou hast found favour with God. And, behold, thou shalt conceive in thy womb, and bring forth a son, and shalt call his name JESUS. He shall be great, and shall be called the Son of the Highest: and the Lord God shall give unto him the throne of his father David: and he shall reign over the house of Jacob for ever; and of his kingdom there shall be no end.' You see, it is a repetition of the covenant as it was given to David; the promise is safe; here is the One who is to carry this on, and there will be no end to His kingdom.

But also in that first chapter of Luke we read the statement made by Zacharias. You remember he has been punished by dumbness for a number of months because of his unbelief; but now the child, John the Baptist, has been born and his tongue is loosed, and old Zacharias begins to speak, and this is what he says: 'Blessed be the Lord God of Israel; for he hath visited and redeemed his people, and hath raised up an horn of salvation for us in the house of his servant David; as he spake by the mouth of his holy prophets, which have been since the world began: that we should be saved from our enemies, and from the hand of all that hate us; to perform the mercy promised to our fathers, and to remember his holy covenant; the oath which he sware to our father Abraham, that he would grant unto us, that we being delivered out of the hand of our enemies might serve him without fear, in holiness and righteousness before him, all the days of our life. And thou, child, shalt be called the prophet of the Highest: for thou shalt go before the face of the Lord to prepare his ways; to give knowledge of salvation unto his people by the remission of their sins, through the tender mercy of our God . . .'

So there is that glorious statement which people read and recite especially at Christmas-time. But I wonder whether they realize what they are saying; do they really get the glory and the thrill of it all? We have taken time with this because I want you to enjoy these things. We use these glorious phrases but do we know their meaning? Can you not see what it is? This man is rejoicing; he says in effect, 'What God has been promising for centuries has come; the covenant which He made, His holy covenant, here it is now being brought to ultimate fruition. Here is the One long promised, promised indeed back in the garden of Eden itself in Genesis 3 : 15 – the seed of the woman that should bruise the serpent's head – and now He has arrived!' And so when you come to consider the importance of the Davidic covenant – or the renewal of the covenant to David – you see its significance.

Now there are people who think that the hallmark of spirituality is to say, 'I am of course a person who reads only the four Gospels, I like to keep to the Lord Jesus. I do not like the Epistles so much, and of course I do not know much about the Old Testament.' But they say that in their folly and ignorance. What do they make of these expressions in the Gospels when they read about 'the seed of David'? What do they think made that poor blind man shout out and cry, saying, 'Son of David, have mercy upon me'? Why did he call Him that? Why does the Gospel according to Matthew start off as it does at the very beginning, 'The book of the generation of Jesus Christ, the son of David, the son of Abraham'? Why pick out David and Abraham? And remember the angels; what do they say? 'Unto you is born this day in the city of David a Saviour, which is Christ the Lord.' No, you cannot understand the Gospels unless you are familiar with the meaning of these terms.

Oh, the importance of knowing something about the covenants! You see, dear Christian people, the Apostle here is referring to these covenants made in time past to their forefathers, but now we have been brought into them! There was a time when as Gentiles we were all outside. This is what happens when we become Christians; we are brought into this, and the God who has carried out His ancient covenants is still the same God and He has pledged Himself; His character is behind it, His sovereignty is behind it. We have seen all that at the end of chapter 8: nothing 'shall be able to separate us from the love of God, which is in Christ Jesus our Lord'. That is it!

Then, finally, let us deal briefly with the next thing which Paul mentions – 'the giving of the law'. What does this mean? Now here again we must be careful. There are some people who think that it means the possession of the law; that they were

the people who had had the law given to them; it was not given
to the Gentile nations. That is perfectly true, of course. But the
Apostle goes out of his way to say 'the giving of the law', and
that is a right translation. This word translated 'giving' is a word
that is found only here in the whole of the New Testament. It
was an old word and the Apostle deliberately chose it. If he
meant to say that to them 'pertained' the law, he would have
said so, but he chose this word, because he obviously wanted to
emphasize the 'giving' of the law, not the possession of it; it was
not that they were the custodians of the law.

As we have seen, the actual law itself came under the
covenant as repeated and as re-emphasized through Moses; but
what Paul is concerned to emphasize here is the way in which
the law was given to them. Why is this? Well, because that was
one of the occasions on which, as it were, God came near to
these people with an audible voice. In other words, what the
Apostle is trying to tell them is that they do not realize their
privileges. They have been elevated to this position; God has
actually spoken to them with a voice that could be heard. It is
described in the nineteenth chapter of Exodus, but a summary of
it is to be found in Deuteronomy 4 : 32–36. Here is Moses
speaking: 'For ask now of the days that are past, which were
before thee, since the day that God created man upon the earth,
and ask from the one side of heaven unto the other, whether
there hath been any such thing as this great thing is, or hath
been heard like it? Did ever people hear the voice of God
speaking out of the midst of the fire, as thou hast heard, and live?
Or hath God assayed to go and take him a nation from the midst
of another nation, by temptations, by signs, and by wonders, and
by war, and by a mighty hand, and by a stretched out arm, and by
great terrors, according to all that the Lord your God did for you
in Egypt before your eyes? Unto thee it was shewed, that thou
mightest know that the Lord he is God; there is none else beside
him. Out of heaven he made thee to hear his voice, that he might
instruct thee: and upon earth he shewed thee his great fire; and
thou heardest his words out of the midst of the fire.'

Now that is more than sufficient to justify our exposition of
this term. It is the way in which God gave the law that the
Apostle is remembering. Oh, the receiving of the law is a
marvellous thing; it is a part of the covenant, but remember the

way in which He gave it! Listen to this tremendous challenge: 'Did ever people hear the voice of God speaking out of the midst of the fire, as thou hast heard, and live?' this has never happened before. This is the only people that has ever existed to whom God has spoken with an audible voice, and He did it when He gave them the law, and so it is not surprising that you get a reference made to this in Hebrews 12 : 18–21.

So, then, this is a part of the Apostle's argument and in all these statements he is simply concerned to do this one thing – to show that these people are absolutely unique in every respect. But the thing that is common to all the respects is that God has made Himself known to them and has pledged Himself to them in a way that He has never done with any other nation. We can only stand in amazement at what God did to those ancient people. And remember that it was these very people who, in spite of all this, rejected and crucified their own Messiah. 'He came unto his own, and his own received him not'.

'Let him that thinketh he standeth take heed lest he fall.'

Six

*

Who are Israelites; to whom pertaineth the adoption, and the glory, and the covenants, and the giving of the law, and the service of God, and the promises; whose are the fathers, and of whom as concerning the flesh Christ came, who is over all, God blessed for ever. Amen.

Romans 9 : 4–5

In the previous chapters we have considered some of the terms which Paul uses to show us the privileges given to the Jews, and the tragedy, therefore, of the fact that they of all people should have rejected the Lord Jesus Christ. We come now to the next of these terms, which is 'the service of God'.

Now this is the phrase which Paul uses in order to indicate how they worshipped God. We ourselves employ the term in the same way when we talk about 'a religious service', a service, as it were, which is rendered unto God. Undoubtedly the best commentary on this particular statement is found in Hebrews 9 : 1–4: 'Then verily the first covenant had also ordinances of divine service, and a worldly sanctuary. For there was a tabernacle made; the first, wherein was the candlestick, and the table, and the shewbread; which is called the sanctuary. And after the second veil, the tabernacle, which is called the Holiest of all; which had the golden censer, and the ark of the covenant overlaid round about with gold, wherein was the gold pot that had manna, and Aaron's rod that budded, and the tables of the covenant; and over it the cherubims of glory shadowing the mercy-seat; of which we cannot now speak particularly.' The writer there is giving us a summary of what he has called the 'ordinances of divine service'. What he meant is that one of the

[65]

peculiar and special privileges of these people was that God Himself had taught them how to worship Him, how to approach Him, and how to enter into His presence.

Now that had not happened with any other nation at all. All the other nations of the world, as the Apostle Paul reminded the learned Athenians – the Stoics and the Epicureans – were all seeking the Lord, 'if haply they might feel after him, and find him' [*Acts* 17 : 27]. But they did not know how to do it. They felt that over and above all their gods, Hermes, Zeus and the rest, there was still some other great power that seemed to be greater than them all. But they did not know Him; He was an 'unknown God'. They built a temple to Him, but they did not know how to approach Him; they had never had any instruction. So the Apostle says, 'Whom therefore ye ignorantly worship, him declare I unto you.' 'Ignorantly worship'! They were trying to worship Him but they were doing it in ignorance.

But the case of Israel was entirely different. They were not left in ignorance. God Himself had taught them how this service was to be rendered. That is what the Apostle is emphasizing here, and there is a great account given of it in the Old Testament. We are told how God called Moses up into the mount and gave him the most detailed instructions as to how He was to be served and worshipped. The building of a tabernacle, the measurements, the specifications of the different departments, how it was to be furnished, the colour, the type of wood – he provided instructions for them all. It is tremendously important. That is why we must never neglect a book like Leviticus, which is just an elaborate statement of the instructions that God gave to Moses in this whole matter of how He was to be worshipped; how there was to be a great high priest and various priests under him, how the Levites were to perform certain other tasks; how this building was to be moved and carried – everything that was necessary is there. Nothing was left to chance, nothing was left to their own invention or imagination.

This is all summarized for us in Hebrews 8 : 1–5: 'Now of the things which we have spoken this is the sum: We have such an high priest, who is set on the right hand of the throne of the Majesty in the heavens; a minister of the sanctuary, and of the true tabernacle, which the Lord pitched, and not man. For every high priest is ordained to offer gifts and sacrifices: wherefore it is of necessity that this man should have somewhat also to offer' – he is referring, of course, to our Lord – 'For if he were on earth, he should not be a priest, seeing that there are priests that offer gifts according to the law: who serve unto the example and shadow of heavenly things' – now this is the point – 'as Moses was admonished of God when he was about to make the tabernacle: for, See, saith he [God] that thou make all things according to the pattern shewed to thee in the mount.' So that all that was done in the erection of the tabernacle and later on of the temple was not something that came out of the mind or the imagination of Moses; everything was told him in detail. And here in Romans the Apostle is reminding us that all this was true of the children of Israel.

Now this again is very significant. There is nothing more important for every one of us than to know how to approach God, and how to enter His presence and take our petitions and prayers to Him. There is nothing higher than that; it is most wonderful, and God had given that very instruction to these people. So it is not surprising that in this list of privileges that Paul records here he puts 'and the service of God'. All that was represented by what took place in the tabernacle is summed up in these few words.

But the point that Paul keeps on making and emphasizing and which we must grasp hold of is that God has had direct dealings with this people and that He has given them the necessary knowledge and information to enable them to know His mind and His will, and to understand His way and His great plan and purpose of salvation. And that is seen most clearly in the 'service' of the tabernacle, the method of worship and of communication with God.

We must not stay with this, but this was so important that when the children of Israel in their supposed cleverness tried to deviate from it they were given a very terrible lesson. Four men, Korah, Dathan, On and Abiram, very important princes in Israel, met together one day and had a conference. They said, 'Why should this matter of going into the presence of God be confined to Moses and Aaron? Who are they? We are as good as they are! This is wrong.' They said, 'We have as much right to do these things as they have.' So they agreed about this, and persuaded the people that they were right, and there followed the so-called rebellion of Korah.

But what happened? They were punished in a terrible manner; the earth opened and they were swallowed up and disappeared. It was a terrible thing. Yes, but what they had done was a terrible thing, and that is why God punished them in that way. And you remember the method that He adopted in order to impress this upon their minds. It is recorded in Hebrews 9 : 4, where the author reminds his readers of the contents of the ark of the covenant, including 'Aaron's rod that budded'; that was the reminder of that incident. God fixed this point once and for ever in their minds by the miracle which He performed when He made Aaron's rod bud and bear blossoms upon it, in order to show that it was he, and he alone, who was the high priest, and that it was he, and he alone, who had the right to go into the presence of God as the representative of the people.

The point is this: It is God who decided and who has revealed how He is to be worshipped, not man, and they should have observed God's way instead of turning to their own inventions. And this is as important today as it was then. There is only one way into the Holiest of all; it is 'by the blood of Jesus'. There is no other. We have been taken into Israel, and God has taught us the only way whereby He can be served. 'The service of God' is something that is still determined by God Himself, and we vary it or try to add to it or modify it or ignore it or neglect it at our terrible peril. The rebellion of Korah and the punishment, and Aaron's rod that budded, should be a permanent reminder to us of that. There, then, is the meaning of 'the service of God'.

So we go on to the next item, which is 'and the promises'. What does Paul mean by this and what is the difference between the promises and the covenants? It is, surely, the difference between a general announcement of something and the details of that announcement. In the covenants, as we have seen, the great plan and purpose of salvation were revealed – how through Abraham and his seed all the nations of the earth would be blessed; it is in this way that God will do His great work of salvation. That is the essence of the covenant.

What then are the promises? Well, they have reference to the particular blessings which are going to result from this great plan and scheme of salvation. We can sum them up like this:

promises have reference to the blessings and the glories of the age of the Messiah; here you have the detailed blessings which will be given to all who belong to the Messiah and to His reign.

Now we must remember that the reign of the Messiah has already started in His people, the church. The kingdom of God has come already in that sense in the hearts of all believers; it has come in the church, though it is yet to come in a visible, external form. But the kingdom of God has already come, so that some of these promises are already fulfilled, while there are others yet to be fulfilled.

That is the meaning, then, of this term 'promises' and, of course, in the Old Testament you find an account of them in great profusion. That is why we Christian people should read the whole of our Old Testament and know it all. It is not enough just to read certain parts and portions only; we should read the whole Bible at least once every year, because you will find these promises and prophecies and adumbrations of what is true of us today, and of what is yet to come, even in the Old Testament. These are prophecies concerning the glory of the age of the Messiah; take Genesis 49 : 10, for instance. Here is Jacob, an old man, on his deathbed and he calls his family together and gives them his blessing. This is what he says concerning Judah, 'The sceptre shall not depart from Judah, nor a lawgiver from between his feet, until Shiloh come; and unto him shall the gathering of the people be.' 'Shiloh'! Here He is, the Messiah! And there is a promise concerning something of the characteristics of His age.

There are many others; we cannot consider them all, but let me give you one of the most remarkable, the story of how one of these promises came through a hireling prophet called Balaam. You will find it in Numbers 24 : 17. Balaam did not want to give the right message, but he had to do so – he could not refrain from doing it. And this is what he said: 'I shall see him, but not now: I shall behold him, but not nigh: there shall come a Star out of Jacob, and a Sceptre shall arise out of Israel, and shall smite the corners of Moab, and destroy all the children of Sheth.' There it is; Balaam, the hireling prophet, prophesying concerning something of the glory of the age of the Messiah.

Of course the book of Psalms contains a great deal of this. There are psalms specifically prophesying and predicting the coming of the Messiah: Psalm 72, for instance, and Psalm 45 – a wonderful psalm about something of the glories of the age of the Messiah, and His bride the church. You find it in the Song of Solomon, and then, of course, when you come to the prophetic books, the great prophets and the minor prophets all have this; they tell us in different ways of the blessings that are going to come under the reign of Messiah: 'the lame man shall leap as an hart', 'the blind shall see, the deaf hear'. It is all there. Isaiah 35, the end of Isaiah 53, Isaiah 55, Isaiah 60, 61 and 62 – all these are just promises of the glories of the age of the Messiah. And the Apostle Paul sums it all up in 2 Corinthians 1 : 20 when he says, 'For all the promises of God in him are yea, and in him Amen, unto the glory of God by us.'

Now here, too, the Apostle Paul is referring to all that; it is to the Jews, he says, that these promises were given. They were having a hard time, they were living a hard life, but you see God did not leave them to themselves. He not only made the covenant; He not only gave them the instruction as to how He was to be worshipped, and how they were to live and so on; He also gave them these great promises. However badly things might go, they were able to look forward to the coming age of the Messiah. It was the promises that sustained this people throughout the running centuries; but they alone had them. In Ephesians 2 : 11–12 the Apostle reminds the Gentiles, who have now become Christians, that earlier they did not have this: 'Wherefore remember, that ye being in time past Gentiles in the flesh, who are called Uncircumcision by that which is called the Circumcision in the flesh made by hands; that at that time ye were without Christ, being aliens from the commonwealth of Israel, and strangers from the covenants of promise' – Paul there has blended together the covenants and the promises. And the result was – 'having no hope, and without God in the world'. Paganism is hopeless; and paganism is as hopeless today as it was in the Old Testament days. The unbeliever, the non-Christian, is entirely without hope. He has no promise at all. He listens to the promises of men because he has not got the promises of God, and he is constantly being disappointed. But the children of God do have the promises.

And the children of Israel had these amazing promises – the golden age, the age that was to come. What a privilege! What a special people they were! Small in number, small in country, with these great nations round and about them, but they had the promises, and whatever might happen to them these held them. They saw dynasties rising and falling and they were not surprised; they knew that ultimately the promises of God would be fulfilled to them. God had given them and God had confirmed them by His oath. 'The promises'!

And the last thing Paul tells us is that they also had 'the fathers' – 'the service of God, and the promises; whose are the fathers . . .'. Now why, do you think, does Paul put that at this point particularly? Is this an anticlimax, or is he working up to a climax? Who are these 'fathers'? Well, there is no doubt that he is referring primarily to Abraham, Isaac and Jacob, and I imagine that he is also including Joseph, Moses and David. They were the particular fathers to whom the children of Israel constantly referred. And this is not surprising, because Abraham after all was the founder of the whole race. It was with Abraham that God set this process going, and it was continued in Isaac and in Jacob, in the giving of the covenant. Joseph, too, was absolutely vital in the whole story, and so were Moses and David, as we have seen.

So why does Paul single out this fact that 'the fathers' belonged to them? It is not merely that they were great men. They were that, incidentally, and great men are always to be honoured, as we find in the Scriptures. But of course it is not only that – and this is where you see the difference between the spiritual and the natural. I think the reason why Paul mentioned these men is that they had had unique experiences of God: that is why he is interested in them.

God had dealt with these people in a very intimate manner; He had not done that with everybody; He had not done that even with everybody in the nation of Israel, but these men were exceptions. Abraham was the friend of God. God came very near to him and spoke to him intimately and with Isaac and with Jacob. Read again in Genesis 28 the story of Jacob that night when he was leaving home, running away from his brother Esau, how he put his head down on that pillow of stones, and then saw the traffic of the ladder to heaven. That was God coming very near to him and speaking to him, and that is what makes these 'fathers' so exceptional.

And this is in line with everything that Paul has been saying in all the other headings. He has emphasized all along that God has dealt exceptionally closely with these people. That is the theme right through the Bible, and it is seen very clearly in the story of all these men. Take Jacob, again at Peniel, in Genesis 32, and the struggle that night, and the giving of the new name, and so on. It is all a part of this same thing. The same is true in the story of Joseph; it is particularly true in the case of Moses; and of course it is obvious in the case of a man like David. 'The fathers'! The outstanding men in the story of the nation.

This is a privilege, says the Apostle, that the Jews ought to have realized. It was through these fathers that God was speaking most distinctly about what He was going to do when He sent His Messiah. That is why he singles them out. This is true of every one of the other phrases which he uses but here it is in persons; God had made this statement in particular to these men. Even a man like Isaac comes in, because the covenant was repeated to him, and Isaac knew God in this intimate way because he was in this line – Abraham, Isaac, Jacob. That is why you find the repetition of that phrase, 'I am the God of Abraham, of Isaac, and of Jacob.' What does He mean by that? It is not simply that He was the God of these three. He says, I am the God who dealt so directly and intimately with these men. That is the emphasis. And so on, of course, with the others.

And these men, therefore, are picked out as those to whom God had granted particularly clearly the revelation of His grand and glorious purpose concerning the coming of the Messiah, the very thing these Jews were too blind to see when it happened. You see how Paul works up his argument. These men were men who had had unusual experiences with God. They were also men of great faith, men who were sensitive to the truth, and to the will of God; and all their descendants should have been the same. But they are so no longer. They are blind, they have turned a deaf ear, as he says later on: 'All day long I have stretched forth my hands unto a disobedient and gainsaying people.' That is what Israel had become. Abraham was not like that, nor were Isaac, Jacob, Joseph, Moses or David. 'You have forgotten your fathers,' Paul says to the Jews, 'these very men whose names you honour, you do not understand them.'

And so the Apostle has been going step after step and going higher as he goes along, and in the words which follow he reaches his climax: 'Whose are the fathers, and of whom as concerning the flesh Christ came, who is over all, God blessed for ever.' Here is the ultimate peak. Of all the privileges enjoyed by the Jews this was the greatest and the most wonderful of all, that the Messiah, the Saviour of the world, should have come out of them, that He should have been a Jew. These are His people, and it is out of them that He has come, 'the root of Jesse', 'seed of Abraham', 'son of David'. There is nothing higher than this, the Saviour of the world comes out of this nation. Here is the highest of all privileges, and yet this is the very thing that they have missed!

Now, of course, all the preceding things that he has mentioned really are true because they lead to this. That is the point and the purpose of all these things – Israelites! The adoption! The covenants! The giving of the law! The service of God! The promises! The fathers! Why has all this been true of them? Simply that they might be the nation out of whom the Messiah should come. That is why Abraham was called out of Ur of the Chaldees. That is why God produced a nation out of him in order that out of this nation might come this blessed Redeemer, this Messiah. The seed of the woman, promised in Genesis 3 : 15, is to be also the seed of Abraham; He is also the son of David. 'This is the whole point,' says the Apostle in effect; 'this has been made abundantly clear in the Scriptures, but these people cannot see it.'

Consider the argument in Galatians 3 : 16 for instance: 'Now to Abraham and his seed were the promises made. He saith not, And to seeds, as of many; but as of one, And to thy seed, which is Christ.' You see, these people had become so blind that they had not noticed the difference between seed and seeds. They had missed this tremendous emphasis upon the singular, 'to thy seed'. One! They had not got it. But here it is, says the Apostle, it is perfectly clear in the Scriptures, it has now happened in actual fact. It was out of you, out of the Jews as a nation, that Christ came according to the flesh.

Now that is what he says here in the first part of this great statement, and it would be good if we could just leave it at that and simply read the words, 'and of whom as concerning the

[73]

flesh Christ came, who is over all, God blessed for ever. Amen.'
But unfortunately we cannot. How tragic it is that this
magnificent statement, which ought to be enough in and of
itself, has become a matter of controversy; and so much a matter
of controversy that we must deal with it. What is the controversy? It concerns the last part of the verse – 'who is over all,
God blessed for ever. Amen.' The whole question is, To whom
does that refer? Does it refer to the Lord Jesus Christ, or is it just
a doxology addressed to God Himself? Now everybody is agreed
about the first part: 'Of whom as concerning the flesh Christ
came'. It is from there on that disagreement comes in. The
famous commentary written by Sanday and Headlam actually
says that this statement has probably been discussed at greater
length than any other single verse in the whole of the New
Testament! Why should that be? The controversy has arisen in
this way. To start with, people are in difficulties over this phrase
'over all', so let us look at that first. What does 'all' mean here? It
literally means everything. It ought not to be limited to mean
over all people, or over a certain number of people; it means over
heaven and earth, the sea, hell, everything – over all things in
the whole universe and cosmos. So the question is, To whom
does this refer? Who is 'over all, God blessed for ever'? There are
those who say that this is the Lord Jesus Christ, while others
maintain that this is God the Father

Now it is important that we should look at this, because we
live in an age when many different translations of the Bible are
sold, and people buy them in their innocence often without
realizing what they are doing. So that is one of my reasons for
calling your attention to this and for dealing with it thoroughly,
in order that we may see what these translations have to say
about this. We are also living in an age in which theologically
there is a very marked and obvious devilish tendency to detract
from the glory of the Son of God, to rob Him of His unique deity,
and to reduce Him to the level and the measure of manhood. It
started in the last century and it has been going on throughout
this century.

Furthermore, we are living in days when there are all sorts and
kinds of 'religions' propagating themselves, plausible salesmen
coming to our doorstep, selling their books to us, appearing to be
believers in the Bible, and apparently knowing the Scriptures.

And there are many innocent people, housewives in particular, who become the innocent prey and victims of these, and help to propagate their nefarious doctrines by buying the books, so swelling the coffers, and enabling them to indulge more than ever in their propaganda, simply because they do not realize the importance of knowing the truth concerning these matters.

So it is in the light of all this that it is absolutely essential that we should be clear about the exact meaning of this statement that we are considering together. Now the Authorized Version reads, '. . . and of whom as concerning the flesh Christ came, who is over all, God blessed for ever. Amen.' That is quite clear, is it not? It is talking about the Lord Jesus Christ right the way through. What about the Revised Version? It is much the same, and so is Weymouth's translation. What of the others? Well, take the New English Bible. It does not describe Christ as 'God over all, blessed for ever'. No, here is the translation: 'From them, in natural descent, sprang the Messiah. May God, supreme above all, be blessed for ever!' You see what that means? That is the Father – not the Son. There is the difference, and you can see why I am calling your attention to it. 'The New English Bible' – people say – 'wonderful, marvellous, everybody can understand it! Here is the book to buy, here is the Bible to read, none of your difficulties that you have in your Authorized Version; here it is in a language we can understand.' Exactly! That is the bait, but here's the hook – concealing, robbing the Son of God of this title and of this glory.

But how did all this come in? Well, the people who really began this were the translators of the Revised Version; they are the ones who first introduced it into this matter of translations. It started originally, of course, with that higher critical movement in theology in Germany from about 1840, but it first appeared in translations openly and popularly with the publication of the Revised Version. Because though the Revised Version translates this phrase correctly, it also puts in notes at the bottom of the page – 'alternative translations' – and it is there that this whole business began. It gave three alternative translations:

1. 'and of whom Christ came according to the flesh. He who is God over all be blessed for ever.'

2. 'and of whom Christ came according to the flesh. He who is over all is God blessed for ever.'
3. 'of whom Christ came as concerning the flesh, who is over all. God be blessed for ever.'

In other words, in this third translation, they are granting that Christ is over all but then they put the full stop, followed by 'God be blessed for ever'.

So in each one of the three possibilities, you notice, this blessedness is ascribed as a doxology to God the Father and is taken from God the Son.

Then what of the Revised Standard Version of America which has been very popular since the last war and has sold very extensively? This is how the Revised Standard Version translates it: 'and of their race, according to the flesh, is the Christ. God who is over all be blessed for ever.' It is exactly the same thing again, and also in the Moffat translation which runs: 'and theirs too (so far as natural descent goes) is the Christ. (Blessed for ever more be the God who is over all.)'

There is also another translation and I regret having to introduce this one but I am constrained to do so. It is the business of a teacher, as the Bible shows us very plainly, not to be content with giving positive information and instruction; the wise teacher is to warn people against error, and against danger and heresy. Scripture is clear about this, and a pastor who does not safeguard his flock and look after their interests and try to warn them beforehand against dangers is an hireling pastor and is unworthy of the name of pastor. The Apostle Paul, in bidding farewell to the elders of the church at Ephesus, prepares them and warns them; he says, There are men who will rise amongst yourselves, and false teachers will come in who will rob the flock; they are going to teach dangerous, damnable heresies – he uses similar language.

It is, therefore, my business to call attention to this. I referred in the last study to Dr William Barclay, Professor in the University of Glasgow and again I mention him because many evangelical people regard him as reliable. Now let me be fair to Dr Barclay. He is an expert linguist, and he is very good on the meaning of words. But you can be very good on the meaning of words and still detract from the truth. There is a difference between an expert linguist and a good theologian. There are many men who are good at the mechanics of Scripture who do not understand its teaching, and Professor Barclay is an avowed 'higher critic' of the Scriptures. He does not believe in the doctrine of the atonement as evangelicals do; he is a universalist and says that everybody will be saved. And in his commentary on the Epistle to the Romans this is how he translates this passage: 'and from them on His human side came the anointed one of God. Blessed for ever be the God who is over all. Amen.' He leaves it at that; and his meaning is perfectly plain and clear.

Let me give you one other translation, that of Professor C. H. Dodd, one-time professor of New Testament in Oxford, since then in Cambridge and again the author of a commentary on the Epistle to the Romans which has sold very popularly. How does he translate it? 'Theirs is the God who is over all blessed for ever.' Our Lord is finished with, you see! He makes a new sentence of the phrase, again carrying on this same idea. But he goes further in his commentary and attempts to give us an explanation as to why the Apostle suddenly introduced this doxology, this ascription of praise and of blessedness to God. Professor Dodd says: 'Moved by the thought of the immeasurable favour of God to His people, Paul breaks out into an ascription of praise.' So he not only translates it like that, he tries to justify his new translation.

Why is it that all these people object to the Authorized Version translation? The answer is this – again to quote Professor Dodd – 'such a direct application of the term "God" to Christ would be unique in Paul's writings; even though he ascribes to Christ functions and dignities which are consistent with nothing less than deity, yet he pointedly avoids calling Him "God".' That is the Professor's reason, and so he says that we must vary this translation.

That, then, is the problem which we are facing. Why is this important? Why should we stay with this? Why should we answer all these alternative translations? Why should we defend the Authorized Version's translation and how do we do so? We shall answer those questions in our next study.

May God have mercy upon us all, and may God especially in these times give to His people the spirit of discrimination. We are living in loose and flabby days, when people say, 'What do these things matter? We are all Christians together, let us all work together. Let us even bring Rome in, yes. What matters as long as we are all against Communism?'! We are living in that kind of climate of opinion and that atmosphere, and it seems to me that because of that some of the most precious truths are being sold, and often through sheer ignorance on the part of God's people, because they do not know and because they do not see the subtlety.

So let us go on protesting, and holding up the truth while God gives us breath and energy. Let men and women say what they will, we cannot remain silent while in various ways like this they are trying to rob our blessed Lord of some of His eternal prerogatives.

Seven

*

Who are Israelites; to whom pertaineth the adoption, and the glory, and the covenants, and the giving of the law, and the service of God, and the promises; whose are the fathers, and of whom as concerning the flesh Christ came, who is over all, God blessed for ever. Amen.

Romans 9 : 4–5

We have been considering the argument put forward for the new translations which turn the last part of verse 5 into a doxology addressed to God instead of being a description of the Lord Jesus Christ. We have seen that we must face this because so many of God's people today are being misled and misguided by various false religions and cults, that we really cannot afford to be uncertain with regard to this matter. How, then, do we deal with this argument?

My first answer is that it is very interesting to observe that these people who would refuse to ascribe those words to the Lord Jesus Christ, and who ascribe them only to God as a doxology, do not attempt to base their position on grounds of grammar. Now, much of the change in modern translations from the Authorized Version is done on such grounds – they say that because of the grammar alone, we are compelled to do this and that, and so to change the great teaching of the New Testament. But here they do not say that, for the very good reason that they cannot possibly do so. They have to fall back, therefore, on this more general statement, that this is something which the Apostle Paul does not do in his writings. So that is a general argument instead of a particular one in terms of grammar – indeed we shall find that the grammar is most certainly against them and on the side of the Authorized Version translation.

Secondly, this variation in the translation is not based either on a question of the various manuscripts of the New Testament. Commentaries often refer to those manuscripts and compare them, so it is important that we should know something about them. This is textual criticism and there is a great difference between textual criticism and what is called higher criticism. Textual criticism means that these various ancient manuscripts should be examined and compared. It is important for the purposes of translation that we should get as accurate a manuscript as is available and, beyond any question, much excellent work has been done in that direction during the past one hundred and fifty years or so.

Higher criticism, on the other hand, is the approach to the Bible which says that the Bible is only a book like any other book. It is a view that denies a unique inspiration, and that certainly denies infallibility. It says that the Bible must be approached in its historical setting and from the grammatical standpoint, and that in this way you will find that you must arrive at conclusions different from those of the men who translated the Authorized Version and different from the teaching of the church throughout the long centuries of her history.

Now I refer to all this just to indicate that here, in verse 5, the proposed variations in the translations are not based upon a matter of manuscripts. We must always pay serious attention to manuscript evidence, but here there is no such evidence, because what decides the translation here is ultimately a question of punctuation – whether you put a full stop after 'flesh', or whether you put a comma. So it has nothing to do with the manuscripts, because the punctuation of the Scriptures did not come in until the third century. The oldest manuscripts of all have no punctuation, so that nobody can say, 'It must be translated like this because that is how it was done in the earliest manuscripts.' The moment, therefore, you have this punctuation, you are already in the realm of the opinion of some particular person.

It is important then that we should see that the argument for these modern translations is not at all a question of 'scholarship'. How over-awed we are by 'scholarship'! But grammatical literary criticism does not come in here, nor, especially, does textual criticism because there is no evidence from that line at all. So it cannot be justified in those terms.

Now lest somebody should think that I am merely giving my own opinion here let me quote from some great authorities. Here is what the commentary written by Sanday and Headlam says – and neither of these men was an evangelical Christian – 'It may be convenient to point out at once that the question is one of interpretation and not of criticism.' Now that is a statement by two great authorities on the whole matter of criticism, so that we are in the happy position that we cannot be over-awed and frightened by the words 'scholarship' or 'criticism'. They do not apply here. So those who would dispute the Authorized Version translation have to fall back upon this general statement, that it is not the custom of the Apostle to describe our Lord as God.

So we can now come to the particular arguments. Why should we contend for this Authorized Version translation? Well, looking at it superficially and generally, one reason is that it would be quite unnatural to introduce a sudden doxology to God at this point because there is nothing that leads up to it and nothing that calls for it. The Apostle is expressing his sense of sorrow and so on, and he is referring here to the Lord Jesus Christ. So that there is nothing that indicates any reason for suddenly uttering a doxology to God.

'But', somebody may say, 'does he not do that very thing in the first chapter in verse 25, where we read, "Who changed the truth of God into a lie, and worshipped and served the creature more than the Creator, who is blessed for ever. Amen"?' But that is not a parallel, because in Romans 1 verse 25 the Apostle is referring to God the Father – the Creator. And having referred to the Creator he says, 'who is blessed for ever.' He is not changing from one person to another, so that that does not make any difference whatsoever to our argument. That, therefore, is the first reason, especially coupled with the fact that the Apostle here, because of the very subject with which he is dealing, is obviously not in a state or mood which would suddenly cause him to burst forth into a doxology to God the Father.

Then secondly – and here we are dealing with grammar – look at this word 'who': '. . . of whom as concerning the flesh Christ came, *who* is over all . . .'. Or, if you take the other way of translating it, 'of whom Christ came according to the flesh, who is over all, God blessed for ever'. Now 'who' means, 'the one who'. And, surely, by all rules of grammar which indicate that a relative pronoun should always refer to the nearest antecedent, then this 'who' clearly refers to the Lord Jesus Christ; He is the nearest antecedent. The Apostle is writing and talking about Him, and when he says 'who' you naturally take it to mean the same person; the One who as concerning the flesh came from these people. That is the One to whom he is referring and about whom he is now going to say certain further things.

This is something that is done very commonly in the Scripture. Let me give you one illustration of it to show the value of the argument. You find it in John 1 : 18: 'No man hath seen God at any time; the only begotten Son, *who* [translated here "which"] is [or who exists] in the bosom of the Father, he hath declared him.' The One who is in the bosom of the Father is the One about whom he has been speaking, so the 'who' is referring to the nearest antecedent, and the nearest antecedent is the Son. And here in Romans, it is exactly the same: 'of whom Christ came according to the flesh, *who* is over all'. That is the grammatically reasonable way of considering this, and before you reject that there must be some very powerful reason.

Then we add to that a third argument, and this is a very important one. The Apostle in the first part of the statement tells us something about the Lord Jesus Christ: 'of whom as concerning the flesh Christ came'. So you would expect that if he has put emphasis upon 'according to the flesh' or 'concerning the flesh' then he has a contrast in his mind – what is the other side of Christ? Christ has two natures in one person; so then Paul goes on to complete it – 'concerning the flesh' He has come of the children of Israel, but on the other hand he is God over all, God blessed for ever. Now this is not only a natural parallel here to complete a balanced statement; it is of course an exact repetition of what we find the Apostle saying about Him at the very beginning of the Epistle in chapter 1. Here are the first four verses: 'Paul, a servant of Jesus Christ, called to be an apostle, separated unto the gospel of God, (which he had promised afore by his prophets in the holy scriptures,) concerning his Son Jesus Christ our Lord.' Then he speaks of Christ like this – 'which was made of the seed of David according to the flesh; and declared to be the Son of God with power, according to the spirit of holiness, by the resurrection from the dead'. You see, he starts off like that. He is anxious that we should know that in this blessed Person there are these two natures. He is truly man, but He is also truly God. There is something which is true of Him 'according to the flesh', there is something which is true of Him 'according to the spirit'. And here in Romans 9 you have a repetition of exactly the same parallel, the two sides of the same statement; the antithesis – 'flesh', 'spirit'; natural, human, divine, eternal, spiritual. It seems to me that that in itself really ought to have been quite sufficient without going any further at all. When Paul puts his emphasis on 'concerning the flesh', you say, 'Now then, there must be something also "concerning the spirit".' You expect it and it is here.

Then the fourth argument, again, is a very interesting one. Notice the relative position of the words 'God' and 'blessed'. 'Christ came, who is over all, God blessed for ever. Amen.' What is the significance of the relative position of these two words? Well, in doxologies, the order of the words is the exact opposite of what it is here! This is a typical doxology – 'Blessed be the God and Father of our Lord Jesus Christ.' The 'blessed' comes first, 'God' follows it. Charles Hodge went into this matter very thoroughly and others have done the same. Charles Hodge says that there is no exception to that order in the Greek or the Hebrew Scriptures. But here it is, 'God blessed' – there is only one doubtful exception to that rule and that is in Psalm 68 verse 19 – and even there the authorities tend to agree that it is not a doxology at all but a simple affirmation.

This is a very important and interesting point. There was a man called Socinus who lived in the period of the sixteenth century. Socinus was a Unitarian; in other words, he did not believe in the Trinity or in the deity of the Lord Jesus Christ. He was, indeed, the man who popularized Unitarianism, so much so that those who hold his views are sometimes referred to as Socinians. Now the Trinitarian position is that we believe in 'God in Three Persons, blessed Trinity': God the Father, God the Son, God the Holy Spirit, co-equal, co-eternal! But Socinus was a Unitarian so why am I so interested in him? Because this argument about the relative positions of the 'blessed' and 'God' – 'God blessed' instead of 'Blessed be God' – that argument convinced even Socinus that the Apostle Paul in this statement was clearly referring to the Lord Jesus Christ.

Now that is a very powerful argument. If even Socinus had to admit that, how much more should his followers admit it? But they do not, they are not as consistent as Socinus, and not as honest perhaps. But it would seem to me that in itself this argument again is enough, almost, to persuade us that this is not in any way a doxology but a declaration concerning the Lord Jesus Christ.

So far, we have been dealing with this point purely in terms of grammar and syntax; but what about the other argument, that the Apostle never refers to the Lord Jesus Christ as God, and that that teaching only comes later? It is said, also, that it is not customary to describe our Lord as 'over all' because He was subservient to the Father and submitted Himself to the Father's will; and that the whole tenor of the teaching in the New Testament is that the Son is subordinate to the Father, and the Spirit subordinate to the Son and to the Father. What of this argument?

Well, there is a great deal to be said in reply to this contention also. The first is that the Apostle Paul very frequently does describe the Lord Jesus Christ as the Head of all creation. Take, for instance, 1 Corinthians 11 : 3: 'But I would have you know, that the head of every man is Christ; and the head of the woman is the man; and the head of Christ is God.' There Paul reminds us that simply for the purposes of our salvation the blessed Holy Trinity has divided up the work between them. We often describe this as the 'economic Trinity'. But in 1 Corinthians 11 the Lord Jesus Christ is described as 'the head of every man'. That is the important point there.

Then we find exactly the same thing in 1 Corinthians 15 : 28: 'And when all things shall be subdued unto him, then shall the Son also himself be subject unto him that put all things under him, that God may be all in all.' Again the two ideas come in, but the point is, that Paul is teaching there that everything is put under Him. You also have the same in Philippians 2 : 5–11 especially in verses 10 and 11: 'That at the name of Jesus every knee should bow, of things in heaven, and things in earth, and things under the earth; and that every tongue should confess that Jesus Christ is Lord [Jehovah], to the glory of God the Father.'

The same truth exactly is found in Colossians 1 : 15–17: 'Who is the image of the invisible God, the firstborn of every creature: for by him were all things created, that are in heaven, and that are in earth, visible and invisible, whether they be thrones, or dominions, or principalities, or powers: all things were created by him, and for him: and he is before all things, and by him all things consist.' There is a perfectly clear, plain and explicit statement of the fact that He is 'over all', and it is characteristic of New Testament teaching.

Not only that; there is a second argument under this heading. Take the term which is used with respect to Him which describes Him as 'the image of God'. Now that term is used to describe an identity and it is chosen quite specifically in order to bring out that notion. We use that language in our ordinary parlance, do we not? When we say, 'He is the living image of his father', we mean that he is exactly like him. Now that is the kind of language that is used here in the Scripture. Let me give you some illustrations of this. In 2 Corinthians 4 : 4, for instance, we read, 'In whom the god of this world hath blinded the minds of them which believe not, lest the light of the glorious gospel of Christ, who is the image of God, should shine unto them.' It was also there in Colossians 1 verse 15: 'Who is the image of the invisible God.'

Then take again that tremendous statement from Philippians 2 : 6: 'Who, being in the form of God, thought it not robbery to be equal with God'. This means that in this equality with God which was true of Him, He did not consider it to be a prize to be clutched at and held on to at all costs. No, instead, He made Himself of no reputation. But the statement is, that He was equal with God. It means nothing else, and it is a very powerful argument. Notice the terms: 'form of God' and 'equal with God'.

Notice, too, the statement in Colossians 2 : 9: 'For in him dwelleth all the fulness of the Godhead bodily'. You cannot get anything beyond that. Hebrews 1 : 3 says the same thing: 'Who being the brightness of his glory, and the express image of his person'. Again you get the notion associated with it, that the Son is the 'heir of all things, by whom also he made the worlds', and who upholds 'all things by the word of his power'. There, then, are terms which should satisfy us that here there are expressions used with respect to Him which clearly indicate that He is God, that He is equal with God; the same form, the same appearance as God. There is only one meaning to these statements.

And then we come to that other argument which says that actually in practice the Apostle Paul does not refer to Him as God directly and explicitly. We are told that this only happens in the writings of the Fathers who came later in the second century. The reply to that argument is that you find in the New Testament that terms are used interchangeably with respect to the Father and to the Son and to the Holy Spirit. Now there are people who would have us believe that the one term is only used of the Father, that 'God' always means the Father, and that the term 'Lord' always means the Lord Jesus Christ. But this is wrong.

Take for instance what Paul writes in 1 Corinthians 3 : 5–6: 'Who then is Paul, and who is Apollos, but ministers by whom ye believed, even as the Lord gave to every man? I have planted, Apollos watered; but God gave the increase.' Now 'Lord' there refers to God the Father and not to the Lord Jesus Christ. Then there is a famous example in 2 Corinthians 3 : 16 and 17, where we read, 'Nevertheless when it shall turn to the Lord, the vail shall be taken away. Now the Lord is that Spirit: and where the Spirit of the Lord is, there is liberty.' There can be no doubt that there we have this term used with respect to the Spirit. Paul is not saying that the Lord Jesus Christ *is* the Holy Spirit. We must not be rigid in this. The terms are used interchangeably.

There is also another important example in Acts 4 : 29; here are the members of the early church gathered together after Peter and John have been set free. They go back and report to their own company and they begin to pray to God, and this is how they pray – starting at verse 24: 'Lord, thou art God, who hast made heaven, and earth, and the sea, and all that in them is' – they are praying to God the Father. And then they go on and quote the second Psalm: 'The kings of the earth stood up, and the rulers were gathered together against the Lord, and against his Christ' – 'the Lord' refers to God the Father – 'For of a truth against thy holy child Jesus, whom thou hast anointed, both Herod, and Pontius Pilate, with the Gentiles, and the people of Israel, were gathered together, for to do whatsoever thy hand and thy counsel determined before to be done. And now, Lord', –

they are not praying to the Lord Jesus Christ, they are still praying to the Father – 'now, Lord, behold their threatenings: and grant unto thy servants, that with all boldness they may speak thy word.' I quote all this to show you that the terms are used interchangeably.

Then let me give you a final illustration from Acts 5 : 3 and 4: 'But Peter said, Ananias, why hath Satan filled thine heart to lie to the Holy Ghost, and to keep back part of the price of the land? Whiles it remained, was it not thine own? and after it was sold, was it not in thine own power? why hast thou conceived this thing in thine heart? thou hast not lied unto men, but unto God.' The Holy Ghost is God. You see, the terms are used interchangeably of the Three, exactly, surely, as we would expect, as the Three are co-equal and co-eternal. So though normally the terms are different they are interchangeable, and it is, therefore, unjustifiable to try to introduce any kind of rigidity into this matter.

Now it is perfectly true that at the beginning and quite naturally, the Jews were somewhat hesitant about this. Even Jewish Christians were hesitant to refer to the Lord Jesus Christ as God. They had been brought up under their strict monotheism; they were almost afraid to mention the name 'Jehovah', and here was someone standing before them as a man in the flesh, and one can well understand their hesitation about calling him 'God'. But we have evidence to show that even at the very beginning they already began to do so, and I want to give you some illustrations of this also. And, of course, as we have seen, by the beginning of the second century, they commonly referred to Him as God.

But now let me give you the evidence that is to be found even in the Gospels. Take for instance what we have in Matthew 1 : 23: 'Behold, a virgin shall be with child, and shall bring forth a son, and they shall call his name Emmanuel, which being interpreted is, God with us.' There it is surely plain enough. The Son is 'Emmanuel', and that means, 'God with us'. In the Prologue of John's Gospel the same thing is quite clear: 'In the beginning was the Word, and the Word was with God, and the Word was God. The same was in the beginning with God. All things were made by him; and without him was not anything made that was made' [*John* 1 : 1–3]. There it is, surely as plain as anything could be. Then again in John 20 : 27–28 we read the confession of Thomas. The Lord said to him, 'Reach hither thy finger, and behold my hands; and reach hither thy hand, and thrust it into my side: and be not faithless, but believing. And Thomas answered and said unto him, My Lord and my God.' Now this is all before Paul began to write, and here are Jews who do not hesitate to refer to Him as God!

But again in Acts 20 : 28, we read, 'Take heed therefore unto yourselves, and to all the flock, over which the Holy Ghost hath made you overseers, to feed the church of God, which he hath purchased with his own blood.' That is a reference to the Lord Jesus Christ. It is He who has purchased the church with His own blood. And then in Titus 1 : 3 Paul says, 'But hath in due times manifested his word through preaching, which is committed unto me according to the commandment of God our Saviour' –'God our Saviour'! – and he goes on to say in chapter 2 verses 13 and 14, 'Looking for that blessed hope, and the glorious appearing of the great God and our Saviour Jesus Christ; who gave himself for us.' So the Apostle does refer to Him as God, and you have the same thing by implication in other places also, such as Philippians 2 verses 5 to 8, and 2 Thessalonians 1 : 12.

And our last answer is that doxologies are addressed to the Lord Jesus Christ! In 2 Timothy 4 : 18 we read, 'And the Lord shall deliver me from every evil work, and will preserve me unto his heavenly kingdom: to whom be glory for ever and ever. Amen.' That is the Lord Jesus Christ. Or 2 Peter 3 verse 18: 'But grow in grace, and in the knowledge of our Lord and Saviour Jesus Christ. To him be glory both now and for ever. Amen.' That, too, is a doxology ascribed to Him. And in Revelation 5 : 13 we find: 'And every creature which is in heaven, and on the earth, and under the earth, and such as are in the sea, and all that are in them, heard I saying, Blessing, and honour, and glory, and power, be unto him that sitteth upon the throne, and unto the Lamb for ever and ever.' The same exactly is ascribed to the Son as is ascribed unto the Father. And Revelation 15 : 3 tells us, 'And they sing the song of Moses the servant of God, and the song of the Lamb, saying, Great and marvellous are thy works, Lord God Almighty; just and true are thy ways, thou King of saints'; the doxology is ascribed unto Him.

Those, then, are the important answers to the arguments that are brought against this translation that we have in the Authorized Version. So let me close this study by quoting in full the comments made on this verse by Sanday and Headlam, who as we have seen had no axe to grind, Sanday in particular. Neither of these men was by any stretch of the imagination an evangelical believer, but they were great scholars and this is their conclusion. Here you have two professors belonging to the University of Oxford, a university which is famous for its carefulness, for its balance, for its fearfulness to commit itself, rejoicing in 'the balanced mind'. So notice how careful they are! 'Throughout there has been no argument which we have felt to be quite conclusive, but the result of our investigations into the grammar of the sentence and the drift of the argument is to incline us to the belief that the words would naturally refer to Christ, unless God is so definitely a proper name that it would employ a contrast in itself: we have seen that that is not so. Even if St. Paul did not elsewhere use the word of the Christ, yet it certainly was so used at a not much later period. St. Paul's phraseology is never fixed, he had no dogmatic reason against so using it. In these circumstances, with some slight – but only slight – "hesitation"' – notice the qualification of the qualification of the qualification! – 'we adopt the first alternative and translate: "Of whom is the Christ as concerning the flesh, Who is over all God blessed for ever. Amen"!'

Then there is the testimony of history with regard to this. Almost unanimously throughout the centuries until towards the end of the last century when the higher criticism began to do its devastating work, practically everybody took these words as they are in the Authorized Version. Here are some of the names: Irenaeus, Tertullian, Origen, Cyprian, Athanasius, Chrysostom, Basil, Augustine, Jerome, Ambrose, Hilary, Luther, Erasmus, Calvin, Beza, Philippi, Tholuck, Delitzsch, Alford, Wordsworth; not to mention Charles Hodge and Robert Haldane.

Now is it not interesting that on such a flimsy basis these modern translators do not hesitate to go against what has been believed throughout the running centuries? What makes them do it? It is a theological interest alone. There is something in them that makes them jump at any opportunity of detracting from the certainty of the fact that Jesus of Nazareth was the eternal Son of God. There is no other reason. They cannot do it on grounds of grammar, or of scholarship or of textual criticism. There is only that reason left, and, therefore, we should have no hesitation in adopting this Authorized Version translation and realizing that the Apostle is saying here that the supreme privilege that was given to the nation of Israel was that out of them according to the flesh came the One who is God over all, blessed for ever, the Messiah, the Lord Jesus Christ.

Eight

*

Not as though the word of God hath taken none effect. For they are not all Israel, which are of Israel: neither, because they are the seed of Abraham, are they all children: but, In Isaac shall thy seed be called.

Romans 9 : 6–7

We start here a new subsection of Romans 9. You remember that in our general analysis of it we indicated that the first five verses constitute a subsection on their own and that here another section starts which runs on to the end of verse 13. It is at this point that the Apostle proceeds to take up the real argument; in verses 1 to 5 he has merely been introducing the subject. So, as we come to this sixth verse, we must remind ourselves of what in general that argument is; and this applies not only to these verses and to this chapter, but also to chapters 10 and 11 as well.

Paul is here dealing with an objection which was actually being brought against him and his teaching, an argument which was also being brought against the preaching of the gospel in general. It was an objection in particular to what the Apostle had just been saying at the end of chapter 8 especially from verse 28 to the end. There, you remember, in that glorious passage, he had been dealing with the final perseverance of the saints and the eternal security of the Christian believer, and he based it ultimately upon this one great thing, the purpose of God. Verse 28 reads: 'And we know that all things work together for good to them that love God, to them who are the called according to his purpose.'

The Apostle's argument was that nothing could make God

forgo His purpose, nothing could frustrate it. 'I am persuaded,' he wrote in that tremendous climax, 'that neither death, nor life, nor angels, nor principalities, nor powers, nor things present, nor things to come, nor height, nor depth, nor any other creature, shall be able to separate us from the love of God, which is in Christ Jesus our Lord' [*Romans* 8:38–39].

But immediately the objection, the difficulty, arises: That is all right, but what about the case of the Jews; are they not an immediate example of the very failure of God's purpose? Because here are people who were set in this unique position by God, and with whom, as he has been reminding us, these covenants were made; who had 'the adoption, and the glory, and the covenants, and the giving of the law, and the service of God, and the promises; Whose are the fathers, and of whom as concerning the flesh Christ came, who is over all, God blessed for ever'. But at the moment, according to this Christian preaching these people are outside, they are 'cast away', they are unbelievers. Does not this therefore prove either that God's purpose can change or else that something can frustrate it?

Now that is the point with which the Apostle proceeds to deal. It looks on the surface as if God has abandoned His own people and all the promises that He has ever made to them. The Apostle has been introducing that whole matter in the first five verses, and we have seen how he puts the case with great sympathy and with great sorrow, and how anxious he is to show that he knows all about the promises to the Jews and their privileged position.

So then what is the answer and the explanation of this? Can Paul still maintain this doctrine of his that the purpose of God never changes and that nothing can ever hinder it or frustrate it? Can he still go on saying that, in the light of the position of the Jews? It is very interesting to notice that in these verses the Apostle does not immediately describe in detail the actual position and 'casting away' of the Jews. He reserves that until he is almost finishing his argument in the eleventh chapter. This is a striking point and one from which we should all learn a great lesson. We observe again the delicacy, the sensitive nature and character of the great Apostle and his tenderness. And the lesson which we must all learn is that when we are handling a difficult matter like this, we should always do so in a manner which is calculated to win people and to persuade them. We do not start with denunciation. Our Lord in His ministry showed exactly the same care. He did not start by denouncing the Pharisees though He knew all about them; that, again, is reserved until towards the end. You will find the great denunciation of the Pharisees in chapter 23 of Matthew's Gospel, not in chapter 1 or chapter 3. In other words, state the case with tenderness, with affection, with love and with a desire to win people.

Nevertheless the Apostle makes it quite plain and clear; his great heaviness and continual sorrow really tell us everything. And it is quite enough; he does not need to bring out the ultimate truth about the Jews. He is in great heaviness, continual sorrow because of them, and because of their condition. But the point that he is concerned about is not even their case and condition, but rather how he can justify his preaching about the purpose of God. This ninth chapter, let me remind you, is a theodicy, a defence of God and a justification of His ways to men. So how does Paul do it?

It is in the sixth verse that we have the key to this particular section; indeed it is the key to the whole section right through to the end of chapter 11. It is a most important verse. 'Not as though the word of God hath taken none effect. For they are not all Israel, which are of Israel.' There, if you like, is the text. Then in verses 7 to 13 he expounds and elaborates it. That is his method. We have seen it so often, and it is the ideal method. Put down your principle, make your big statement, then demonstrate it, illustrate it and establish it, then gather it all together and wind it up again at the end.

Furthermore, verses 7 to 13 are an exposition especially of the last phrase in verse 6 in which Paul says that they are not all Israel that are of Israel. There he is giving us the true meaning of the term 'Israel', and his argument, to put it briefly, is that God's word has done, and is doing, and will do what it is meant to do. It has not failed in its purpose. The question, therefore, is, What is it meant to do? What is its purpose? And the answer is that it was only meant for the 'elect' in Israel and not for all who are in Israel. That is what he is setting out to prove and that is the reply to the contention that is brought against him. Now let us follow him as he works out his argument.

The first thing he does is to make a statement, and the statement is just a categorical assertion: 'Not as though the word of God hath taken none effect.' Now let us be clear about the translation of that. Incidentally let us observe that here he is more or less repeating what he has already said in chapter 3 verse 3. Having proved in the first two chapters, and especially in chapter 2, that the Jews were in as bad a case as were the Gentiles, he then raises the question: 'What advantage then hath the Jew? or what profit is there of circumcision? Much every way: chiefly, because that unto them were committed the oracles of God.' Then: 'For what if some did not believe? shall their unbelief make the faith of God without effect?'

And that is more or less what he is going to do again here. In chapter 3, he just threw it out, as it were, leaving it to be worked out in detail when he comes here to this ninth chapter: but it is the same essential point. And what he says is this: having described the condition of the Jew, the privileges, in verses 4 and 5, and his terrible heaviness and constant sorrow because these people are not believers and are indeed cast out, he says, 'Not as though the word of God hath taken none effect.' Or you can translate it like this: 'The case is not as though the word of God has taken no effect.' But, perhaps the most literal translation is: 'But the thing' – that is to say the state of the case – 'is not such as this.'

So then, he says, the fact that I am troubled about them does not mean that the word of God has had no effect. What does he mean here by 'the word of God'? It is important that we should be clear about this. Everywhere in the New Testament you will find that with one exception apart from this, 'the word of God' stands for the gospel. Take for instance 2 Corinthians 2 : 17: 'For we', he says, 'are not as many, which corrupt the word of God: but as of sincerity, but as of God, in the sight of God speak we in Christ.'

You have exactly the same thing in 2 Corinthians 4 : 2: 'But [we] have renounced the hidden things of dishonesty, not walking in craftiness, nor handling the word of God' – that is to say the gospel – 'deceitfully; but by manifestation of the truth commending ourselves to every man's conscience in the sight of God.' And you find the same use of it in 2 Timothy 2 : 9; Titus 2 : 5; Hebrews 13 : 7; Revelation 1 : 9; 6 : 9 – and everywhere in the book of Acts.

The only other exception in addition to the one that we have before us is Mark 7 : 13, where Christ is also dealing with the Jews and he says, 'Making the word of God of none effect through your tradition, which ye have delivered: and many such like things do ye.' Now, there, the context makes it quite plain that in that verse 'word of God' refers to the Old Testament Scriptures and does not mean the gospel.

And here, quite clearly, 'the word of God' at this point means the declared purpose of God; whether it be promise or threat or decree, or whatever it is; that is, the word of God – something that God has stated and proposed to do. It includes the covenants, the promises and all these other things that we have been looking at together. So that when he says here, 'Not as though the word of God hath taken none effect', he is not saying that the gospel has had no effect. What he is arguing about here is this great purpose of God which he started dealing with in the twenty-eighth verse of the eighth chapter.

Furthermore, when he says, 'none effect', he is using a striking word. It means, 'It has not fallen to the ground or been ineffective or ineffectual.' And what is again interesting is the tense which he uses – 'hath taken.' He uses the perfect tense, which means, 'Not as though the word of God has failed in the past or is now failing.' The particular tense that the Apostle uses quite deliberately is a tense that carries a double meaning in it – it includes the past and the present.

So then this is the Apostle's great fundamental statement and proposition. But let us be clear about it, and here again is a very valuable point for us to observe as we in turn are put to it, by modern detractors or those who come to us asking questions, to defend the truth of God. Paul is not saying that the word of God cannot fail, but that it has not failed. Why do I take the trouble to point that out? I do so for this reason: If somebody tackled us along these lines and said, 'You say that this purpose of God is absolutely sure; you quote Toplady and say that nothing "can make Him His purpose forego, or sever my soul from His love"; how do you prove that?' – what would be our answer? Well, the tendency of so many of us would be to fall back at once upon the sovereignty of God and say, 'Because God is God it cannot fail.' But that is not what the Apostle is actually saying. He believes that, of course, but he is not saying it here. He is going to prove it in another way, in a very much stronger way, especially in view of the fact that he is dealing with and arguing with Jews. So the lesson, therefore, I would suggest, is that we should always try to answer the people who are putting the question. If you are dealing with a Jew, as the Apostle is primarily doing here, then try to give it in a form or to use an argument which will be particularly effective with Jews. Of course, this was Paul's method. He preached like that and he did everything like that – 'Unto the Jews I became as a Jew ... to them that are without law, as without law ... I am made all things to all men, that I might by all means save some' [*1 Corinthians* 9:20–22]. So he does not just fall back on the general argument of the sovereignty of God; he meets them on their own ground, and takes that ground from beneath their feet. He does believe in the absolute sovereignty of God, and that is a final answer; but in addition to that he works it out in this way. The state and the condition of the Jews, he is going to show them, does not imply any change whatsoever, still less any failure, with respect to God's eternal purpose.

So how is he going to do this? Well, immediately, he puts it all in a nutshell: 'Not as though the word of God hath taken none effect. For they are not all Israel, which are of Israel.' There, then, is the fundamental proposition. Now a more literal way of translating it, perhaps, would be something like this: 'Not all those who are out of Israel as a source, these are Israel, the true Israel,' or 'Not all those who are out of Israel, these are Israel.' So that the Authorized translation here is quite a good one and really does convey the meaning.

Here then is a crucial and fundamental statement. Paul said it before at the end of chapter 2 in verses 28 and 29, where we read: 'For he is not a Jew, which is one outwardly; neither is that circumcision, which is outward in the flesh: but he is a Jew, which is one inwardly; and circumcision is that of the heart, in the spirit, and not in the letter; whose praise is not of men, but of God.' It is the same point exactly. Let us try to learn from this man how to conduct an argument. There was no need to say more at that juncture; he was just dealing with this one great point of justification. So he asserted it as a truth but he did not elaborate it. It is here he is going to elaborate it, where he deals with this whole question of the Jew.

In the same way he has hinted at it in chapter 4, verses 11 to 13, where he is dealing with the whole question of Abraham, a case that he took up from the standpoint of justification: 'And he received the sign of circumcision, a seal of the righteousness of the faith which he had yet being uncircumcised: that he might be the father of all them that believe, though they be not circumcised; that righteousness might be imputed unto them also: and the father of circumcision to them who are not of the circumcision only, but who also walk in the steps of that faith of our father Abraham, which he had being yet uncircumcised. For the promise, that he should be the heir of the world, was not to Abraham, or to his seed, through the law, but through the righteousness of faith.' Again it is essentially the same point, but it is now that he is really going to give it a very thorough and exhaustive treatment.

Now why do I say that this is such a vital and all-important statement? Well, I do not hesitate to assert that if we want to understand Old Testament history properly, then in many ways this is one of the most crucial statements in the whole of the Scriptures. It is so easy to get lost in that history and to fail to understand it exactly. We see God choosing one and not another, and in genealogical tables we find one line being worked out while others, which have been mentioned, are dropped and we hear no more about them. Now all this can be very confusing, and here is the key to the understanding of it.

It is also the key to the understanding of the chequered history of the children of Israel; their constant disobedience, their constant complaining and grumbling to God; here is the explanation of why eventually they found themselves in the captivity of Babylon. It was all due to the fact that they kept on assuming that because they were the children of Israel nothing could go wrong with them and that God must always bless them. So that when He did not, they could not understand it, and they suggested that God was going back on His promises. It was all because they did not realize that 'they are not all Israel, which are of Israel'.

But it is also a vital principle in the understanding of the four Gospels in the New Testament. Have you ever noticed the amount of time and space that is given in the Gospels to the various arguments and wranglings in which our Lord had to be involved with the Jews – the Pharisees and scribes and Sadducees and doctors of the law? People have often complained

about them. 'Why can we not have the simple teaching?' they
say, 'Why can we not have the direct message? Why must we
have all this about the Jews and their questions and their
opposition; what is it all about?' People do not understand it and
that is because they do not understand this principle. The key to
the understanding of all the attitude of the Jews, especially their
religious leaders, to our Lord Himself, is to be found in this
phrase: 'They are not all Israel, which are of Israel.'

The first man to make this point, of course, was John the
Baptist. He was the forerunner, the first preacher; and this is
how he puts it. Here he is, out in the wilderness, preaching a
baptism of repentance for the remission of sins, and the people
come crowding out from all parts to listen to him, and this is
what we find him saying. He faces a congregation of Pharisees
and scribes and all sorts of people, and he says to them, 'Bring
forth therefore fruits worthy of repentance, and begin not to say
within yourselves, We have Abraham to our father: for I say
unto you, That God is able of these stones to raise up children
unto Abraham' [*Luke* 3 : 8]. You see, John with his spiritual
insight knew their attitude, their mentality and their whole
outlook. He knew that they were saying in their hearts, 'Why do
you call us to repentance? We are the children of Abraham; go
and preach that, if you like, to Gentiles but not to us.' And his
response to them, in effect, is this: 'I know that you are children
of Abraham, I know that you are Israelites – but "they are not all
Israel, which are of Israel".'

And then there is another illustration of it in John chapter 8
where our Lord puts it very explicitly; indeed He has to do this
because of what the people say to Him. He has been preaching,
and we are told, in verse 30, that 'As he spake these words, many
believed on him. Then said Jesus to those Jews which believed
on him, If ye continue in my word, then are ye my disciples
indeed; and ye shall know the truth, and the truth shall make
you free.'

But instead of thanking Him and thanking God, this is their
response: 'They answered him, We be Abraham's seed, and were
never in bondage to any man: how sayest thou, Ye shall be made
free?' So He answers them, and among the things He says to
them is this statement in verse 37: 'I know that ye are
Abraham's seed; but ye seek to kill me, because my word hath

no place in you.' And then we read further, 'They answered and said unto him, Abraham is our father. Jesus saith unto them, If ye were Abraham's children, ye would do the works of Abraham. But now ye seek to kill me, a man that hath told you the truth, which I have heard of God: this did not Abraham.' 'I know that ye are Abraham's seed' – and then at the same time, 'If ye were Abraham's children, ye would do the works of Abraham'; all that, too, is just another way of saying, 'They are not all Israel, which are of Israel.' So it is essential to an understanding of all the disputation and misunderstanding that takes place right through the pages of the four Gospels.

In exactly the same way it is the key to the understanding of what we read in Acts about the treatment that was meted out to the Apostles as they went around preaching the gospel – the trouble they had when they eventually had to leave the Jews and go to the Gentiles. The problem was that the Jews, at the time of our Lord and the time of the Apostles, were making the same fatal assumption that they had made right through the Old Testament. They were assuming that the mere fact that they were Jews and descendants of Abraham saved them in and of itself. They thought that they needed no new salvation; they had no need to believe on Jesus of Nazareth as the Son of God, the One who had to die for them; they were already saved! Hence the fury of the Pharisees when He convinced them of sin and promised them that He would set them free. That is the whole explanation. They said, 'We are the children of Israel and you must not speak to us like that.' It is still the trouble with Pharisees, whether they be Jews or Gentiles. It is the cause of the 'offence of the cross'; it is why such people always get annoyed. It is what makes them say, 'This man preaches to us as if we were sinners!' while, for various reasons, they do not think they are sinners. So we must realize how important this verse is.

Then, in the fourth place, this great principle laid down here by the Apostle is absolutely essential to the whole doctrine of salvation. Now this is where it becomes very urgent and practical for us, and that is why I am elaborating it in this way. Somebody may say, 'What has all this got to do with me? All right, it may have been a wonderful argument with respect to the Jews at that time but where is its relevance to me?' Let me try to show you. Here is the key to two questions. First: How is the salvation that has been worked out by the Lord Jesus Christ applied to anybody? Secondly: To whom is that salvation applied?

Let me subdivide that second one by asking four further questions. First: Is there such a thing as a Christian country? Does the fact that you are born and brought up in a country that is called Christian mean that you are a Christian; whereas people born and brought up in what are called pagan countries are not? Do we believe that? Many people do, and that is what this principle deals with.

Secondly: Are the children of Christian parents of necessity Christians? There are many who believe that they are, and that there are promises to this effect; and some would maintain that this is why these children should be baptized – because they are already Christians. People have argued that in the past and are still doing so.

Thirdly: Are baptized children of necessity Christians because they have been baptized? The Jew argued that anybody who had been circumcised was therefore an Israelite and therefore saved. And there are people who still say that every child that is baptized is of necessity a Christian. That issue is raised here; these people have all been circumcised, but 'they are not all Israel, which are of Israel'.

And so the fourth question is this: Are all who have been baptized, whether as children or as adults, and are all who are church members, of necessity Christians?

Those are the questions and they are very important and relevant. I was reading recently an article by an evangelical writer in which he referred to the many people in this country today, who never darken the doors of a place of worship but who were baptized when they were infants, as 'lapsed Christians'. 'Lapsed Christians'! They have no interest in Christianity at all, they never go near a place of worship, and they say they do not believe in it; but because they were baptized when they were infants they are described in that way. So this is a tremendous question, and a most urgent one at this very time. I am putting it in its modern form now, but it is exactly the same principle as the Apostle is laying down here.

So how does he deal with it? In this way: He shows that the important thing to concentrate on is the meaning of the term

'Israel', and so he says the following things. The term 'Israel' has two meanings or connotations, a general one and a particular one – 'all Israel', 'Israel'; external, internal; physical Israel and spiritual Israel. That is Paul's first point. The whole confusion has arisen, he says, and people say that God's purpose has gone astray or that it has fallen to the ground, simply because they have not understood the meaning of the term 'Israel'.

So, secondly, Paul says that there are two Israels; one is the nation as a whole; the other is those who are the true spiritual descendants of Jacob, the first Israel, and the true heirs of the promises made to Abraham, Isaac and Jacob, as we have already seen.

Thirdly, all belong to the former, to the general, to the external, to the physical, but only some belong to the latter. All the children of Israel belong to the physical nation, they are all in physical descent from Abraham. But they are not all included in this second meaning, this special, internal, spiritual meaning. This is a most important point. All are in the first, but only some are in the second.

Fourthly, God's purpose and promises, says Paul, have reference only to the second group, to this inner Israel, this special, spiritual Israel – not to the Israel according to the flesh. That is the real scope of the promises and the purpose of God.

So the Apostle arrives at his fifth and final deduction which is this: the promises of God have never failed with regard to the true Israel, and they never will. 'Not as though the word of God hath taken none effect. For they are not all Israel, which are of Israel.' God's promises were never meant to apply to the generality who are merely of Israel. They were meant for this peculiar group only, and they never will fail.

Let us, then, apply this to the four questions that I put to you earlier.

1. Is there such a thing as a Christian country? The answer is, No.
2. Are children of Christian parents of necessity Christians? The answer is, No.
3. Are baptized children of necessity Christians? The answer is, No.
4. Are all who are baptized, whether children or adults, and all who are church members of necessity Christians? The answer is, No.

Why? Because there is this essential and vital distinction which the Protestant Reformers rediscovered in the Scriptures and re-emphasized as over against the Roman Catholic Church and her teaching: the distinction between the visible and the invisible church. All belong to the visible church, but all do not belong to the invisible church. That is the distinction. All are not Israel, which are of Israel. All who belong to the visible external, organized church are not of necessity in the church of God and truly members of the body of Christ.

Therefore, we must realize that our whole position as Christians depends, in many senses, upon this – not only with regard to the case of the Jews at that particular time nearly two thousand years ago, and not merely in its precise relevance with regard to the argument about the purpose of God. There are many who go to a place of worship regularly every Sunday and hear the gospel, but they have never believed it, and it is generally because they have never seen that they need it, and they resent it. It is because they have not realized this truth. There are many relying upon birth, upon baptism at any age; there are many relying on parentage, there are many relying upon church membership. Here once and for ever the principle is laid down that ought to disabuse our minds of all such error: 'They are not all Israel, which are of Israel.'

And, thank God, the Apostle goes on to show us the difference between the two, and what it really means to belong to the true Israel of God, and in whose case the purpose of God is operating, and in whose case alone the purpose was ever designed and meant to operate. The word of God has not fallen to the ground. Let us be clear as to what it was meant to do, and the moment we are clear about that, we shall see that it has done it, it is doing it, and always will do it to the glory of God the Father.

Nine

*

Not as though the word of God hath taken none effect. For they are not all Israel, which are of Israel: neither, because they are the seed of Abraham, are they all children: but, In Isaac shall thy seed be called. That is, They which are the children of the flesh, these are not the children of God: but the children of the promise are counted for the seed. For this is the word of promise, At this time will I come, and Sara shall have a son.

Romans 9 : 6–9

We are here beginning to deal with the Apostle's great argument in reply to the objection that is brought against the gospel particularly by the Jews. He has made his great proposition, that 'they are not all Israel, which are of Israel', and now immediately he goes on to show that this is a fact which can be clearly demonstrated in the history of the children of Israel themselves. Now this is very important. He does not merely lay down a proposition, he says that this can be proved from the very history of those who object to this teaching of the gospel.

This, of course, is a masterstroke. Paul uses the *ad hominem* argument which really cannot be refuted. It is a particularly powerful argument, as we shall see, to use to Jews, because he meets them on their own ground and shows how the things in which they boast so much are the very things that prove the wrongness of this criticism which they bring to the Christian gospel. He does it like this. He takes up two instances which prove his whole point and which are of particular value when you are dealing with Jews. The first, in verses 7 to 9, deals with the case of Abraham and his two sons, Ishmael and Isaac. And then from verse 10 to verse 13 he takes up the second case of

Isaac and his two children, Esau and Jacob. So let us consider the first case, in verses 7, 8 and 9.

Paul begins by using the general covenant name 'Israel'. They were known as the children of *Israel*, but, of course, the story of these people goes back beyond Jacob. He was the man who was given the name of Israel, but before that the covenant was actually made with Abraham, Jacob's grandfather. The covenant made with Abraham was repeated to Isaac and repeated to Jacob but Abraham was the real father of the nation and it is with him that the whole story really begins. So that is why you have these frequent references to Abraham.

The prophets make use of this argument; as we saw in our last study, our Lord Himself made use of the same argument; and we saw, too, that the Jews themselves were ever ready to describe themselves as 'children of Abraham'. The Jews revered the name of Abraham, so that anything that can be demonstrated in the case of Abraham is a powerful argument that not only meets them on their own ground, it meets them on one of their most tender points.

Now the Apostle has already done this selfsame thing in chapter 4.[1] There, he takes up this whole case of Abraham. 'What shall we say then that Abraham our father, as pertaining to the flesh, hath found?' [*Romans* 4:1]. Having given his great argument about justification in chapters 1, 2 and 3, he then asks how all this applies to Abraham, because if the Jews could show that it did not apply to him, then the whole argument as far as they were concerned would be useless. But Paul is able to turn the tables on them and to show that if there is any one case in which the whole doctrine of justification is seen more clearly than any other it is in the case of Abraham. 'Abraham believed God, and it was counted unto him for righteousness' [*Romans* 4:3]. He is the supreme illustration of justification by faith only. So Paul has used the argument of Abraham early in the Epistle and he is doing the same thing again, knowing full well what a powerful argument it will be.

'The point that I am making,' says Paul in effect, 'that "they are not all Israel, which are of Israel", is shown very strikingly in the case of Abraham himself.' As all Jews knew perfectly

[1] See *Romans: An Exposition of Chapters 3:20–4:25: Atonement and Justification*, 1970.

well, Abraham had two sons; the elder of the two was called Ishmael, and then there was the second son whose name was Isaac. 'Here, then, is the case', continues the Apostle, 'that I want to put before you. So far as "natural" descent was concerned there was no difference at all between the two sons. Ishmael was as much the son of Abraham as was Isaac, and yet, the whole point is that a division was made immediately, that Ishmael and his descendants formed one group, while Isaac and his descendants formed another. And what is so perfectly clear', says Paul, 'is that this whole matter of God's promise and covenant comes down the line of Isaac only, not through the line of Ishmael, though Ishmael is by nature, by natural physical descent, as much a child of Abraham as is Isaac.' That is the statement in verse 7: 'Neither, because they are the seed of Abraham, are they all children: but, In Isaac shall thy seed be called.'

Let us work out the Apostle's argument. The first thing he points out is that there are two meanings to the word 'seed'. You notice that he repeats it twice: 'Neither, because they are the seed of Abraham, are they all children: but, In Isaac shall thy seed be called.' Now it is obvious that 'seed' does not mean exactly the same thing in both instances, but it is the same word, not only in the English translation but also in the Greek. Yet obviously there is a difference, and we can put it like this. The first use of the word 'seed' is in a natural sense, meaning a descendant after the flesh, as any child of any father is the seed of that father.

But in the second use of this word in this verse, it is clearly something different. Here, it is used only in the sense of one through whom the covenant that God made with Abraham will be carried on. It is, God says, in Isaac that your seed continues in the matter of this 'promise', this 'covenant', this special relationship. Isaac and Ishmael are both natural seed, but it is only Isaac who is seed in this sense. In other words, there is a natural seed and there is a spiritual seed. Though you call them both the seed of Abraham there is that essential difference. It is exactly parallel with saying, 'They are not all Israel, which are of Israel.' All are 'of Israel', but only some are true Israel. This is Paul's first point – the double use of the word 'seed'.

But then, in exactly the same way, he points out that there are two meanings also to the word 'children'. 'Neither, because they are the seed of Abraham, are they all children.' Now Isaac and

Ishmael were obviously both children of Abraham, but Paul says that they are not both children. There is a common, a general, natural use of the word 'children', which just means that they are descended from the same father. But there is also a particular and a special meaning, a spiritual and a covenant meaning to this word 'children' and in this sense it is Isaac alone who is a child. In this special sense, in this matter of the promise and the covenant, only some are children.

Then there is a very interesting statement at the end of this verse. 'Neither, because they are the seed of Abraham, are they all children: but, In Isaac shall thy seed be *called*.' Now this word 'called' helps us. This is the word that God spoke to Abraham when he was in trouble over this whole matter of sending Ishmael away. You will find the account of that in Genesis 21 : 10–12. Sarah had seen Ishmael 'mocking', and Sarah was jealous: 'Wherefore she said unto Abraham, Cast out this bondwoman' – Ishmael's mother, Hagar – 'and her son: for the son of this bondwoman shall not be heir with my son, even with Isaac. And the thing was very grievous in Abraham's sight because of his son [Ishmael]. And God said unto Abraham, Let it not be grievous in thy sight because of the lad, and because of thy bondwoman; in all that Sarah hath said unto thee, hearken unto her voice; for in Isaac shall thy seed be called.' Now when God puts it like that He is saying in effect, 'The seed in this matter of the promise that I have made to you – in what I have told you is going to happen through you, of how nations and kings will come out of you – all that is in terms of Isaac; "In Isaac shall thy seed be called."'

But what is the meaning of the word 'called'? Well, I think you will find that the majority of commentators want to regard this as just 'reckoned' or 'counted'. They say that it means to bear a name or a title; and the name comes down by inheritance from father to son, the eldest son. He is the heir, and it is 'reckoned' to him as the one who is called by the name or the title. Sanday and Headlam, for instance, make a great point of this and show that 'called' in Romans 9 : 7 does not mean the same as it does in verse 11, where we read, 'For the children being not yet born, neither having done any good or evil, that the purpose of God according to election might stand, not of works, but of him that calleth.' They say that there, obviously, it means election and choice and so on, but that here in verse 7 it means simply that in Isaac shall thy seed be 'counted' or 'regarded'. It is a question of a name or a title and it just means 'designated'.

Well now, if you look up these words you will find that the same word is used in verse 7 as in verse 11, and, as the authorities say, very rightly, it is a word that can be used in one of two senses. It can mean 'reckoned' or 'called' and no more. But I suggest to you that we must look at the other possible meaning in the Greek, and that is the word 'vocation'. Not designation, but vocation; something including designation but going beyond it. And I want to put in a plea for this second use of the word, because it is stronger than merely reckoning or designating; and my reason for doing this is what we have already found in chapter 4. What makes me feel that this is so important is that there the Apostle is dealing with precisely the same matter as here. He is dealing with this whole case of Abraham, so he says in verses 16 and 17, 'Therefore it is of faith, that it might be by grace; to the end the promise might be sure to all the seed; not to that only which is of the law, but to that also which is of the faith of Abraham; who is the father of us all, (as it is written, I have made thee a father of many nations,) before him whom he believed, even God, who quickeneth the dead, and calleth those things which be not as though they were.'

The meaning of the word 'called' here is not merely designation or reckoning, it really means 'call into being'. God calls into being those things which are not, as though they were. In other words He is the Creator. He speaks of things which are non-existent as if they were existent. That is His way of showing that He is going to bring them into existence. In other words He is going to 'call' them into existence.

We must not make too much of this but at the very minimum we must take the two meanings into consideration. It is not merely the name that is going to be carried on by Isaac and his seed; there is more than that: 'In Isaac shall thy seed be *called into being*.' In other words it will be produced through Isaac and not through Ishmael. We need to make this point even at this stage, because what follows really only has true meaning as we attach this particular sense of vocation to the word 'called' here at the end of verse 7. So if you like you can put it like this: 'In Isaac shall thy seed be brought into being and reckoned and named.'

Let me give you two arguments for saying this. The next verse supports this contention. 'That is,' Paul says, expounding what he has been saying, 'They which are the children of the flesh, these are not the children of God: but the children of the promise are counted for the seed.' Now then, that is 'reckoned' or 'counted'. But there the Apostle uses a different word. That is not the word that he uses in verses 7 and 11. He uses the word in both 7 and 11 which has this extra idea of 'calling into being'. That is not present at all in verse 8, as we shall see. It is rightly here translated as 'counted'. So that is one argument.

But then, in addition to that, verse 9, it seems to me, also supports this contention: 'For this is the word of promise, At this time will I come, and Sara shall have a son', and when we come to expound that, I think you will see the force of that verse. So we are arguing that verses 8 and 9, when properly taken, support the contention that 'called' at the end of verse 7 really means 'produced', 'called into being by God'. So then, the point that is emphasized in verse 7 is that it is God's choice and calling that matters; it is God who determines in which of the two – Ishmael and Isaac – the seed is to be carried on, and the great purpose is to be brought to pass.

There is no difficulty at all about this, is there? The story itself makes the thing abundantly plain and clear. It was not Abraham's choice, we have absolute evidence of that. Abraham was most unhappy about it all, and we are told that twice over, lest anybody might think that it was his choice. We can see that in Genesis 17. When God makes the announcement that a child is to be born of Sarah, we read in verse 18, 'Abraham said unto God, O that Ishmael might live before thee!' Ishmael was obviously a favourite of Abraham for some reason. But, 'God said, Sarah thy wife shall bear thee a son indeed; and thou shalt call his name Isaac: and I will establish my covenant with him for an everlasting covenant, and with his seed after him. And as for Ishmael, I have heard thee' – and He tells Abraham the lesser blessing that is going to be given to him. But Abraham, if he had had his way, would have seen to it that this great blessing and the promise and the covenant should have come down not through Isaac but through Ishmael.

And strangely enough the whole thing is repeated in Genesis 21 verses 9 to 13, as we have seen. At the banishment of Ishmael and Hagar, Abraham was very unhappy because of his son, and God had to say to him, 'Let it not be grievous in thy sight because of the lad . . . And also of the son of the bondwoman will I make a nation, because he is thy seed.' He is your natural seed, so I am going to make a great nation of him, but I am not going to give him this peculiar, special blessing which attaches to the covenant and all that comes from it. That blessing is to be through Isaac. He only is the seed in the special sense.

What, then, does Romans 9 : 7 establish? It establishes this: that the moment that God makes His covenant with Abraham, there is a particularizing, there is a selection, and all the seed of Abraham are not the seed or children in this special sense of being the ones that are to carry out God's purpose and in whom God's word is to be established and held firm. There is a purpose being carried out in the one; and the other, as far as that is concerned, is placed on one side. And the selection is made by God Himself. It is God who is speaking.

But let us go on. Verse 8: 'That is' – in other words Paul is going to explain what he has just been saying. 'That is' actually should read, 'This is', which means, 'This means'. He says, 'This statement, "In Isaac shall thy seed be called", means this . . .' He is going to put it explicitly, so that nobody can be in any difficulty with respect to it; he is going to open out the matter before us. He is going to make clear what he put in summary form in verse 7; he will explain the meaning of both the word 'seed' and the word 'children', and he will bring the two together. He will show us that the two things really mean the same.

And he does that by putting it now in terms of 'children'. 'That is [this means], They which are the children of the flesh, these are not the children of God.' Or putting it the other way round, which makes it more natural for us – the children of God are not merely the children of the flesh: 'but the children of the promise are counted for the seed.' Now you see what he is establishing here. There are children of the flesh, there are children of God, and what he is saying is that not all the children of the flesh are the children of God and the children of the promise.

That, says Paul, is what I meant by my statements in verse 7. When I say that they are all 'children', the important thing that matters is this – which of them is the child of God? Natural descent makes us children of Abraham – yes; but it does not make us children of God. It is 'the children of the promise [who] are counted for the seed'. They are the children of God. The children of God and the true seed, the spiritual seed, are synonymous.

Furthermore, as we saw earlier, this word 'counted' is a good translation here in verse 8. It does not mean the same as the word 'called' in verse 7; it does not carry that extra meaning of 'calling into being'. This is an interesting point. The word that was used by the Apostle for 'counted' is a numerical word, it means a numerical calculation. It means eventually therefore 'considered' – you count, as it were, out of a number, and put on one side a certain number out of your calculation. So it is very rightly translated 'counted', 'considered', 'regarded as', 'reckoned as' the children.

So that what Paul establishes in verse 8 is that the purpose, the important thing, is to be children of God. Here, he has introduced the term. He has put it generally earlier, and he has to say 'seed' and 'seed', and 'children' and 'children', and we are not quite sure what he is talking about, but here all doubt goes. What I mean by 'children' in this real sense, he says, is 'children of God', and that is also what I mean by 'seed'. He has brought the two terms together – 'children of God', that is the thing that matters.

What is it, then, that determines this? What makes me a child of God? Well, Paul says, negatively, it is not to be 'of the flesh', it is, rather, to be 'of the promise'. Now this word 'of' is important. It means 'in virtue of' or 'resulting from'. It is not the children who result from the flesh and its activities that are the children of God. No, it is those who result from the activity of 'the promise'.

Let us see, then, what he is saying. Look at it in terms of Isaac and Ishmael. Ishmael and Isaac both result from the flesh, but only Isaac results from and is brought into being by the promise. They both had the same natural father, Abraham. Ah, but the thing that matters is birth according to the promise. This, and this alone, is what makes us children of God. This means that the promise that God gave and made to Abraham concerning his seed, and the blessing that should come through the seed, does not come just as the result of natural descent, and it does not apply to all Abraham's natural progeny and descendants.

That is what Paul is setting out to prove, because the Jews argued for the opposite. They maintained that they were all descendants of Abraham, and that everything, therefore, applied to them; they were already saved. But here, the Apostle is establishing that they were not. The promise that God gave with regard to salvation, with regard to the covenant, with regard to His great purpose – the promise given to Abraham and his seed, and all the great blessing that was to come in this way – this is not a matter of natural descent. It does not work itself out along that line at all. It does not apply to all of Abraham's children, otherwise Ishmael would be in, but he is not – 'In Isaac shall thy seed be called.'

So then we are entitled to make this most important statement: the promise produces its own children! That is clearly stated in this eighth verse. The children of the promise – not the ones produced by natural descent, but the children that result from the promise – they are the ones who are counted for the seed; these are the children of God. Now this is where, to me, it gets really exciting. Have you ever noticed this, I wonder, as you have read Romans 9? Verse 9 proves what Paul says. 'For' – he is working out the argument; now here is the proposition: it is the children who are produced by the promise who are the seed, and they alone. 'For this is the word of promise'; this is the statement made in the giving of the promise. What is it? 'At this time will I come, and Sara shall have a son.'

Now here is a crucial matter. The Apostle in that statement is not making an exact quotation from the Old Testament; he is taking Genesis 18 : 10 and Genesis 18 : 14 and, as it were, conflating the two and making a resultant statement. That is something that he does quite frequently. He takes it as it was translated in the Septuagint, and he therefore is fully entitled to put it as he puts it here.

But if we are to get the full significance of this, we really must consider the statements that were made in detail in the book of Genesis about the promises that God made to Abraham. First, Genesis 17 : 21 says, 'But my covenant will I establish with Isaac, which Sarah shall bear unto thee' – note this – 'at this set time in the next year.' Here in Romans 9 : 9 we have: 'At this time will I come, and Sara shall have a son.' Then in Genesis 18 : 10 we read, 'And he said, I will certainly return unto thee according to the time of life; and, lo, Sarah thy wife shall have a son.' Verse 14: 'At the time appointed I will return unto thee, according to the time of life, and Sarah shall have a son.'

So what does this 'according to the time of life' mean? That to me is very interesting, because most people take this statement here in Romans 9 : 9 as meaning 'this time next year Sara shall have a son', and that it means no more than that. But I want to show you that it does mean more, and I do so by quoting 2 Kings 4 : 16 and 17 where we find the wonderful story of the great woman of Shunem. Elisha, you remember, used to pass by her house and she recognized that he was a 'holy man of God', so she made a little room for him on the wall where he could go and rest and meditate. Elisha was so pleased that he asked her whether there was any blessing she would like. And she said that she dwelt among her own people and did not want any gifts. Then it was discovered that what she really did want was a son because she had no children. Then we read: 'And he said, About this season, according to the time of life' – the same expression – 'thou shalt embrace a son . . . And the woman conceived, and bare a son at that season that Elisha had said unto her, according to the time of life.' It is the same expression.

What, then, does it mean? It seems to me that there is only one conclusion at which we can arrive. It means 'according to the period of gestation'. It is not simply a general reference to 'this time next year'. No. God is saying, 'Next year, according to the time of life' – after the period of gestation, nine months, have passed – 'Sarah shall have a child.' It includes that further meaning. This, of course, is not of any doctrinal importance but I think it helps the whole argument.

Now I make such a point of this because, clearly, we are here face to face with a miracle. What is a miracle? A miracle is never something that contradicts or breaks the laws of God. Many people do not believe in miracles because they say that they break the laws that God has implanted in nature. But a miracle never does that, and the whole case of the birth of Isaac is a wonderful illustration of this. 'The time of life', the normal period of gestation, still operates. But nothing would have happened if God had not acted. That is what makes it a miracle. A miracle does not break the laws of nature or dismiss them or set them aside; it acts above them and puts power into them. It uses them, but it uses them with all the power of God and therefore shortens everything and makes the impossible possible.

That, then, is the statement set out before us. Now we must examine the deductions and here we have something truly wonderful. The first deduction is that the promise was made with respect to Isaac not only before he was born but even before he was conceived in the womb. That is a very important point.

Secondly, the child Isaac was born because of the promise. The promise was not given because the child was born, but the child was born because the promise was given. That is the clear statement that is made. We must get rid of this notion that the two children are there before us and God, now looking at the two, selects this one and rejects that one. That is quite wrong.

Thirdly, Isaac is something more than the son of Abraham. He *is* the son of Abraham; Abraham produced (forgive the term) Isaac, but also, in a sense, he did not, because Isaac is really produced by the promise! He is the child of the promise, as we saw in verse 8. The children of the promise, the children resulting from and brought into being by the promise, are counted for the seed. Remember the term, 'At this time will I come'. It is God speaking. And when you take that in the light of Genesis 21 : 1 and 2 you see what it means! 'And the Lord visited Sarah as he had said' – notice the term – 'and the Lord did unto Sarah as he had spoken. For Sarah conceived, and bare Abraham a son in his old age, at the set time of which God had spoken to him.' 'At this time will I come' – yes, Paul is summarizing here, it is a kind of précis of Genesis 21.

In other words, it is God who produced Isaac in order that His promise might be carried out. And this, of course, we know full well, because the facts are given to us. Abraham was ninety-nine years old, Sarah was over ninety. The thing was impossible to them by natural generation. That is the whole wonder of it all. In one sense Abraham and Sarah produced Isaac. In another sense, they did not, because they could not. But God enabled them to do it. It is God who visited Sarah and it is God who did something to her. It is a miracle. The ordinary process is used, yes, but that could do nothing. It is God who makes it do something.

So that then our next deduction is that God elected Isaac as the seed and produced him because He had elected him. Is that clear to you? God had chosen Isaac to be the one through whom this covenant and promise were to be worked out. Because He had decided on that, He then acted and worked His miracle, and so Isaac was born of Sarah with Abraham as his father. It is the election of Isaac that comes first. The production is something that follows. He does not elect him, in other words, after he has arrived. That is the teaching.

But let us go still further. Isaac then, we can say, is really born of the Spirit. Oh, I know that in a sense he is born of the flesh, but the important thing about Isaac is that he is born of the Spirit. Do you think I am going too far? Well, let the Apostle support me, not only in Romans but in Galatians as well. In Galatians 4 : 22 we read, 'For it is written, that Abraham had two sons, the one by a bondmaid, the other by a freewoman. But he who was of the bondwoman was born after the flesh; but he of the freewoman was by promise.' The opposite to being born of the flesh is to be born of the promise. 'Which things', he says, 'are an allegory: for these are the two covenants; the one from the mount Sinai, which gendereth to bondage, which is Agar. For this Agar is mount Sinai in Arabia, and answereth to Jerusalem which now is, and is in bondage with her children. But Jerusalem which is above is free, which is the mother of us all. For it is written, Rejoice, thou barren that bearest not; break forth and cry, thou that travailest not: for the desolate hath many more children than she which hath an husband.' Then notice this: 'Now we, brethren, as Isaac was, are the children of promise. But as then he that was born after the flesh persecuted him that was born after the Spirit, even so it is now.' So there is a specific statement saying that Isaac was born after the Spirit, and not only after the flesh. He was born after the flesh, but the thing that makes him what he is, the thing that makes him the seed, is that he was born of the Spirit as well. That is the important thing to hold on to.

So that my final deduction is this: Nothing matters in this connection except the spiritual birth, and that spiritual birth is always 'of God'. It is never 'of the flesh'. The case of Isaac proves it. Abraham and Sarah, as we have seen, could not produce Isaac; it was God who produced him. He is born 'of the Spirit'. And this spiritual birth is always of God, and, as in the case of Isaac, says Paul in Galatians 4, it is always something that is determined beforehand, even before we are born. It depends upon nothing in us in any shape or form, but is entirely God's determination and

God's production. So that it is not surprising that the Apostle has already said in Galatians 1 : 15 and 16, 'But when it pleased God, who separated me from my mother's womb, and called me by his grace, to reveal his Son in me, that I might preach him among the heathen; immediately I conferred not with flesh and blood . . .'

That, then, is our exposition of this first case that the Apostle puts before us, and you see what he has established. Natural descent is not the thing that matters. The thing that matters is that we are born of the promise, born of the Spirit. God's purpose does not apply to everybody, it does not apply to all the seed of Abraham. God's purpose applies to and is worked out in only those who are 'born from above', 'born again', 'born of God'. The natural must not come in at all. The case of Ishmael and Isaac proves and establishes that once and for ever. God brought Isaac into being by His own action in order that His purpose might be carried out in him and through him. And as the Apostle argues in Galatians 1 and 4, it is the sole explanation also of anybody who is a Christian, anywhere and at all times.

So we have seen again the importance of taking every word in the Scripture. 'At that season will I come.' 'The children of promise'! Produced by the promise, born of the promise, not of the flesh. These, and these alone, are the seed.

Ten

*

*And not only this; but when Rebecca also had conceived by one,
even by our father Isaac; (for the children being not yet born,
neither having done any good or evil, that the purpose of God
according to election might stand, not of works, but of him that
calleth;) it was said unto her, The elder shall serve the younger.
As it is written, Jacob have I loved, but Esau have I hated.*

Romans 9 : 10–13

Paul's great object here, let me remind you, is to demonstrate
that the purpose of God, stated in His word, with regard to His
people has not broken down or failed in operation – 'Not as
though the word of God hath taken none effect.' There were
those who thought that the case of the Jews seemed to
contradict that, and that Paul in Romans 8 had gone too far in
emphasizing the final perseverance of the saints and the
absolute certainty of the fulfilment of God's purpose. So Paul
takes up the argument here in these verses, and his fundamental
proposition is that 'they are not all Israel, which are of Israel';
and he proves this by putting actual facts before them. We
considered the first fact of Ishmael and Isaac in our last study
and we saw that all to whom the promises apply in all ages and
generations are of necessity therefore, clearly as Isaac was,
children who are born of the Spirit. And so any believer, any
Christian, is ultimately only to be explained in terms of God's
action and God's activity and God's interference in the natural
process whereby they have become human beings. It is not the
natural, therefore, that matters, it is God's supernatural intervention in the natural.

The Apostle now continues with his argument in these

[116]

words: 'And not only this . . .'. He says that that is not his only case; he has something further to say, and here he introduces the case of the two sons of Isaac and Rebekah, Esau and Jacob. This will add to the proof that he has already given.

We need to ask at this point why he adds something further; why does he not content himself with the case of Isaac and Ishmael, which seems to prove conclusively that 'they are not all Israel, which are of Israel'? Why then add this further case? The answer, of course, is that the Apostle Paul was a master debater, and he was also the incomparable teacher. It is a part of the business of any teacher to try to forestall difficulties and problems that will arise in the minds of those who are listening to him. It is a very poor teacher who just makes a positive statement and leaves it at that. The test of a good teacher is the number of negatives he uses; and, furthermore, the number of possible objections that he deals with before people have even thought of them. And the Apostle is in a category entirely on his own, because he is supreme in both respects. He never takes any risks in these matters. He states his case, then he puts up the difficulties, the opposition, the objections, and deals with them and demolishes them. We have seen him doing that at great length already in earlier parts of the Epistle, and we saw it particularly at the end of chapter 8.

And now he is doing the same thing again. What are the difficulties or the objections that he anticipates? Well, somebody might come forward and say, 'That is all right; we know about Isaac and Ishmael, but that does not prove anything, because though they had the same father they had not the same mother, and after all Ishmael's mother, Hagar, was not an Israelite at all. She was a pagan and, furthermore, she was a servant and a slave. So that it was quite obvious that Ishmael, being the child of this pagan slave, and not in the true line of "Israel" – mother as well as father – it was obvious that he should be set aside and not chosen, and that Isaac should be chosen because he was born of Sarah who was in the same line and belonged to these special people of God. That is perfectly clear,' they would say, 'but our argument is, that all who are descended of Isaac come in the true line and most surely will be the people of God.' It was the case of the Jews that they were the descendants of Isaac as well as of Abraham; their boast was of their fathers, Abraham, Isaac, and Jacob.

So the Apostle, here in these verses, deals with this objection, and he deals with it in a manner that is complete and quite final and conclusive. And it is very interesting to notice that he does it by adopting precisely the same method as he does in the previous argument in verses 7, 8 and 9. You remember that he does three things there. He states a fact, he quotes an explicit statement of God and he deduces the doctrine. He takes up this statement of fact in dealing with the two children of Abraham. He also quotes, 'In Isaac shall thy seed be called', and also, 'At this time will I come, and Sara shall have a son.' And then he has his own doctrinal explanation, 'They which are the children of the flesh, these are not the children of God: but the children of the promise are counted for the seed.' That is the doctrine. And it is interesting to notice that he puts that in the middle.

Now he does exactly the same thing here. 'Not only this,' he says, 'but when Rebecca also had conceived by one, even by our father Isaac . . .' There is the fact. Then he gives the explicit statement of God in verses 12 and 13: 'It was said unto her, The elder shall serve the younger. As it is written, Jacob have I loved, but Esau have I hated' – two quotations of statements made by God. And then in between them, in verse 11, the Apostle presents his doctrine which he deduces from the facts and the word of God as he has put them before us.

Let us follow him then as he makes these three points here. First of all, the facts – he reminds them that Rebekah had two children. Now there were two mothers in the previous case, Sarah and Hagar. But now there is only one, Rebekah. But notice the interesting details that we are given about Rebekah in Genesis 25. We are told in verse 21: 'And Isaac intreated the Lord for his wife, because she was barren: and the Lord was intreated of him, and Rebekah his wife conceived.'

You see the parallel with the case of Sarah, who also was barren, and who was troubled by that fact. But God intervened, and she had a son called Isaac. Here is exactly the same thing. The conceiving was the result of the Lord being 'intreated' and acting by way of reply to the prayer that was offered to Him. So that we can say again of the birth of these two sons, Esau and Jacob, what we were able to say about the birth of Isaac, that it is as the result of the intervention of God.

That, then, is the general statement of how Rebekah ever had a child at all. Then Paul says, in order to bring out his point, of course, 'Rebecca also had conceived by one . . .' In the case we are considering, there was one and the same mother, but also one and the same father. He troubles to say that solely for the purpose of his argument. He might have said, 'Rebecca conceived by our father Isaac', but he wants to emphasize this 'one' because of the people's objection that there were two mothers in the first case. All right, he says, in this case there was one father for the two boys and the same mother also. 'One' in both instances is something that is emphasized.

It is another interesting point, in passing, to notice how Paul again includes himself in the argument. He is anxious to try to win these Jews if he can, so he says, 'by our father Isaac'. He was a Jew himself, so he includes himself with the Jews and there reminds them that they always prided themselves in the fact that they were not only the children of Abraham, but also of Isaac and of Jacob. The three fathers were always mentioned together, as we have seen, and that was the proud claim of the Jews. So the Apostle is anxious to state the case as pleasantly as he can, and in as appealing a manner as he can, in order that his argument will be still more effective.

But then there is another wonderful point here, which makes the case still more interesting. It is that they happened to be twins, they were in their mother's womb at the same time. In the earlier case, Ishmael had been born a number of years before Isaac, but here, in order to emphasize this fact of the unity of the natural, the fact is that they were actually in the same womb, and born from that womb of Rebekah at the same time; though, inevitably, one, Esau, was actually born just a little before the other. Nevertheless though of the twins Esau was the one who first appeared in the world, Jacob is the one through whom the seed is to be perpetuated.

Now, of course, the Apostle here has a powerful and striking case, because Esau was the father of the people who became known as the Edomites. Those who are familiar with the Old Testament will know the trouble that the Edomites constantly gave to the Jews, and, too, the attitude of the Jews towards the Edomites. They despised them and they hated them. The Apostle knows this and what he is really saying in effect to them is this: 'You see, the Edomites, who were old traditional hated enemies, were born of exactly the same father and mother as your father, Jacob.'

So he sets the facts before them in that way, and the conclusion that is implied is, of course, quite inevitable; it cannot possibly, therefore, be a matter of natural descent. There is an Israel and an Israel: 'they are not all Israel, which are of Israel', they are not all truly of Isaac who are the children or the sons of Isaac. This case of Esau and Jacob proves it quite conclusively. The Edomites and the Jews appeared as opposites though they came ultimately and originally from precisely the same father and mother, and were in that mother's womb at precisely the same time.

But then we must look at the specific statements of God that Paul quotes. Now do not ask me why it was that here in verse 11 he pushed in his doctrine in brackets! He did that sort of thing and he did it quite often. It may be a defect in style, but that is how he has done it. But in order to get this clear in our minds let us take it another way; let us look at his quotation of God's specific statements first. He reminds us first of what God said to Rebekah. Rebekah, you remember, did not understand what was happening to her, so God told her, 'Two nations are in thy womb, and two manner of people . . . and' – now this is the most striking thing of all and this is Paul's quotation – 'the elder shall serve the younger' [*Genesis* 25 : 23]. And do not lose sight of this fact, that God said that to Rebekah before the children were born.

But then the Apostle has a further quotation: 'As it is written, Jacob have I loved, but Esau have I hated.' This is added in order to give us an explanation of the first quotation, and here he is quoting from the prophet Malachi: 'The burden of the word of the Lord to Israel by Malachi. I have loved you, saith the Lord. Yet ye say, Wherein hast thou loved us? Was not Esau Jacob's brother? saith the Lord: yet I loved Jacob, and I hated Esau, and laid his mountains and his heritage waste for the dragons of the wilderness. Whereas Edom saith, We are impoverished, but we will return and build the desolate places; thus saith the Lord of hosts, They shall build, but I will throw down; and they shall call them, The border of wickedness, and, The people against whom the Lord hath indignation for ever. And your eyes shall see, and ye shall say, The Lord will be magnified from the border of Israel' [*Malachi* 1 : 1–5]. This is a particularly pregnant and pertinent quotation for the Apostle to make.

Now let us examine the terms: 'Jacob have I loved, but Esau have I hated.' It seems perfectly clear that these words must not be taken in their absolute sense, but people have often stumbled at this term 'hated'. This is surely a term that must be interpreted here in the light of what we read, for instance, in a statement made by our Lord, recorded in Luke 14 : 26. We are told there that our Lord 'turned, and said unto them' – the great multitudes that followed Him – 'If any man come to me, and hate not his father, and mother, and wife, and children, and brethren, and sisters, yea, and his own life also, he cannot be my disciple.' That is the same word, and obviously that is not meant to be taken in its literal and absolute sense of hatred.

What our Lord is indicating is a relative attitude. He means that if you put anybody before Him, you cannot be His disciple. You have, as it were, to regard even your nearest and dearest in a lesser light, and even as a hindrance and an obstacle to you, if they would insinuate themselves between you and Christ. You hate what they are doing, you hate what they are in that respect only; you do not hate them as persons. Charles Hodge puts this perfectly. He says, 'Hate means to love less, and to regard and treat with less favour.' It is in that sense that this word must be interpreted here in Romans 9.

That is the explanation, then, of why it is that Esau will serve Jacob, though Esau is actually born before Jacob. It is because of God's attitude towards him. God's favour is on Jacob, not on Esau. That is the relative position that they occupy face to face with God. I do not stop to indicate here, because I have to do so later, that this is not a reference merely to the subsequent history of the descendants of Esau and those of Jacob and to the fact that God blessed the Jews and not the Edomites. It includes that, but it all starts way back when Esau and Jacob were actually in Rebekah's womb. It is because of what God had determined there that Esau and Jacob are in their relative positions and that there is this striking difference between the Edomites and the Israelites in all their subsequent history.

Now that is the whole purpose of what Malachi says; and the whole argument that he is putting before the children of Israel.

He says to them, 'Why are you behaving like this? You are the people that God has loved, you are the descendants of Jacob, and God has set His affection upon you. Why do you treat Him as you do?'

So we have considered the two quotations and we draw this conclusion. It is the same once more. The distinction between Esau and Jacob, Edomites and Israelites, is a distinction that has been drawn by God Himself. He tells us what He is doing; He made His statement to Rebekah, He made His statement through Malachi, and He makes it quite clear that He is doing this in order to carry out His great purpose. There, then, is the second argument which Paul uses, the specific statements made by God not only with respect to what He is doing but as to why He is doing it.

That brings us, then, to the third argument, which is the doctrine or the theological significance of the facts, and God's statements with respect to them. This is the sentence that the Apostle puts in brackets in verse 11. It is an extraordinary statement and it is what is called an anacoluthon. In other words, the Apostle sets out to make a complete statement, but he does not do so. He interrupts himself and says something else and it is on this ground that he is often criticized as being a bad stylist.

Now there is no need for me to defend the Apostle Paul, but the defence is that he really does tell us what he wants to say, though he does not put it in the form of a balanced statement as he originally intended. Let me explain. When he starts off by saying, 'For the children being not yet born, neither having done any good or evil, that the purpose of God according to election might stand . . .' – then you expect some further statement to balance that. But he does not give it to us; he says, 'not of works, but of him that calleth'. Of course, if you are interested primarily in style and in eloquence, balanced statements and form, then you can say that the Apostle is a little defective in that respect. But the Apostle was not concerned with that; he was concerned with truth and with the statement of truth. And the statement of truth, of course, is sufficient and quite complete in and of itself.

So let us look at it, as he gives it to us here, in these brackets. We can say, first, that there is no absolute necessity for him to give us this doctrine at all. If he is simply out to prove that 'they are not all Israel, which are of Israel', then he has done so to the hilt. The details are simply illustrations to prove and to show the outworking of the purpose, this is the big thing. But we must have doctrine. Paul never stops at facts alone. He is always interested in our understanding the truth, the principle, and now he is going to put it before us, and what he says is this: What God did in the case of Esau and of Jacob was not something haphazard or something that He did merely out of whim. He did it, Paul tells us, because it was a part of His great purpose and plan, which is always carried out by means of the principle of election or choice.

That, therefore, is what he is really telling us here. 'The children', he says, 'being not yet born, neither having done any good or evil, that [in order that] the purpose of God according to election might stand . . .' Then he is simply saying it again in a negative form – 'not of works, but of him that calleth'. The fundamental proposition is that God carries out His great purpose by means of and through this process of election. He is saying nothing new here. He is only repeating what he has already told us in chapter 8 verses 28, 29 and 30. What matters, he says there, is God's purpose. All things are going to work together for good to those who are in God's purpose. But how do we know this, how can it be guaranteed? Well, he says, you can be certain that these people are in God's purpose because God has foreknown them, He has predestinated them; and because He has predestinated them He has called them; and because He has called them He has justified them; and because He has justified them He has glorified them. We have already considered that in detail, so we need not stay with it now.[1] But that is the statement and Paul is saying exactly the same thing here in smaller compass.

Let me then expound it to you. Notice first the way in which he puts it – the children being 'not yet' born. The time element is a vital factor in the argument. Something happened to these before they were born – 'neither having done any good or evil'. That makes it still stronger. And what Paul says is that God chose Jacob rather than Esau, and he told Rebekah that the elder would serve the younger, before either of them was born, and

---

[1] See *Romans: An Exposition of Chapter 8:17–39: The Final Perseverance of the Saints*, 1975.

before either of them had a chance of doing either good or evil. That is the statement.

But now the question is – Why did God do this? Why did He set His affection on Jacob rather than Esau in that way? And Paul gives us the answer: 'that . . .' – which means 'in order that'. He did it in order that His purpose and object might be carried out. How? Well, you can look at it like this: God's purpose is something that is worked out through this process of election; 'the purpose of God according to election'. Now, 'according to' means 'by means of', or 'through'. God's purpose is worked out by using this principle of election or choice or selection. That is what Paul is saying.

Now the word 'election' is an interesting one. It is a word, we are told by the authorities, that had been used previously in Jewish literature in only one book, *The Psalms of Solomon*. It means a process of choice, a process of selection and I make this point about the word because it is perfectly clear here that we are dealing with something that was very specially revealed by God through the Spirit to the Apostle Paul. This is something that has been given to him in a peculiar way, so he uses this word in order to bring out his teaching.

What, then, is the object? Paul says that God works out His purpose through this method because it is the only way whereby this process and purpose can be made certain and sure: 'that the purpose of God according to election might stand'. Now, 'might stand' is a very good translation, and I say this because many people use the translation known as the Amplified New Testament, which, speaking generally, I would not hesitate to say is excellent. But this is one of the few instances in which it is really poor and misleading. It translates this phrase as 'in order further to carry out God's purpose'. But that is not what it means at all! It means 'in order that God's purpose *might stand*'!

Grimm and Thayer in their Lexicon are quite clear about this; they say the word means 'to continue', 'to continue to be'. It means to last, to endure, to remain firm – and of course it means that it is the exact opposite of what Paul has put into the mouth of the objectors, at the beginning of verse 6. Here is the beginning of the whole statement: 'Not as though the Word of God had fallen down.' So what is it that makes certain that the word of God will not fall down but will stand and be firm and secure? Oh, it is, Paul says, that God's purpose is always carried out through the process of election. That is the argument.

That, then, is Paul's most important statement, and in order to make quite sure that none of us is still muddled about this, he goes on, and does not complete what he obviously originally intended to say. But, again, as a good teacher he says, 'Look here, let me make it clear and certain to you – "not of works, but of him that calleth".' He uses there a negative and a positive. It is not of the works of man, so this shuts out once and for ever the thought that the purpose of God through election is something that works out simply through God foreseeing that certain people are going to do good works.

Now there are those people, as we saw in our studies on Romans 8,[2] who try to get over 'foreknowledge' by saying that. They maintain that when Paul says, 'whom he did foreknow, he also did predestinate', it means that God having all knowledge was able to see ahead of time what certain people were going to do – that some were going to do good works and believe, others were not. It is not that, says Paul; this process of selection has nothing to do with works at all; they are entirely shut out. And in any case, it cannot be, he says, because these two, Esau and Jacob, were not capable of doing anything; they were not yet born, and they had done neither good works nor bad.

And then to emphasize his argument further the Apostle puts it positively – it is not of works, but it is altogether and entirely 'of him that calleth'. In other words this purpose of God is worked out through election entirely as the result of the action and the activity of God Himself. It is completely independent of anything in us, our birth, our nationality, our good works or anything else whatsoever. And the cases he has given us, of course, prove it to the hilt. It was God who produced Isaac; it was God who produced both Jacob and Esau. But then having produced the two, He had already selected the one even before either was born, so the purpose of God is carried out in the case of Jacob. It is 'not of works, but of him that calleth'. It is of Him that calls things that are not, as if they were; it is nothing of man at all. It is God's free choice, and it is an absolute and a sovereign choice. That God should act in this way and choose and produce

[2]See *Romans: An Exposition of Chapter 8:17–39: The Final Perseverance of the Saints*, 1975.

His own people, is the only way in which His purpose could be surely and infallibly carried out and stand. That is what Paul is saying.

And, of course, he has already said this before.[3] He said it in chapter 4 verse 16. Winding up his great argument about justification by faith only, he makes this most vital statement: 'Therefore it is of faith, [in order] that it might be by grace; to the end [with the object, the intention] the promise might be sure to all the seed . . .' – that the promise might stand, that the promise might not be of none effect. That is why it is of faith, in order that it all might be of grace. And it is all of grace in order that it may be sure and in order that it may be certain.

And his argument is the same here. If it depended upon anything in us, if our salvation and our ultimate glorification at any point or in any way were dependent upon us or upon anything that we have done or can or ever will do, it would certainly fail. But, says Paul, it does not depend upon us. In order that the purpose of God according to election might stand, God chooses Jacob and not Esau before either of them was born, and before either of them had done any good or evil. It is an entirely independent action of God, and it works like this, because this is the only way in which we can be certain and sure that we are going to be finally glorified. So what guarantees it to every single member of this family of God is that it is God who is working it out, that it is entirely the result of the free sovereign action of Almighty God. And that is what Paul has been proving by his two cases.

3See *Romans: An Exposition of Chapters 3:20–4:25: Atonement and Justification*, 1970.

Eleven

*

And not only this; but when Rebecca also had conceived by one, even by our father Isaac; (for the children being not yet born, neither having done any good or evil, that the purpose of God according to election might stand, not of works, but of him that calleth;) it was said unto her, The elder shall serve the younger. As it is written, Jacob have I loved, but Esau have I hated.

Romans 9 : 10–13

Having gone carefully through the actual statements found in these verses, we are now in a position to draw certain conclusions with regard to the case of the two sons of Isaac. We are also in a position to draw conclusions with regard to the whole section, the argument which begins at verse 6 and which is to prove that 'they are not all Israel, which are of Israel'. It is most important that we should draw these conclusions, because we must be clear what the Apostle is saying. For if we are not clear about this, then we cannot possibly understand the section that follows. Now, judged by any standard this is a most important statement. It is also an extremely difficult one. It is one of the most difficult statements in the whole of Scripture, so do not be discouraged or blame yourselves if you have found it difficult to follow. But, on the other hand, do not give up and say that because it is difficult you cannot be bothered with it. You should never say that about any portion of Scripture. Christian people, who do not apply what mind and understanding they have to a passage of Scripture because it is difficult, are sinning very grievously.

'But', you say, 'this is a very controversial passage and people argue about it and have always done so, and I do not want to be involved in such disputation.' But you have no right to back out of argument. Whatever God has given us He has given *us*, and we are meant to apply our minds to it, whether it is comparatively simple, or whether it is comparatively difficult, as this is. We have no right to ignore Scripture, and if we do, we do so at our peril. Indeed it is an insult to God, who raised up men to write these very Scriptures for our instruction, for our enlightenment, and for our establishment in our most holy faith.

So then, we must consider it. This seems to me to be one of the great causes of trouble in the church at the present time. Christian people have become lazy; they pick and choose in the Scriptures. They have their favourite passages and they avoid others and thus there is great ignorance concerning certain fundamental and essential doctrines. There is nothing more glorious than this truth that we are considering and that is partly why it is so difficult. We must, therefore, apply ourselves to it, but we must do so, of course, in the right spirit. We must be humble and we must be ready to learn.

Let me add one other thing. What we are doing is to try to understand what the Apostle Paul said. I am not here giving a lecture on election. Now some people, I know, want to go off into an argument on election on both sides but I am not here to do that. I am here to try to discover and to expound what the Apostle Paul has actually written. If you like at the end to disagree with him, that is your responsibility. My responsibility is to make clear and plain as far as I can what the Apostle has said, and I do appeal to you to listen to him before you begin to talk about your own opinions.

Is that not, generally, the trouble in most arguments? You watch the next time you see two people having an argument! If you just sit and listen to them, you will notice that neither is really listening to the other; he is waiting for the other to stop; indeed he is ready to interrupt him. And that is precisely what so many people do with the Scriptures. They have never really allowed the Scriptures to speak to them; they are so anxious to give their opinion. So be wise, listen to the Apostle Paul, make sure that you know what he is saying, and then you will be able to follow his great argument as he develops it from verse 14 onwards.

We are now, therefore, in a position to draw conclusions and deductions. So let me try to summarize what the Apostle is saying to us in these most important verses.

First, the promise and the purpose of God have respect to certain people only. This is as true of the nation of Israel as of anybody else. That is just another way of saying, 'They are not all Israel, which are of Israel' – contrary to the fatal wrong assumption of the Jews. That was the reason why ultimately they crucified the Son of God Himself. They had not realized that. The promise of God is not universal, not even universal with regard to Israel, the Jews. It is only to certain people.

Secondly, these people, to whom the purpose and the promises of God apply, are, and become what they are, not because of anything in themselves. They are the people of God, they are this 'seed' that Paul talks about, not because of their birth, not because of their nationality, not because of anything that they do, not even their believing the gospel. They are what they are because God calls them into being, because of the supernatural element in their birth, as we have seen in the case of Isaac who was born, as Paul tells us in Galatians 4: 28–30, 'after the Spirit'.

Thirdly, God's purpose, in other words, is being carried out, and always has been and always will be, by means of this process of election or selection, and we saw how Paul demonstrates this by the cases of Ishmael and Isaac, Jacob and Esau.

Fourthly, God brings His purpose to pass and carries it out by means of this process of selection and election for one reason only – because it is the only way which guarantees that His purpose and His plan will certainly and surely and infallibly be carried out and brought to a final fruition: 'that [in order that] the purpose of God according to election might stand'. It does not depend upon us at all, but upon God Himself, His character and His action.

Now, of course, in putting it like this, the Apostle is simply giving in a summary form what he argued at length in chapter 8 from verse 28 to the end. That was the whole point there – that God's purpose is certain and sure. He says, 'If God be for us, who can be against us? He that spared not his own Son, but delivered him up for us all, how shall he not with him also freely give us all things? Who shall lay any thing to the charge of God's elect? It is God that justifieth.' And so on right to the very end, to the triumphant conclusion: 'In all these things we are more than conquerors through him that loved us. For I am persuaded, that neither death, nor life, nor angels, nor principalities, nor powers, nor things present, nor things to come, nor height, nor depth, nor any other creature, shall be able to separate us from the love of God, which is in Christ Jesus our Lord.' That is it! It is the purpose of God; He is carrying it out Himself, nothing can frustrate it. And God, he says here, does it in this way through this process of election and selection, in order that it may stand, that it may never fall.

Those, then, are the main conclusions. But there are certain aspects of this which we must emphasize in particular, because they are emphasized by the Apostle. The first – and in a sense it is just another way of putting the same point – is that God's choice is absolutely free and sovereign. It is His choice and entirely independent of us, of anything we are or of anything we do. It is determined by one thing only, and that is by God's own nature and His own eternal will. Paul says in Ephesians 1 verse 5, '. . . according to the good pleasure of his will', and he keeps on repeating that. It is according to His own will; it is the only explanation and we are given no other.

The two cases we have been considering emphasize that completely. The choice of Isaac was altogether the choice of God. It was not Abraham's – we have seen in the story in Genesis what Abraham's views on the subject were. He said, 'Look, here is Ishmael, why do You not use him?' 'No,' said God, 'that is not My purpose.' Isaac would never even have been born had it not been God's will. And it was exactly the same with Jacob and Esau, as we saw in our last study. It is entirely in God and not in us at all. That must be emphasized, because you will not follow the argument that begins at verse 14 if you do not understand that. I am not interested in whether you like it or not. I am trying to expound Paul's argument, and what he says is that it is God's free and sovereign choice.

Secondly, this choice of God involves a rejection as well as a choosing. 'Esau have I hated' as well as 'Jacob have I loved'. God does not so much hate a person as hate the sinful condition of the person, the sinful attitude of the person and all that that is going to lead to. God, as we are told in the Sermon on the Mount, 'maketh his sun to rise on the evil and on the good, and sendeth rain on the just and on the unjust' [*Matthew* 5 : 45]. The statement here in Romans 9 is from the standpoint of His view of sin, and of man in sin. So there is a rejection as well as a selection. God hates evil, God hates sin – that is the second principle.

Then we come to the third and the most important principle. This choosing and electing on the part of God is something that we must view in the right way; in other words, in the way in which the Apostle puts it before us. Many people, it seems to me, get into trouble over this whole doctrine because they view it in a wrong way. According to the Apostle's teaching, God's electing and selecting is not a matter of an arbitrary selection out of a mass of humanity. Yet I am sure that many have always thought of it like that – that God is confronted by the whole of humanity and that what the Apostle is teaching here is that God looks at all those people and says, 'I am going to choose some of them; I am going to forgive them and give them salvation; and I am going to reject the others.' Now I assert that that is not what the Apostle says; it is, in fact, to misunderstand what he is saying.

I put it like that because I think that both the cases which the Apostle has used prove that that is not what God does. What God does is to produce a people for Himself. We saw that it was God who produced Isaac. It was a miraculous birth. It was not a case of Isaac and Ishmael being born and God looking at the two and saying, 'I am going to take this one and not that one.' That is quite wrong! God produced Isaac because He had already decided that it was through this man whom He was going to bring into being that the seed was to be carried on. So we must get rid of this notion of God looking at a humanity or a collection of people who have already arrived, in an utterly arbitrary and unfair way, taking out one and leaving another, though they are both equally sinners and equally hopeless. It is not that. This is a very positive process.

Now the Apostle has made that perfectly clear in the case both of Isaac and of Jacob. But later on in the chapter he again makes it clear. Read what he says from verse 22: 'What if God, willing to shew his wrath, and to make his power known, endured with much longsuffering the vessels of wrath fitted to destruction: and that he might make known the riches of his glory on the vessels of mercy' – notice this! – '*which he had afore prepared unto glory,* even us, whom he hath called, not of the Jews only, but also of the Gentiles?' He had prepared them beforehand unto this glory! That is what Paul is saying. It is exactly the same thing as he has told us in the case of Isaac and of Jacob. Then, in verse 29 he quotes Isaiah: 'And as Esaias said before, Except the Lord of Sabaoth had left us a seed, we had been as Sodoma, and been made like unto Gomorrha.' It is always God who brings this seed into being and preserves it. If the Lord of Sabaoth had not done this it would not have been there at all. That is another way of saying what the Apostle has put so plainly before us in the two cases that he has cited, both of which prove that it is not a matter of an arbitrary selection out of a mass of humanity, but rather a matter of God producing a people for Himself. It is all determined beforehand, and we who are Christians are produced to that end as a part of that purpose.

Now the right way of looking at this statement is to take it in terms of what Paul has already told us in chapter 5 verses 12 to 21. All humanity was in Adam, who was also the representative of the whole of humanity. God dealt with him, and through him He dealt with the whole of humanity. Then Adam fell, and all humanity fell with him. Now that is the explicit statement of verse 12 in chapter 5: 'Wherefore, as by one man sin entered into the world, and death by sin; and so death passed upon all men, for that all have sinned . . .' We have considered that in great detail in earlier studies, and you see the importance of doing things thoroughly.[1] I am in no difficulty about chapter 9 because of our careful interpretation of what has gone before. But if you have not grasped that you are bound to be in trouble here.

So, then, the position is that all humanity is lost in Adam, and is under the wrath and the condemnation of God. We can go further; we can say that all are rejected in Adam – all, because all have sinned in Adam's sin. That is the position of everybody who has ever been born after Adam, from one standpoint. What, then, is God's way of salvation? It is this: It is not so much to select people out of the fallen race of Adam for salvation. It is not to take some people and reform them. No! God is doing something entirely new. There is a new, a second Man, there is a

---

[1] See *Romans: An Exposition of Chapter 5: Assurance,* 1971.

last Adam. That is the whole teaching of Romans 5 – and you have the parallel teaching in 1 Corinthians 15. Jesus Christ is the first of a new humanity and the Head of a new race. Did you realize that? Here is the whole key. God's way of salvation is to produce a new race. It is not a selection out of the old race; it is not just a question of some of Adam's race being forgiven and others not; it is the production of a new humanity in Christ.

In other words, we must always think of salvation, God's way of salvation, as a positive process. It is a new people, a spiritual people, produced by a spiritual birth. We can go further: These people are brought into the world and are born and are prepared for that end and object. We have established that in the case of Isaac. Here it is repeated in the twenty-third verse of this chapter: 'And that he might make known the riches of his glory on the vessels of mercy, which he had afore prepared unto glory.'

But we must be clear about the place of the natural in all this, because this is crucial. God does not do away with the natural; He uses it and He intervenes in it in a supernatural manner. Both the cases cited prove that. You remember that in the case of the birth of Isaac, Abraham was ninety-nine and Sarah was ninety, so the question of having a child was a sheer impossibility. Yet they had a child! The natural process came into it, God used it; but the supernatural came into it, a miracle was brought about as well. So God used the natural supernaturally and my contention is that He always does that. We saw that He did exactly the same with Jacob. We are all born, therefore, in a natural sense as the children of Adam. As Ishmael and Isaac were the natural children of Abraham, and as Jacob and Esau were the natural children of Isaac, so we are all the natural children of Adam. But the teaching is that nevertheless, as Christians, we are all of us separated from our mother's womb in a spiritual sense.

Now the exact time when this spiritual fact is made manifest is irrelevant. Take the case of the Apostle Paul, which will illustrate this for us perfectly. What does he say about himself? 'But when it pleased God, who separated me from my mother's womb, and called me by his grace, to reveal his Son in me, that I might preach him among the heathen . . .' [*Galatians* 1 : 15–16]. Notice what he says – that he had been separated from his mother's womb as a Christian, as a servant of God, and as an

Apostle. Yes, but we all know that for a number of years he was a persecutor, and a blasphemer; he was reviling Christ and doing everything he could against Him. But what Paul says is that though all that was true, nevertheless it was also true that he had been separated from his mother's womb. He was by nature a child of Adam, but God, even in bringing that man into this world, had done this supernatural, spiritual thing. It only shows itself in time on the road to Damascus but it was there, he tells us, from the moment of his conception.

So this is a most important point. What happened in the case of Isaac and of Jacob happens in the case of every Christian. God produces this new humanity, not by scrapping the natural process but by using it, and by so acting in it and upon it and through it as to bring His own purpose to pass. The others? – well, they are just left. Ishmael was just left as the natural child of Abraham. Esau was left as the natural child of Isaac. And all the unredeemed, the unsaved, the non-Christians, are left as they were, as the natural children and progeny of Adam.

Now this appears to us to be entirely something that happens in time, but this is only the manifestation of God's great and eternal purpose. Our being convicted of sin, our repentance, our calling by the gospel, the changed life and so on – all that is something that happens to us in time, and we say, 'I was converted at such and such a date or at such a particular period.' That is all right; that is nothing but the manifestation of it. There is Saul of Tarsus on the road to Damascus. But the thing has happened in his mother's womb! Go back further. Certain things became obvious about Isaac and about Jacob at a given point in time – yes, but it was all determined before they were born. That is the argument of the Apostle.

So the natural is used by God in this way, and what Paul is trying to get us to see here is that we must not look at it from our natural angle in terms of the time process; we must learn to look at it from eternity in the purpose and the plan of God, and so we will see how it works itself out. Take the statement of it that we find in Ephesians 1 verses 3 to 5: 'Blessed be the God and Father of our Lord Jesus Christ, who hath blessed us with all spiritual blessings in heavenly places in Christ: according as he hath chosen us in him before the foundation of the world, that we should be holy and without blame before him in love: having predestinated us unto the adoption of children by Jesus Christ to himself, according to the good pleasure of his will.' There is the same truth again in a summary form.

And this is true of everyone who is a Christian. We are all the children of Abraham, the children of faith; we are all born in a spiritual manner as was Isaac himself. And there is a further very interesting case of this in the Old Testament; it is that of Jeremiah. His prophecy begins, 'The words of Jeremiah the son of Hilkiah, of the priests that were in Anathoth in the land of Benjamin: to whom the word of the Lord came in the days of Josiah the son of Amon king of Judah, in the thirteenth year of his reign. It came also in the days of Jehoiakim the son of Josiah king of Judah, unto the end of the eleventh year of Zedekiah the son of Josiah king of Judah, unto the carrying away of Jerusalem captive in the fifth month. Then the word of the Lord came unto me, saying, Before I formed thee in the belly I knew thee' – is it not an exact parallel? – 'and before thou camest forth out of the womb I sanctified thee, and I ordained thee a prophet unto the nations' [*Jeremiah* 1 : 1–5]. God produced him for that purpose. But it only actually happened in time, 'in the days of Josiah the son of Amon king of Judah, in the thirteenth year of his reign'.

Do not get mixed up with this time element. You see, the Son of God really began His public ministry at the age of thirty, but He had been sent into the world to do it. There were thirty years when people just looked at Him and thought that He was a man like everybody else; suddenly He bursts forth in His ministry. The same was true of Jeremiah. For all those years, nobody knew that he was to be this remarkable prophet of God, but God had known it: 'Before I formed thee in the belly I knew thee.' You notice it is God who forms him. Of course! This is what He does with all His people. So, let me emphasize it again, God actually brought us into the world through the natural process in order that we might become a part of this 'new humanity' in Christ. We appear to be exactly like everybody else, and yet according to this teaching we were always different. We did not know we were different and nobody else knew that we were. Jeremiah did not know that he was different, nor did Isaac and Jacob – these things are not known. Nevertheless it is still the fact. Christian people were never exactly equal and identical with others. There was always this vital and essential difference – not yet

[135]

manifested, but it was there. Before the foundation of the world, before our mother's womb even, there was always this difference. According to the flesh, according to nature, we are all the children of Adam, and yet we are not only that. We are children whom God has produced and brought into being in order that this purpose and plan of His might be carried out in us.

Salvation, according to the Apostle, must be viewed positively. God has to 'produce' a new humanity. He does it through the mechanism of the old humanity coming down from father to son, as He does with Isaac and Jacob; but the vital thing is the new humanity, the new production. So that there is no cause for complaint; no one has a right to say anything. All humanity in Adam is condemned, and deserves to be, as Ishmael and Esau were; such people do not desire God, they are not interested in Him, and are God-haters. There is no complaint. It is not an arbitrary selection; it is God producing something quite new.

So let me summarize it all by putting it like this. The purpose and the promises of God apply only to those people whom God has produced for Himself by a spiritual birth. That is what Paul says and he leaves his evidence at that point, although he could have gone on to say this: Out of the twelve sons of Jacob, God selected Judah and not the other eleven. Out of this house of Judah He then selected the house of David in particular. In other words, this process of selection is to be found running right through the Old Testament. That is what makes the genealogical tables so fascinating! They are there to show us God's process and purpose worked out through election. Look, for example, at the book of Ruth and see how God did it. This is God's action altogether and you cannot explain it in any other way. Again God uses the natural but He intervenes in this miraculous manner to produce His people, and so He is producing a new humanity.

Now I do trust that this is plain and clear to you. Meditate about it – and in this way. Check my exposition. Remember that the test of any exposition of Romans 9 verses 6 to 13 is that the exposition must lead to the question that is asked in verse 14; and if it does not, it is a wrong exposition. The question is this: 'What shall we say then? Is there unrighteousness with God?' So that as you check my exposition make certain that your exposition, if it does not agree with mine, leads to that question. Whatever the interpretation of this statement is, it must lead certain people to say, 'Very well, if you say that, if Paul says that, there is unrighteousness with God.'

So then think about it in those terms. Go through the cases again, watch what Paul says, notice these extraordinary expressions: 'This is the word of promise, At this time will I come, and Sara shall have a son.' God said that. Go back, turn it up in Genesis, read all about it. Do the same with the case of the two children of Isaac and of Rebekah; take this great statement: 'that the purpose of God according to election might stand, not of works, but of him that calleth'. Any exposition must give full weight to all these statements, and I suggest to you that there is only one way to interpret it; it is the one that I have attempted to put before you. God guarantees the production of this people, this 'seed'. So that at the end there will be a perfect new humanity, complete and entire in Christ. He is the Head, we are the body; He is the first-born among many brethren, something entirely new. He is the second Man, He is the last Adam. That is how God saves, that is God's plan of redemption. Does it not help you to understand the incarnation as you have never done before? It is not taking out of the old mass of humanity and doing something to it; it is the production of something entirely new. May God give us understanding in this glorious mystery, and may He so apply it to us that we shall be lost in a sense of 'wonder, love and praise'.

Twelve

*

What shall we say then? Is there unrighteousness with God? God forbid. For he saith to Moses, I will have mercy on whom I will have mercy, and I will have compassion on whom I will have compassion. So then it is not of him that willeth, nor of him that runneth, but of God that sheweth mercy. For the scripture saith unto Pharaoh, Even for this same purpose have I raised thee up, that I might shew my power in thee, and that my name might be declared throughout all the earth. Therefore hath he mercy on whom he will have mercy, and whom he will he hardeneth. Thou wilt say then unto me, Why doth he yet find fault? For who hath resisted his will? Nay but, O man, who art thou that repliest against God? Shall the thing formed say to him that formed it, Why hast thou made me thus? Hath not the potter power over the clay, of the same lump to make one vessel unto honour, and another unto dishonour? What if God, willing to shew his wrath, and to make his power known, endured with much longsuffering the vessels of wrath fitted to destruction: and that he might make known the riches of his glory on the vessels of mercy, which he had afore prepared unto glory, even us, whom he hath called, not of the Jews only, but also of the Gentiles?

Romans 9 : 14–24

We come now to the section which starts at chapter 9 verse 14 and goes on to the end of verse 24. I should rather say sub-section, because this is a subsection of the greater whole which runs from the beginning of the ninth chapter right until the end of the eleventh chapter.

The Apostle has been demonstrating that God carries out His great purpose of salvation by means of election and here now, at verse 14, he goes on to consider the objection to that teaching. He states it in his customary manner and he answers it in several different ways. Now as we come to look at this objection and his manner of dealing with it the first thing that strikes us is the form in which the Apostle puts the objection before us; he says, 'What shall we say then? Is there unrighteousness with God? God forbid.'

Now we must improve a little on this translation. In the Authorized Version the words 'is' and 'there' are in italics, which means that they have been supplied by the translators because they are not in the original. The translators supply them in order to help us to understand, but they really might have done better here. What the Apostle actually said was this: 'What therefore shall we say? Not unrighteousness with God?' He has the word 'not' before 'unrighteousness', and I think that it throws a significant light upon his whole argument. 'What therefore shall we say? Not unrighteousness with God? May it not be.' That is the true way of translating 'God forbid'. We have had an example of that before, in the third chapter. In a sense it means 'God forbid', but the actual words used by the Apostle were 'May it not be' – the thing is unthinkable.

So, then, why is it interesting to note the way in which the Apostle presents this difficulty, this objection, that arises in the minds of certain people? It is because the very form in which he puts the objection helps us to decide whether our exposition up to date has been the wrong one, because it is quite clear that the objection with which the Apostle is going to deal is one which arises as a direct result of what he has been saying; and, as I have indicated, if our exposition of what has gone before does not lead to this objection, then of necessity it has been wrong. Whatever it is the Apostle has been saying from verse 6 to verse 13 about God's purpose and the way in which He carries it out, it must be something that, on the surface, at any rate, makes some people think that God has been unrighteous and that He is unfair. So before we go on to deal with the argument, we must be quite certain in our minds that we are clear as to what the Apostle actually has been saying.

Now I have to put it like that because if you read the commentators you will find that there is a good deal of confusion about it. Commentators are human after all and some of them do not like what the Apostle says, so what they try to do is to say that he has not said it. That is nothing but sheer

God's Sovereign Purpose

confusion. Whenever we are confronted by a portion of Scripture which is different from our own ideas there are always two
things to do. The first, obviously, is to try to make sure as to
what the passage is saying, and it is only then that we proceed to
consider our own personal reaction to what is being said. If we
confuse the two, if we bring in the second in trying to decide the
first, then, obviously we are going to go astray. If, because we do
not like a conclusion, we go back and try to manipulate what
has led to that conclusion, in order to make it lead to another,
then we are just guilty of a dishonest study of the Scriptures and
of dishonest exposition.

Now I am not charging commentators who do not agree with
what I have been saying with deliberate dishonesty but I do
suggest that they are unconsciously dishonest. If ever we try to
manipulate the Scripture to make it suit what we believe, we are
guilty of dishonesty. We must never manipulate the Scripture,
we must allow it to speak for itself. So, then, we must first be
quite sure of what exactly the Apostle says, and that is where
this question in verse 14 is of great value to us. What the Apostle
has been saying obviously raises in the minds of certain people
this question of God being unfair, or unjust, or unrighteous, so
the Apostle puts it before us.

This helps us therefore to check the exposition which we
have given and the conclusion at which we have arrived.
Furthermore, this question of Paul's, it seems to me, automatically excludes certain expositions that people have put forward,
and these are the popular ones today in the so-called 'liberal'
school of theology, among the liberal interpreters, the people
who really do not believe in the divine inspiration of the
Scriptures, the people who trust their philosophy rather than
the teaching of the Bible, and who put philosophy before
revelation. Some of them are popular writers and therefore tend
to make people think that what they say is right and true.

Here, for instance, is one of their expositions. There are those
who say that the Apostle, in this whole section from verse 6
onwards, is really dealing with the problem not of individual
salvation but of nations – that his only interest is in the position
of the Jews as a nation. And they try to argue that the whole of
the chapter is only contrasting the Jews with every other nation.
Paul, they say, is interested in Isaac as the head of one nation and

[140]

in Ishmael as the head of another; he is interested in Jacob as the head of a nation and in Esau as the head of the Edomites and so on. They get rid of the individual aspect, and, of course, they do that because they do not like the idea and the teaching of personal election to salvation.

Now our reply to that is that, obviously, Jacob and Esau were first and foremost individuals before they became heads of nations, and that Jacob is the saved man while Esau is described as the 'profane' man – not just the nation that came out of him, but the person himself. But, still more important, the Apostle's whole object, in this chapter and the subsequent chapters, is to give us a final proof of the absolute certainty of individual salvation. Everybody agrees that until the end of chapter 8 he has been dealing with individuals, and my argument is that he is still doing so, and that he is supporting the argument for that absolute certainty by dealing with this objection; to show that whenever God sets His affection and heart upon an individual, then that individual's final salvation is sure and absolutely guaranteed – and this is one of his ways of proving that. That, as you remember, we have shown all along is the real way to approach these chapters 9, 10 and 11.

But furthermore, it is perfectly clear that all along he is dealing with individuals. Look at it in verse 15: 'For he saith to Moses, I will have mercy on whom I will have mercy, and I will have compassion on whom . . .' As we shall see, Moses was trying to plead on behalf of the whole nation, and God's reply to him is, 'No, I have mercy on whom I will have mercy; on some individuals but not on others.' This is a division within the nation of Israel, so he is clearly dealing with individuals.

We also find exactly the same statement in verse 18; this 'on whom' corresponds to the famous 'whosoever' in John 3 : 16. It is the individual! But there is a final proof of this in verse 24 where Paul says, 'Even us, whom he hath called, not of the Jews only, but also of the Gentiles'. He is not dealing with nations there; he is speaking of individuals who have been called, some out of the Jews, some out of the Gentiles, for salvation into the kingdom of God.

Then another exposition that is put forward by some people is that the Apostle here is not considering personal or eternal salvation at all, but simply what they call 'election to position

and privilege'. They say he really was only thinking of Jacob as
the one who was called to be in this privileged position as the
head of this particular nation, this theocracy, with which God
was going to have dealings.

We need not spend any time with this. All that we have said as
an objection to the first exposition applies equally well here.
And as we go on with the argument, and especially when we
come to chapter 10, we see that all along the Apostle is dealing
with the individual. Take chapter 10 : 13: 'Whosoever shall call
upon the name of the Lord shall be saved' – he is dealing with the
whole question of how an individual becomes a believer. There
is nothing at all about position or privilege or the theocracy of
Israel or anything of the sort! He is concerned about individuals
out of any nation becoming Christian believers.

Then a third attempt to evade the difficulty of this doctrine is
to say that all the Apostle is really doing in this section is to
justify this way that God has chosen to save people – namely,
justification by faith, as against justification by works. The
famous Arminius, the real father of all Arminians, when dealing
with this passage, says that God here is revealing His plan, and
that this plan was to extend His mercy to those who had
responded to Him when He 'called' and who believed on Christ,
not to those who sought salvation by works. The passage that
follows – verse 14 and following – shows that God has decided to
give His mercy in His own way and on His own plan. That is, to
give it not to him who runs – who strives after it by works – but
to him that seeks it in the way that He has appointed, by faith.
But people object to that, says Arminius; they want to earn their
salvation by works, so Paul here is vindicating God's use of this
method of justification by faith for those to whom He is going to
show His mercy.

The answer to that is very simple. The Apostle is not dealing
with justification by faith at all. He is dealing with the persons
who are justified by faith, which is a much deeper and a more
profound problem. His whole emphasis here is upon this: Why
is it that one man has faith and another man does not? He
has already dealt with the question of justification by faith alone
at great length, especially in the first four chapters. He has
been carrying on that assumption right through to the end of
chapter 8; there is no need to demonstrate it any further. No, he

is not dealing with God's *way* of showing His mercy, as Arminius would have us believe, rather he is dealing with the *people to whom* God has shown mercy. He is not interested in methods here; he is interested in persons, and that has been the whole point of the argument about Isaac and Ishmael and about Jacob and Esau.

Now what Arminius is doing, of course, is to turn our faith into works. He is saying that what really saves us is our works, whereas the whole object of the Apostle is to say that we are not saved by anything that we do. We are saved entirely by the fact that God, who chose Isaac instead of Ishmael and Jacob instead of Esau, has chosen us! In other words the question before us is this: What is it that leads to faith? Why does anybody at all have faith? It is altogether a deeper and a more profound question than that which is suggested by the exposition of Arminius. But these are the ways in which men try to get over this difficulty. If salvation were by our faith, then there would be no question of unrighteousness in God; it would be a reward of our faith, and the objection that Paul deals with in verse 14 would never have been raised at all. It does not lead to the conclusion of the question that we are now examining together.

And that brings us to the fourth and the last common misinterpretation of this particular section. There are those who would have us believe that all that Paul is really saying here is that God chose Isaac rather than Ishmael, and Jacob rather than Esau, because in His foreknowledge He saw what kind of people they were going to become. He saw that Ishmael was going to be the kind of man he became, and that Isaac was going to be a good and a godly man. He saw all this in His great, eternal omniscience and foreknowledge, and because He knew that, then He decided to choose them, Isaac and Jacob rather than Ishmael and Esau. They say that it is nothing but a question of God's foreknowledge.

But that gives them the credit! That is a reward of their goodness, and if salvation is just the reward of our faith and our belief or for anything else in us, then there is no question of unrighteousness with God; it is a righteous thing, it is what we would expect God to do, and there would be no difficulty and no problem at all. It would mean that we are saved because God foresees that we are going to believe whereas others reject, so we are saved because we believe and the others are rejected because they do not. Nobody objects to that; indeed that is what everybody likes! There would be no need to have this great argument if that were the true exposition of what Paul is saying from verse 6 to verse 13. But you see there is an objection, and so we must reject all those four proffered expositions.

No, what the Apostle is saying from verse 6 to verse 13 is that God, of His own eternal and sovereign will in the carrying out of His own great and eternal purpose, chooses some to salvation and rejects others. That is the conclusion at which we have arrived. That is the only conclusion that leads to this particular difficulty, this charge that people feel in their hearts against God. They say, 'If that is so, then God is unjust. If it is true that God chose Jacob and rejected Esau when they were both still in the womb and had not done any good or bad nor anything at all, if you say it is entirely "of him that calleth" and nothing to do with man, then it is not fair.' That follows, does it not? You can understand the objection and the difficulty which arise. That, therefore, is certainly the exposition and interpretation of what the Apostle is actually saying in these verses. And that this is so will become more plain and clear as we proceed to follow him in the argument that he opens out before us.

We can put it like this: If that is what the Apostle actually says, what do you feel about it? Now that is the second question. I reminded you that there are two questions. (1) What exactly does the Apostle say? (2) What is your reaction to it, what do you make of it? The Apostle lays down this great proposition, that God's purpose of salvation is guaranteed and will be finally successful because it is something that depends entirely upon God's will and purpose, and in no respect upon human response. That is his statement, so how do we respond to it?

Now we are approaching what is, of course, one of the most difficult problems in the whole realm of theology, which means 'knowledge of God'. It is a matter that has been debated throughout the centuries – perhaps in some ways the most difficult matter of all, because it takes us immediately to a consideration of the mind of the eternal and everlasting God – and therefore we must pause for a moment to make certain comments which are essential at this point. One is that again we should thank God for the way in which He used and dealt with His servant Paul; we should thank God for the way in which the Apostle never evades a difficulty, never skirts round it. There are teachers who, when they come to a problem, either say nothing or they make a joke about it and go round it. Never does the Apostle do that; he always puts up the difficulty, examines it, and gives his answer to it. It is one of the most wonderful things of all about the Scriptures.

So I would lay it down as a proposition that because a thing is difficult to understand we must not pass it by. We must not only read those portions of Scripture that we think we understand and that we find easy; we must take the whole of the Scripture and consider it all, otherwise we are insulting God. It is He who has given it to us. And a Christian who does not examine a thing or deal with it simply because it is difficult, is a Christian who is guilty of very grievous sin. It is like a child who throws away a most wonderful gift which has been given it by its parent, and who does not appreciate what is being done for it. Let us be careful then, lest in a kind of superficial impatience and because we do not like doctrine, we say, 'I cannot be bothered with that, I am interested in positive salvation.' I am just cautioning you to be very careful how you speak about the Word of God.

So that brings us to the second point, which is the spirit in which we do this. There is surely no subject concerning which we need to be more careful about our spirits than this. The history of the church unfortunately proves that point to the very hilt. Let us not approach it in a partisan or in a debating spirit. How often has this been used merely for the purposes of debate and people are anxious to prove their point on the one side or the other. That is not the way to approach God's truth at any time.

Still less let us approach it in a bad temper. I have known more Christian people lose their tempers over this subject than anything else. A Christian should never lose his temper, and most certainly he should not lose his temper over God's truth. And if we cannot discuss this great question that is before us without becoming heated, then the thing that we must consider first is our own selves and our own temper. We are not fit to face truth at all! If we cannot consider the truth in a balanced and a controlled manner we are indeed in a very serious condition. So let there be no impatience.

Still less let there be any bitterness. Is it not extraordinary that one has to say these things? And yet they are essential. I have known people who have not only lost their tempers but have displayed bitterness of spirit when they have been discussing this question. I have known people walk out of meetings and leave churches in bitterness over a question like this. But why should there be bitterness? You see, we must realize that we are in a realm where the devil is always ready to be active.

Still less should we approach a subject like this in a spirit of superiority. Dr William Barclay, for example, approaches it like this: 'Inevitably our minds stagger at this argument; it presents us with a picture of a God who apparently quite arbitrarily chooses one and rejects the other. To us' – that is to say, to us twentieth-century people – 'it is not a valid argument because it makes God responsible for an action which does not seem to us to be ethically justified. But the fact remains that strange as it seems to us and unacceptable as it seems to us, it would strike home to a Jew.' So you see Dr Barclay tells us that what we have got here is a Jew arguing with Jews. Of course, to us it is no argument at all because it seems to us to make God responsible for an action which is not 'ethically justified'. 'To us', you see! We are twentieth-century people with our high ethics, we cannot accept this sort of argument. Of course it was all right for Paul to use it with the Jews two thousand years ago when their ethical conceptions were not ours.

And that, I say, is to be superior. Dr Barclay says that what the Apostle is teaching here is wrong. Now let me say this for Dr William Barclay; he is right about what the Apostle is saying. He agrees that in verses 6 to 13 the Apostle is saying what I have been putting before you, but when he comes to this section he only has one thing to say: 'I agree', he says, 'that that is what Paul says', but then he goes on to say, 'I think that Paul was wrong.' That is why I am putting it like this: Do not approach the Scriptures with an air of superiority, because it simply means, in the end, that you imagine that you are superior to the Apostle Paul, that you know more about ethics and about righteousness and about the mind of God! God deliver us from this modern trust in scholarship which does not hesitate to criticize the writings of a divinely inspired Apostle!

What then should our spirit be? Well, the exact opposite of that sense of superiority. Let it be humble, let us approach this passage with reverence. But above all let us recognize, before we begin, that we are not in a position to understand everything. Let us, in the words of the Scriptures, remember that God is in heaven, that we are on earth, and that we are not only very small and finite but sinful in addition. So let us not expect to understand the mind of God fully. Is there anything more ridiculous than a creature such as man is, claiming the right to understand fully everything that God does and everything that God proposes to do?

No, as I approach a passage like this, the word of Scripture that always comes to me is, 'Put off thy shoes from off thy feet, for the place whereon thou standest is holy ground' [*Exodus* 3 : 5]. Indeed, the Apostle himself puts it for us at the end of chapter 11 as he comes to the conclusion of this mighty matter: 'O the depth of the riches both of the wisdom and knowledge of God! how unsearchable are his judgments, and his ways past finding out! For who hath known the mind of the Lord? or who hath been his counsellor? Or who hath first given to him, and it shall be recompensed unto him again? For of him, and through him, and to him, are all things: to whom be glory for ever. Amen.'

In other words I am simply saying this: Do not be too ready to say, 'But I do not understand this, I cannot see that.' Calm down, cool down, realize that there are many things you cannot see. You have a very little brain and you have a very poor spirit within you; do not be surprised that you cannot. But instead of rejecting it because you cannot understand it, get your spirit right, come back to the Word, try to consider it again, pray God to give you understanding and enlightenment. Nothing is more important, as you come to Scripture, than your spirit; it is much more important than your intelligence, or your training. Here are commentators, you see, today, men who have had wonderful training and who are able men, yes, but because their spirits are wrong, their whole exposition goes wrong. So let us be careful!

And the last point is this: notice that the Apostle's method of dealing with this whole question is in terms of Scripture. Having laid down this objection, which is a very real one to

many people, he says: 'For he saith to Moses . . .' He quotes
Scripture: 'For the scripture saith unto Pharaoh . . .' This is a
point which we need to emphasize. The Apostle does not do what
so many of us have often done – and I plead guilty to it myself in
past days. I argued about this particular question before I ever was
a Christian and did so very glibly with others, and they were
equally glib and equally ignorant. Were it not for the mercy of
God we would all be in hell, as we richly deserve to be for putting
up our opinions of God and what He does and what we think He
ought to do.

The Apostle's method is not to engage in a general philosophical discussion; he deals with it in terms of Scripture; and you
notice the way he does so. In verse 17 he makes it quite clear that
to him the Scripture is the word of God, for he says, 'The
scripture saith unto Pharaoh'. What actually happened was that
God told Moses what to say to Pharaoh – 'And say this to him'.
God spoke to Pharaoh through Moses. The Apostle puts it here by
saying, 'The scripture saith unto Pharaoh', by which he means
that the Scripture is the word of God. We have not here merely
the writings of men. The men were the instruments used by God,
but the Scripture is the word of God! That is why we must be so
careful that we do not take a question like this and turn it into a
philosophical problem and then begin to argue as philosophers
and express our opinions. We must not do that. We are dealing
with the word of God, and the writings of the Apostle Paul are the
word of God.

Now we have the authority of the Apostle Peter for saying that.
Do you remember how he puts it in his Second Epistle at the end
of the third chapter? He is dealing with this whole question of the
end of the world and he says, '. . . even as our beloved brother Paul
also according to the wisdom given unto him hath written unto
you; as also in all his epistles, speaking in them of these things; in
which are some things hard to be understood, which they that are
unlearned and unstable wrest, as they do also the other
scriptures, unto their own destruction' [2 *Peter* 3 : 15–16]. Peter
was conceivably thinking about this passage which we are
examining – 'things hard to be understood'.

So we must be very careful that we do not find ourselves
arguing against God. What the Apostle writes here is not the
opinion of a man. He is writing under divine inspiration; he is

writing the word of God. And his teaching, as that of Peter, and of our Lord Himself is that the whole of the Old Testament is the word of God, and therefore we must humble ourselves before it and listen to it very carefully. Says Paul, in effect, 'I am not going to argue with you in terms of what I think; this is what God has said, this is God's word on this matter.' And so he quotes it to them. Therefore you and I must approach it in this way. I have often heard people who claim to believe the Scriptures 'from cover to cover' as they put it, quite unconsciously denying the Scriptures. I have heard them say, for example, concerning what the Apostle teaches about women, 'Oh, that is only the opinion of the Apostle Paul'. So that means, you see, that they think the Apostle is not divinely inspired. If, when you do not happen to agree with him, you begin to say that it is only the opinion of this man or that man who happens to be a writer, you are denying the doctrine of Scripture. Let us be careful what we are doing.

The Apostle submitted himself utterly and absolutely to the Scriptures. He had no other authority than the Scriptures and what was revealed to him as a chosen Apostle. And what applies to the Old Testament applies to the New and to the writings of this Apostle at this particular point. We are not arguing with a man, or looking back at someone who lived nearly two thousand years ago, and who did not have the advantages that we have – our latest developments of knowledge and of science, and our knowledge of grammar. The moment we begin to speak like that, we are denying that the New Testament Scriptures are the inspired infallible word of God. So we must submit ourselves and our judgment to the teachings of the Scriptures, and to the whole of Scripture. We must not only believe the Scriptures when we happen to agree with them, we must believe them when we do not; we must believe them when we do not understand; and if at a point they seem to us to be saying something that implies that there is unrighteousness in God, we say at once, 'That is impossible, there is something wrong with me. Let us go back to it again, let us examine it carefully. Let me, in a spirit of humility, and praying the Holy Spirit to enlighten me, go back again to see if I can arrive at an understanding.' That is the way to do it. Do it scrupulously.

My last point, to encourage us in this particular attitude and approach and spirit is this. History has its place and its value and its importance in this whole matter of interpretation, and if you have a feeling in your heart which says, 'I cannot possibly believe a thing like that. It means that God is unfair, that God is unjust, I cannot understand how God can choose a man before he is born, to me that is . . .', then, in addition to all I have said let this carry a little weight with you – that the greatest teachers in the Christian church throughout the centuries have believed and have taught this doctrine exactly as the Apostle Paul puts it here before us. Be very careful that you do not find yourself standing up against a man like the mighty Augustine of Hippo; be careful that you do not find yourself arguing with the man who is revered by the Roman Catholics above everybody else, Thomas Aquinas, because he interpreted it in exactly the same way as Augustine did. And so did all the great schoolmen and Martin Luther, John Calvin, John Knox, all the mighty Puritans, Jonathan Edwards, Charles Haddon Spurgeon, Charles Hodge, Robert Haldane, and many others.

Now I put it like that because there are people today who are so ignorant that they seem to regard this as some new doctrine which has suddenly come into the church, and they get excited about it and write articles and books and pamphlets about it, as if it were something quite new. Did you know that this doctrine is in the Thirty-Nine Articles of the Church of England? Did you know that until about 1860 all the denominations in this country, apart from the Methodists, believed it? Until then, John Wesley and the Methodists were the very small exception in the history of the church, but now, alas, we have lived in days when those who do not believe this truth are the rule and no longer the exception.

But throughout the running centuries the great expositors and doctors of the church took these words of the Apostles at their face value, and interpreted them accordingly and did their utmost to give enlightenment and understanding to all of us who by nature feel at first that this is something we cannot accept, we cannot believe. So listen to them. Not only be careful about your spirit, not only be careful lest you may be found arguing against the Scriptures or arguing against God, but let this come in as a supporting and as an additional argument. Do not put yourself into the position of the superficial thinkers who, because they cannot understand and explain, therefore reject the plain teaching of the Word of God.

This is a very solemn matter, so let us try to look at it always from this standpoint. What the Apostle is really concerned to do is to show that you and I, in spite of what we are still, in spite of our fallibility, our frailty and inconstancy, our lack of diligence, our ignorance, and our proneness to sin – what Paul is really trying to tell us is that if we are born again at all, if we are children of God, then we will always be that, and nothing and no one in heaven or hell or anywhere else can ever separate us from the love of God which is in Christ Jesus our Lord. He is not having an interesting discussion or an academic debate about election and predestination – that is not what he is doing at all. He is trying to tell us that if we are in the purpose of God, we will always be there. Or, to put it another way, because we are in the purpose of God we are saved, and because we are saved, we are in the purpose of God and always will be. He says that if it depended upon us in any way it would collapse, but it does not because this is entirely something that God does, and because God does it, it is safe, it is sure, it is final, it is certain.

Let us, then, realize what Paul is saying. Election is only a part of this; it is the way in which God carries out His purpose. But the great thing to look at always is the purpose of God which is brought to pass infallibly, absolutely, certainly, in this way and in spite of what is so true of every one of us.

Thirteen

*

What shall we say then? Is there unrighteousness with God? God forbid. For he saith to Moses, I will have mercy on whom I will have mercy, and I will have compassion on whom I will have compassion. So then it is not of him that willeth, nor of him that runneth, but of God that sheweth mercy. For the scripture saith unto Pharaoh, Even for this same purpose have I raised thee up, that I might shew my power in thee, and that my name might be declared throughout all the earth. Therefore hath he mercy on whom he will have mercy, and whom he will he hardeneth.

Romans 9 : 14–18

In our consideration of the great subject that the Apostle deals with in these verses, we have looked first at exactly what the Apostle is saying from verse 6 to verse 13. Then, having agreed about that, we are beginning to consider our reaction to it, and we have emphasized the importance of our approaching such a subject in the true and in the right spirit. But now, before continuing with the subject I want to add just a footnote to our last study. I gave a list of people and the way in which they had interpreted this whole matter of God's sovereign purpose in salvation; and I indicated that there was one big exception – John Wesley. I had already mentioned the case of Arminius, and Wesley was more or less a follower of Arminius. Someone may very well, therefore, say, 'How, then, can you reconcile these things, because Wesley was a man who undoubtedly was blessed of God and was used of God in the salvation of sinners, and yet you say that his whole attitude towards this subject was wrong?'

There are two replies which are to be made to that. The first is

– and I hope we are all clear about this – I am not saying that the understanding of this truth is essential to salvation. It is quite wrong to think that it is. What I am trying to show is that it is essential to a right understanding of the way and the mechanism of salvation, but it is not essential to salvation. And, indeed, I would have thought that the cases of people like Arminius and John Wesley prove this to the very hilt. Though a man may be wrong in his understanding of this particular aspect of the truth he can still be a Christian; he can even be used of God in the propagation of the good news of salvation.

In other words I would argue that this is in itself one of the strongest proofs of this doctrine, that it is not of man. God can use a man in spite of his being in a muddle intellectually. God can even use a man who may be wrong at certain points in his doctrine. Remember it is not a doctrine that is essential to salvation. You have to divide doctrine up in that way. There are certain things that a man must believe before he can be a Christian at all, but that does not apply to every aspect of doctrine. And so I say that the fact that God can use and bless the ministry of men who are actually wrong at this point is ultimately the greatest proof of this doctrine; that it is not the understanding of the preacher that matters, but God, the election of God and the working of His purpose through the word and the Holy Spirit upon it.

Let us, then, keep that clear in our minds and continue to work it out for ourselves. We are not concerned here with doctrine that determines whether people are Christians or not, whether they are saved or not. But we are very concerned about their assurance of salvation, which is a different thing. You can be saved without having assurance. So it is assurance that we are dealing with here.

Now in the previous chapter, we saw the reaction of the Apostle to any suggestion that there is 'unrighteousness with God'. He tells us that it is unthinkable. But Paul does not leave it at that; he wants to give us some further grounds for this expression of utter impossibility. Let us analyse his argument. It runs from verse 14 to verse 24, but let us look at it in general first before we proceed to the details. He puts the question in verse 14. In verses 15 to 18 he states the case in order to answer the objection that is raised on what he has said in verses 6 to 13.

Then from verses 19 to 24 he deals with a further objection which arises now out of that statement. In other words in verse 19 you will find, 'Thou wilt say then unto me, Why doth he yet find fault?', and that arises out of what he has just been saying. So in these verses he deals with this further objection and he answers it finally and completely. There is a general analysis of the passage.

Coming then first of all to the statement of the case in verses 15 to 18, we can further subdivide this also. Paul has two cases to state, because he has been saying two things in verses 6 to 13. The first is that God chooses to show mercy to some people; but secondly, Paul also says that God does not choose to show mercy to others, rather He hates them. 'Jacob have I loved, but Esau have I hated', and that before they were ever born.

So because he has made two statements, there are two objections in verse 14: 'What shall we say then? Is there unrighteousness with God?' – and it appears to be unrighteous in two ways. It seems to be unrighteous on God's part to give mercy to some and not to others, and it also seems to be unrighteous on the part of God to hate and to condemn some even before they are born. So the Apostle takes up both in verses 15 to 18. In verses 15 and 16 he deals with the first case and vindicates and establishes God's sovereignty and absolute freedom in showing mercy to those to whom He shows mercy. Then in verse 17 he deals with the second case, and here he vindicates and demonstrates God's sovereignty and freedom in rejecting some people. And in verse 18 he arrives at a general conclusion which is, 'Therefore hath he mercy on whom he will have mercy, and whom he will he hardeneth.'

That then is the statement of the case in general, so let us now look at the details. First of all, in verses 15 and 16, Paul takes the first case. He says, I justify my statement that God shows mercy to some and not to others in this way: 'For he saith to Moses, I will have mercy on whom I will have mercy, and I will have compassion on whom I will have compassion. So then it is not of him that willeth, nor of him that runneth, but of God that sheweth mercy.'

What does he mean by that? Well, what he is saying is that to show mercy to some, and to do so in the way that God does, cannot be unrighteous, because God Himself has said that He does so. The Apostle quotes from Exodus 33 and his argument, in effect, is this: 'You cannot say that this is unrighteous, because it is not I who am saying this. God Himself has told us, in what He said to Moses on that occasion, that He does this very thing, and,' says the Apostle, 'by implication, that is sufficient in and of itself. What God says is always final. What God says is always just and it is always righteous and when God says deliberately, explicitly, and specifically that He does a certain thing and in a certain way, then that should be the end of all argument.'

Now it is very interesting to notice the circumstances under which God made the statement to Moses in Exodus 33. We cannot go into this in detail but it is a great incident in the Old Testament, that followed what took place when Moses was up on the mount with God, and he came down and found the people worshipping the golden calf. The people had become restive and they felt that Moses had gone, so they went to Aaron, and Aaron had thus made this golden calf for them and there they were worshipping it. You remember what happened. Moses was filled with a sense of consternation and he pleaded on behalf of the people. And towards the end of that thirty-third chapter you will find that Moses, having made many requests of God, goes on in verse 18 to say, 'I beseech thee, shew me thy glory. And he [God] said, I will make all my goodness pass before thee, and I will proclaim the name of the Lord before thee; and will be gracious to whom I will be gracious, and will shew mercy on whom I will shew mercy.'

And what it means is this: Moses was asking not only for a manifestation of God's mercy, but for a manifestation of God's glory also to the whole nation. Not only for himself but for the whole nation. And God's reply to him is, I am not going to do this for the entire nation. 'I will have mercy on whom I will have mercy, and I will have compassion on whom I will have compassion.' Not the whole people, but upon certain members of the company only and not upon the others. Those are the circumstances in which God came to make this great statement to Moses.

The terms of this statement are interesting and important. He talks about 'mercy' and 'compassion'; or, as we have it in Exodus 33 : 19, about being 'gracious' and showing 'mercy'. And the two terms are used because there is a difference in their meaning. 'Mercy' represents the desire to relieve suffering, while 'compassion' (or graciousness) refers to the feelings which are experienced in the view of suffering. In other words, compassion generally comes before mercy. Compassion means that when you see a case of suffering, then there are certain feelings that are kindled within you immediately, a sense of sorrow and a sense of pity. And mercy is what puts that into practice. Mercy is more practical than compassion; it is the desire to relieve the suffering, to do something about it and to remove it.

So it is a matter of very great significance that these are the particular terms with which we are dealing. You see, the objection put forward to the teaching of the Apostle is that it seems to show 'unrighteousness with God'. 'Look,' says Paul, in effect, 'we are not dealing with a matter of righteousness here nor of justice, we are dealing with compassion and with mercy!' And this is absolutely vital to an understanding of the whole argument. If you want to bring in the notion of justice and of righteousness here, then you had better realize what you are saying. 'Wait a minute,' says the Apostle; 'if you want to argue with me in terms of justice and righteousness I will very easily tell you the position. It is this: If God dealt with any one of us in justice and in righteousness, then we would every one of us be damned eternally, because that is what we deserve.'

So it is important to understand our terms. We must not think of it in terms of justice and of righteousness at all, otherwise there is no hope for anybody. The whole world lies 'guilty before God'. 'There is none righteous, no, not one'; everyone deserves hell and eternal punishment. 'No,' says the Apostle, 'I am talking about compassion and about mercy, and, in the very use of the terms, any grounds whatsoever for any complaint against God's action are already removed.' Even if the Apostle had gone no further, therefore, the terms in and of themselves are sufficient to answer this charge of unrighteousness with God.

But we must go on, and you see how I am trying to build up the argument as the Apostle puts it. You start with your terms, then you consider the significance of those terms, and that is what we have just been doing.

Then, thirdly, what God said to Moses is a proclamation of the fact that God is not merciful to all: 'I will have mercy on whom I will have mercy, and I will have compassion on whom I will have compassion.' What He is saying is that He does not have mercy upon all; it is only upon some. Now this is a crucial and most important point. It is a mistake to think that God has to be merciful to all. We must differentiate between some of the attributes of God and others. God is always wise, God is always true, God is always holy, God is always powerful and God is always just in His dealings with all people, but, here, God Himself tells us quite deliberately that He is not always merciful, that He shows mercy not to all but only to some. There is a distinction here.

Now I make this point, because there is a doctrine which goes by the name of 'universalism', which believes that ultimately everybody will be saved. And the argument for that is that God is love and that God is mercy. So in order to emphasize my point let me quote from one of the great Puritan teachers, Stephen Charnock, who wrote a book on *The Existence and Attributes of God*. He puts it like this: 'God is necessarily good [compassionate] in regard to His nature but freely in regard to the effluxes of it to this or that particular subject He pitcheth upon.' Charnock says that there is a distinction between God as 'necessarily good', but God, in regard to the manifestation or the outflow of this goodness, is good with respect to this particular subject that He happens to 'pitch upon', or whom He happens to choose and not, indeed, to all.

Charnock then goes on, 'He is not necessarily communicative of His goodness as the sun is of its light, that chooseth not its objects but enlightens all indifferently.' You see his comparison? He says, Look at the sun. The sun emits the light and it goes everywhere. There is no question of choice involved; it does not choose to show some light here and not there. But God, he says, is not like that. 'This were to make God of no more understanding than the sun, to shine not where He pleaseth but where He must.' That is the point! God *pleaseth* to show mercy, He is not *bound* to show it. The very fact that He says, 'I will have mercy on whom I will have mercy, and I will have compassion on whom I will have compassion', means that He is not bound to. He chooses to sometimes and at other times He does not.

Charnock says that if it were not like that, and God had to show mercy to all, then God would be as mechanical as the sun shining in the heavens. 'But God', he says, 'is an understanding Agent and hath a sovereign right to choose His own subjects. It would not be a supreme goodness if it were not a voluntary goodness.' It would, in other words, be a kind of mechanical goodness. 'But', he says, 'God is absolutely free to dispense His goodness in what methods and measures He pleaseth according to the free determinations of His own will, guided by the wisdom of His mind, and regulated by the holiness of His nature. He is not to "give an account of any of His matters" [*Job* 33 : 13]. He will have mercy on whom He will have mercy, and He will have compassion on whom He will have compassion, and He will be good to whom He will be good.'

So the point that is established is this: God does not, because He is God, show mercy to everybody. Universalism teaches that He does, and it is very popular at the present time. It is the teaching, beyond any question, of Karl Barth, that well-known theologian on the continent of Europe. He teaches 'universal salvation' – that at the end everybody is going to be saved. His particular reason for saying this is that it is all in Christ, that Christ is the only elect person; we are all condemned in Christ; we are all saved in Christ. That is how he arrives at it, but we need not go into that now.

But there are others who teach this same universalism. I quoted Professor William Barclay in an earlier study; he teaches this quite unashamedly in most of his books, and often in his articles. He believes that at the end all humanity irrespectively will have been redeemed. There will be no such thing as anybody finally lost and irredeemable and suffering the torment of eternal hell.

Dr C. H. Dodd, whom we have previously quoted, also has a commentary on this very passage. He can see quite clearly that Paul is here teaching that God chooses some individuals and rejects others, but then he says in brackets, 'We shall see that this selection of individuals is made with a view to the ultimate elevation of all mankind into the new order.'

Now that is typical universalist teaching and it is very common. And, of course, there is only this to say about it: it is an entire contradiction not only of this passage but of innumerable other passages in the whole of the Bible. The Bible clearly divides mankind into the saved and the lost, those who are going to be with God and those who are going to be shut out from His presence eternally, those who are going to heaven and those who are going to hell. It is in the Old Testament and it is here in the New. Our Lord Himself taught it. It is everywhere. But it is entirely rejected by these people.

On what grounds, then, do they believe in their universalism? It is entirely on the grounds of their own thought. Their argument is: If God is love, if God has mercy, it is inconceivable that anybody should be outside it. But that is to reason from philosophy. That is to reason on their own understanding of God, and it is to deny what God Himself said to Moses. God said to Moses, 'I am not going to show mercy to all. I will have mercy on whom I will have mercy, and I will have compassion on whom I will have compassion.' The teaching of universalism is not merely a contradiction of the teaching of the Apostle Paul and of the Son of God; it is a contradiction of the plain teaching of God Himself.

We are handling very high and important and serious matters here. In the end it comes to this: on what are you basing your position? There are only two ultimate bases. You either believe this to be the inspired Word of God and trust yourself entirely to what it says, or else you base your position upon what you think and what other people think with you. It has to be one or the other. So that ultimately it is not an argument about this particular teaching; it is an argument as to whether this is the Word of God or whether it is not. Was the Apostle Paul here controlled by the Holy Spirit when he wrote? Can you trust that report in Exodus of what God said to Moses? If you are a universalist you are rejecting both and you are putting your idea of the love of God and of mercy in God before the plain, explicit teaching of the word of God, this Holy Scripture. I leave it to you. For myself I know nothing apart from what I have in this Book. I have no authority, I have no opinion, apart from what I am told here. And it seems to me that even if we had nothing else, we have here as explicit a condemnation of universalism as can ever be found. Let us be careful lest we insinuate a little bit of our own thinking.

There are other forms which this argument takes; it is not

only universalism. There are those who teach a kind of 'conditional immortality'. It is the same argument. They say, 'I cannot believe that the love of God can finally leave people in that sinful condition and punish them forever.' Now that again is nothing but a human opinion. So let us be careful that we do not contradict ourselves and say that we do believe the teaching of Scripture and then suddenly drop it and introduce our own philosophic conception of God, and, because we are in difficulties, put that before the plain teaching of Scripture itself.

Then the fourth point is that whether we receive mercy or not depends solely upon the sovereign will of God: 'I will have mercy on whom I will have mercy, and I will have compassion on whom I will have compassion.' Now the Apostle is there substantiating what he has already told us in verse 11: 'For the children being not yet born, neither having done any good or evil, that the purpose of God according to election might stand, not of works, but of him that calleth.' It is His will that calls; it is His will that shows the compassion and the mercy; it is entirely a matter of God's will.

But we must go on in verse 16. Paul draws his conclusion from this: 'So then'! 'So then it is not of him that willeth, nor of him that runneth, but of God that sheweth mercy.' You see, he does not take any risks; he knows us so well. He knows that we will wriggle out of an argument, wriggle out of a plain statement. He says, You shall not; let me put it another way round, and here it is explicitly.

Now what does 'it is' mean here? It means participation in the mercy of God, or participation in salvation. What decides whether a man is saved or lost, whether he is in the kingdom of God or outside, is 'not of him that willeth, nor of him that runneth, but of God that sheweth mercy'. Now the will, of course, the willing, is perfectly clear here. 'It is not of him that willeth' means 'it is not of a man's desire'. What decides whether a man is saved or not, is not that *he* desires to be saved. 'Nor of him that runneth', means that salvation does not depend upon a person's works or activities.

Now this is quite plain and explicit; let me put it, therefore, as plainly as I can. The Apostle says that our salvation is not the result of our desiring it, neither is it the result of anything whatsoever that we do about it. He excludes both desire and action. In other words, he excludes everything.

We must be quite clear about this. Paul is not talking here about the self-righteous. There are some who try to get out of this difficulty by saying that the Apostle is only talking about a man who trusts in his own works. No, he is going much further than that, he is including everything that the man is capable of – all his desires, all his wishes, everything. None of them comes in at all. 'But surely', says somebody, 'our faith comes in; surely it is my faith that ultimately matters? What decides whether a man is saved or not is: Does he believe or does he not? The man who believes is saved; the man who does not believe is not saved.'

No, says Paul, because if you say that, you are turning that belief, that faith, into a work; it comes in 'running', it is the man's activity, so in that case he is given the reward of salvation for his faith, for his belief. But this is not reward! If it were a matter of reward nobody would ever bring the charge that God is unjust and unrighteous. The charge arises because God chooses one and not the other when neither of them has done anything at all; he has not desired, he has not willed, he has not done anything at all. God chooses before they are born.

Can anything be more explicit than this? We must never say that our salvation depends upon anything whatsoever in us. The willing and the running exclude every activity on the side of man. 'It is', as the Apostle puts it, 'of God that sheweth mercy', which is just another way of saying what he has said at the end of verse 11: it is 'of him that calleth'. It is entirely, utterly, absolutely, altogether from God. It is God's will; it is God's choice; it is entirely of God. And that is Paul's statement.

Now I generally think that the best way, perhaps, of approaching this and trying to grasp it and to understand it is to look at it in the light of the parable which is found in Matthew 20 : 1–6, the parable of the workers in the vineyard. This always seems to me to be the best commentary on Paul's statement, coming from the lips of our blessed Lord Himself. You see, people have always objected to this doctrine; they have always tried to put up their own works. So take the context of that parable, in Matthew 19 beginning at verse 24. It follows the case of the rich young ruler and we read, 'And again', says our Lord, 'I say unto you, It is easier for a camel to go through the eye of a needle, than for a rich man to enter into the kingdom of God. When his disciples heard it, they were exceedingly amazed, saying, Who then can be saved? But Jesus beheld them, and said unto them, With men this is impossible; but with God all things are possible. Then answered Peter and said unto him, Behold, we have forsaken all, and followed thee; what shall we have therefore? And Jesus said unto them, Verily I say unto you, That ye which have followed me, in the regeneration when the Son of man shall sit in the throne of his glory, ye also shall sit upon twelve thrones, judging the twelve tribes of Israel. And every one that hath forsaken houses, or brethren, or sisters, or father, or mother, or wife, or children, or lands, for my name's sake, shall receive an hundred-fold, and shall inherit everlasting life. But many that are first shall be last; and the last shall be first.' And then comes the parable of the workers in the vineyard. Surely it was a mistake to have divided up the chapters in this way! This parable belongs essentially to the end of chapter 19.

And what is the message of the parable? Surely it is quite plain. Here are men who come and say that they want work, and the master agrees with them that if they go and work in the vineyard that day, he will give them a penny for doing so. But then, later on in the day, even at the eleventh hour, he goes out and sees some people standing idle in the market and he says, 'Why stand ye here all the day idle?' So he said to them, 'Go ye also into the vineyard; and whatsoever is right, that shall ye receive.' He makes no bargain with them; he just tells them that if they are prepared to trust him, then he will give them that which is right. Then the end of the day comes and the lord of the vineyard chooses to pay first those who went in at the eleventh hour; they have only worked for an hour and he gives them a penny.

And then, we are told, 'When the first came, they supposed that they should have received more; and they likewise received every man a penny. And when they had received it, they murmured against the goodman of the house' – Is there unrighteousness with God? You see! – 'saying, These last have wrought but one hour, and thou hast made them equal unto us which have borne the burden and heat of the day.' They say, You are unjust, you are unfair, you have given them the same amount as us and they have only done a twelfth part of the work that we have done; it is not righteous.

'But he answered one of them, and said, Friend, I do thee no wrong: didst not thou agree with me for a penny?' That is justice, that is righteousness; you agreed with me, you would do this work, you would work for twelve hours for a penny. 'Take that thine is, and go thy way.' You have no grounds of complaint; I am dealing with you on the grounds of strict, absolute justice and righteousness and fairness; there is nothing unjust in what I am doing, I am carrying out the bargain. 'I will give unto this last, even as unto thee. Is it not lawful for me to do what I will with mine own?' What are you complaining of? I have paid you what I promised, and it is a fair wage and you have said you would be satisfied. Why do you complain, what right have you to complain, why do you intervene at all? Can I not do what I like with my own money? If I choose to give a penny to this last man who has not earned it as you have, why should I not? 'Is thine eye evil, because I am good? So the last shall be first, and the first last: for many be called, but few chosen.'

And that is a perfect commentary on this very matter. People say, 'Is it right that one should be forgiven and shown mercy, that one should be given it and not another? Is that right, is that fair, is that just?' But that is the argument of the Pharisees, and whoever objects to this teaching we are looking at in Romans 9 is really being a Pharisee. The Pharisees were furious with our Lord for mixing with the publicans and sinners. They said, 'These people are sinners and there He is sitting down with them and eating with them and talking to them. He should only be with us because we are good people; we deserve it, they do not, they have done nothing, and there He is mixing with them. This is wrong; this man is a blasphemer, this man is a sinner.' That was their objection to His teaching and to His conduct and behaviour.

But this is the reply to it: If you want to bring in the notion of justice and of righteousness, very well, you will get your wages, you will get what you deserve, and the wages of sin is death! If it were a matter of justice and of righteousness, as we have already seen, all would be damned; nobody has any claim upon God's mercy. The fact that anybody has ever received mercy is entirely because of the character and the nature of God. The real mystery is not that everybody is *not* saved, but that anybody *is* saved – that is the mystery! God owes nothing to anybody, but if He chooses to do something with what is His own, should our eye be evil because He is good? God has a right to show mercy to whom He will; He has a right to have compassion upon whom He will; there is no ground of complaint whatsoever.

There is no legal opposition, then, that we can erect against this, there is no charge that we can bring against God. If He did nothing, but allowed the whole of mankind to go to everlasting perdition no one would have the slightest ground of complaint. So God is absolutely free to do as He likes and as He pleases. And what He told Moses, and what is repeated by Paul is that He chooses to show mercy to some and not to others. Why? you ask me. I do not know. He does not tell us. That is the mystery. But that He has a right to do it is surely as plain as anything can be. Do not talk about justice and righteousness. This is mercy; this is compassion! It is altogether a free gift of God, and He has a right to do anything He likes. The mystery, the thing that we ought to be amazed about, is not that He has mercy upon some and not upon others, but that He has mercy upon anybody at all, and especially that He has had mercy upon us.

We are not told anywhere in the Bible what determines this in God; we are obviously not meant to know; it is too big for us. God is in heaven and we are on earth. He says, 'My thoughts are not your thoughts, neither are your ways my ways . . . as the heavens are higher than the earth, so are . . . my thoughts than your thoughts' [*Isaiah* 55 : 8–9]. Do not try to understand the mind of the eternal God. You cannot! Recognize what He says, what He does, recognize His right to do so. And if you have ever received mercy, and know you have had it, then if you really examine the whole position you will not feel that there is any unrighteousness or injustice in God in this. You will be filled with this sense of wonder and amazement that He has been able to have mercy on anybody, above all on you. And when you consider the way He contrived in order to show this mercy and to make it actual and practical, even in delivering His only begotten Son up to the death of the cross on Calvary's hill, your amazement and astonishment will be so great that far from asking questions about unrighteousness and injustice you will humble yourself before Him, 'Lost in wonder, love and praise'!

Fourteen

*

For the scripture saith unto Pharaoh, Even for this same purpose
have I raised thee up, that I might shew my power in thee, and
that my name might be declared throughout all the earth.
Therefore hath he mercy on whom he will have mercy, and whom
he will he hardeneth.

Romans 9 : 17–18

We have seen that in verses 15 to 18 the Apostle Paul is dealing
with the two objections to his teaching in verses 6 to 13. In the
first place he establishes God's sovereignty and freedom in
showing mercy to those to whom He shows mercy. Now in verse
17 we come to his handling of the second case, this charge of
unrighteousness in God in the light of this teaching, and he starts
off by saying, 'For the scripture saith'. Now this is an interesting
point because the word 'for' here might very well lead us to think
that verse 17 follows directly on his teaching in verses 15 and
16. But quite patently it does not; it goes back to verses 13 and 14.
Verse 13, as we have just seen, puts the general position like this:
'Jacob have I loved, but Esau have I hated.' Then comes the
objection, 'What shall we say then? Is there unrighteousness
with God?' – for loving Jacob and for hating Esau – 'God forbid.'
Then verses 15 and 16 show that there is no unrighteousness in
God loving Jacob and showing mercy to whom He will show
mercy. Then having dealt with that, Paul says in effect, 'I will
take up the other objection now, What about the hating of Esau?'
– and he introduces that. So that the 'for' at the beginning of this
verse 17 really connects us with the statement in verses 13 and
14. It is the second aspect of this general criticism, or, as we have
put it, it is the statement of the second subsidiary case.

[165]

Now here we really are looking at one of the most difficult problems that can confront anybody who ever reads the Bible, even more difficult than that of our last study. There is nothing, I imagine, in the whole range of the scriptural teaching which causes such offence to the natural man and to many uninstructed Christians as this very statement: 'For the scripture saith unto Pharaoh, Even for this same purpose have I raised thee up, that I might shew my power in thee, and that my name might be declared throughout all the earth. Therefore' – the general conclusion to the two cases – 'hath he mercy on whom he will have mercy, and whom he will he hardeneth.' It is the 'hardening' that is the rock of offence.

So as we look at this statement, the first thing for us to do once again is to take the terms as they are used by the great Apostle. I am taking it for granted that you are studying this because you are not afraid of difficulties and because you do not say that if a thing is difficult then you will not examine it or try to understand it. I take it that you are studying this because you want light on it, that you do not shy off like a frightened horse and, because you do not like a thing, say, 'I do not look at that; I keep to the parts of Scripture that I like.' Of course that is quite fatal. It is dishonouring to God, quite apart from the fact that it is dishonouring also to the Scripture.

Let us see, then, how the Apostle handles it. The first thing we notice is that he says, 'The scripture saith unto Pharaoh . . .' That is an interesting statement in and of itself because if you go back to Exodus chapter 9 verse 16, you will find that it was God who spoke through Moses. But here the Apostle refers to it as 'scripture', which tells us once more something that we must never forget about Scripture. It is God's word, and the terms you will find in the New Testament are always used interchangeably: 'God said'; 'the Spirit saith'; 'the scripture saith'; 'the Holy Ghost saith'.

In other words, we are not dealing here with the opinions of the Apostle Paul. That is something that has been said a great deal, is it not? You hear people saying, when they do not like something, 'Ah, but that is only what Paul says.' Of course, if you start speaking like that, what you are really doing is showing your view of the Scriptures. This man is an Apostle of Jesus Christ; he is divinely inspired, and he has been given a revelation. So when people make such statements, they are denying the doctrine that the Scripture is the uniquely inspired and inerrant Word of God. Let us be careful how we handle the Scriptures. It was Moses who actually spoke to Pharaoh, but here Paul says, 'The scripture saith . . .'; 'God saith . . .' These things are synonymous and they are interchangeable.

But the real argument which the Apostle develops and which ought to settle the matter for us is this: If, as we saw in our last study, the Scripture says a thing, then there is no more to be said, we have just got to accept it. As Christians we are people who submit ourselves to this Book; we know nothing apart from it. We are not philosophers, nor seekers and searchers after the truth. We are children, we say we know nothing, we need to be enlightened and to be taught. We believe that this is God's revelation; here is God speaking, and we submit ourselves to it. So that when you are dealing with a Christian in a matter that is difficult to understand, and you say, 'The Scripture says', then immediately it ought to be the end of all argument and doubt.

Now Paul has used that argument in both these subsidiary cases that he puts forward. We saw before that he says, 'He saith to Moses, I will have mercy on whom I will have mercy.' Very well, if God said that to Moses, there it is; it is not a matter of opinion; God has said it. Here again we have exactly the same thing. Whatever God says is always right, it is always just, and it is always true. The Apostle is saying here, in effect, 'I am not expressing my own opinion; this is what God has said. You say that it sounds as if it is unrighteous that God should say, "Esau have I hated"; you do not like this aspect of rejection as well as favour. 'But', says Paul, 'you should not raise this question, for the Scripture has said, God Himself has spoken.' And then he goes on to quote this statement which God gave to Moses to say to Pharaoh, that great potentate under whose authority the children of Israel were living at that point. It is there in Exodus 9 : 16, and because God has said it, there cannot be any element of unrighteousness about it; this is the end of all dispute!

However, the Apostle is obviously anxious that we should consider the statement, so let us look first at the terms which are used, because people often find difficulty with them. Here is the first statement: God said to Pharaoh through Moses, 'For this same purpose have I raised thee up . . .' Now this term 'raised thee up' is liable to misunderstanding, and because of this people get into trouble. A better translation would be, 'I have caused thee to stand.' The meaning conveyed in the original term is that of allowing someone to appear, or bringing someone forward on to the stage of events. Charles Hodge has, I believe, a very good translation here: 'For this purpose have I raised thee up and placed thee where thou art, instead of cutting thee off at once.'

Now it is a difficult expression but there is this general consensus of opinion among the authorities with regard to its exact meaning. The danger is to assume that it means, 'For this purpose have I created thee.' But it does not mean that. There is no suggestion here of creation. The whole idea is of bringing on to the scene of action at that particular point and juncture in history. So we must get rid of any notion that Pharaoh was made for this purpose.

The second term is the one which is mentioned at the end of verse 18 – 'whom he will he hardeneth' – and it is this hardening process which is a rock of offence to large numbers of people. To harden means to render obstinate, to render stubborn. It does not merely mean to punish; it is more than that, and here, again, there has often been an attempt to say, 'That man Paul was a legalist, a lawyer, and he can think in terms like this, but this sort of thing is remote from God.' But the history in the book of Exodus uses this term ten times over so that there shall be no question or mistake about it at all.

But here is where the difficulty comes in. The record in Exodus not only tells us that God hardened Pharaoh's heart; it also tells us that Pharaoh hardened his own heart. There is an example of that in Exodus 8, in two separate statements: 'But when Pharaoh saw that there was respite, he hardened his heart, and hearkened not unto them; as the Lord had said' [*Exodus* 8 : 15]; and then in verse 32: 'And Pharaoh hardened his heart at this time also, neither would he let the people go.' Here then is the problem which confronts us.

How do we resolve it? Well, there are some who have tried to do so by saying, 'That is quite simple, all it really means is that God allowed Pharaoh to harden himself.' But that will not do. The word used is an active word; it is not a permissive idea at all. The statement, quite definitely, is that God rendered Pharaoh stubborn and obstinate. It was not merely that He permitted him to become thus, as the word that is used here in the eighteenth verse demonstrates: 'Therefore hath he mercy on whom he will have mercy, and whom he will he hardeneth.' There it puts it squarely and solidly, as it were, on to God. God does this.

But quite apart from that we have the statement in Exodus 4, which surely should make this clear to us. Before Moses had ever been sent to Pharaoh, God tells him, 'When thou goest to return into Egypt, see that thou do all these wonders before Pharaoh, which I have put in thine hand: but I will harden his heart, that he shall not let the people go' [*Exodus* 4 : 21]. So you see, it is not God just allowing Pharaoh to react in this wrong way when Moses speaks to him. No, God tells Moses beforehand that He is going to do this, so we must take it in a very active and in a very definite sense. The temptation always is to try to slide out of difficulties by explaining them away. You cannot do that. We have got to face this honestly and squarely.

How, then, do we deal with these two aspects of the statement? The answer is, of course, that they are both true. God hardened the heart of Pharaoh, and Pharaoh hardened his own heart as well. There is no real conflict between the two things. The point the Apostle is establishing is that God ordained that Pharaoh should be there at that particular point and juncture in order that through him and by means of him He might make known His might and His name throughout the whole world. There, then, is the statement. But notice the procedure we have adopted: we take the terms, we make sure of the meaning of each particular term, and then we take the statement as a whole and see what it says. And that is the conclusion we arrive at: that we are being reminded here quite definitely that God did harden Pharaoh's heart in addition to the fact that Pharaoh hardened it himself.

So having clarified what Paul is saying, we now come to its meaning. How do we react to all this? What do we make of it? Let me start with a negative and give you an illustration of how we must not face it. It is a quotation from the *Commentary on the Epistle to the Romans* by Dr C. H. Dodd. It is a commentary in the Moffatt series that was very popular before World War II and still is. This is how Dr Dodd approaches the problem.

Having dealt with verses 15 and 16 he now comes to verses 17 and 18 and this is what we read: 'The next step, however, that Paul takes seems to be a false step. It was not necessary, for his argument, to show that God also creates bad dispositions in those who are not to be saved, that He not only has mercy on anyone just as He pleases, but also makes anyone stubborn just as He pleases. It was enough for Paul's purpose here that the positive working of God's redeeming purpose should be self-determined in regard to its objects. This position is guaranteed by data of the religious consciousness, for the truly religious man knows that any good that is in him is there solely by the grace of God, whatever he may make of this in his philosophy.' Dr Dodd finds no difficulty about that first objection, the religious consciousness has to agree with that. Whatever a man may call himself theologically, when he is on his knees he has to admit and confess that he has had it all from God, and that he is what he is by the grace of God.

'But to attribute one's evil dispositions to God', he continues, 'is a sophistication. One may feel driven to it by logic, but the conscience does not corroborate it. The doctrine of sin which we have met in the earlier chapters of the epistle (particularly chapters 1 and 7) does not admit of this solution of the problem. It was however a good *argumentum ad hominem*, for the Jewish objector would be bound to recognize the authority of the Scripture which said that God made Pharaoh stubborn [*Exodus* 9 : 12, 16], and could not complain if Paul gave it an application of which he had not thought.' You see the argument, he says: Now of course while our conscience cannot corroborate this, Paul was very clever there. He knew he was dealing with Jews who believed the Scripture, and therefore when he quotes the Scripture against them, they cannot answer him. It is a clever debating point but our conscience does not corroborate it.

Then he goes on, 'The Hebrew mind tended to determinism, attributing to the omnipotent will of God, as first cause, all consequences of second causes, and this tendency was strengthened in the rabbinic period by a definite fight against dualism, which might introduce into the universe a "second power" over against the One God. Such dualism was familiar to the Jews through the Zoroastrian religion of Persia. But a fully ethical conception of God makes it self-contradictory to attribute evil to His will. Paul shared the tendency to determinism, but when he had fully in view the revelation of God in Christ as pure love, he could not hold that sin was the result of His action. Here' – in these verses we are dealing with – 'his thought declines from its highest level. And, while the argument is primarily *ad hominem*, it does lead up to a doctrine for which he later makes himself responsible – namely, that by divine decree Israel was blinded to the significance of the Gospel [11 : 8]. That doctrine is set forth with qualifications which partly draw the venom from it. Here he pushes what we must describe as an unethical determinism to its logical extreme, in order to force his opponent to confess the absolute and arbitrary sovereign will of God.'

I have given that quotation at length in order to show how we should not react and how we should not interpret this statement which the Apostle quotes from the book of Exodus. And all we need say about it, is this: Here is a man who does not hesitate to set himself up as a greater authority on ethics and the love of God than the Apostle Paul, a man who does not hesitate to sit in judgment on the Apostle Paul and to say that Paul is quite wrong in saying this and that he has fallen from his own standard. The commentator is a greater man, a greater mind, a greater spirit and a greater saint than the Apostle, and he looks on as a judge. He says, Now the Apostle at other times, of course, has this wonderful conception of the love of God, but in order to score a debating point over the Jews, he has let himself down here.

But when you adopt that attitude you have no authority at all except what you yourself think. If you think you can sit in judgment on the apostles, then you are the authority; it is your religious consciousness; it is what you think and what you feel. And you are left in the position of those who do not submit to the Scriptures; they themselves are the authority and you must believe what they say. If they do not understand a thing or do not like it, they say it is wrong. But, the moment you take that attitude towards the Scripture, what do you believe and what do you not believe? And, of course, Dr Dodd is so wrong in his statement where he says that Paul here attributes any ethical wrongness to God, or says that He puts the idea of ethical wrongness into a man. Paul, as we shall see, does not say that at all.

We have also looked in detail at that quotation because you will find that the bulk of modern commentators take that view. Dr Dodd in this matter is but a typical and representative sample of the way in which men come to the word of God trusting to themselves and their own understanding and not hesitating to arrogate to themselves a superiority even to the divinely inspired apostles. But our view is that our whole faith is built upon the foundation of the apostles and prophets, and that we would know nothing at all were it not for their teaching. It is always wrong to sit in judgment upon the scriptural teaching. That is simply to exalt modern man and to put him above the very word of God, this Scripture which the Apostle equates with the mind and the heart of God Himself.

No, the right way to approach such a passage is this: Whenever you have a difficult passage of Scripture you must compare it with other Scriptures. This is not an isolated statement at all; there are many other statements in Scripture that say almost exactly what we find here. If we go back to Genesis 45 verses 7 and 8, we will find something along the same lines. There is Joseph, down in Egypt, a great man under Pharaoh, a sort of Food Controller, and his brothers, because of the famine, have come down for food – you remember the beautiful story. At last Joseph makes himself known to his brothers, and when they realize that this great man, in whose hands they are entirely, is none other than their own brother Joseph, whom they had sold and treated in such a shameful and abominable manner, they are filled with terror. But this is how Joseph speaks to them: 'And God sent me before you to preserve you a posterity in the earth, and to save your lives by a great deliverance. So now it was not you that sent me hither, but God: and he hath made me a father to Pharaoh, and lord of all his house, and a ruler throughout all the land of Egypt.'

What an extraordinary statement! These brothers of Joseph, in that shameful way, had first of all decided to kill him, but one of them pleaded for him, so when some travelling people came along they decided to sell him to them. It was a most disgraceful action. But Joseph says, 'God sent me before you . . . it was not you that sent me hither, but God.' The evil action of the brothers is attributed to God. And the same point is made again by Joseph in Genesis 50 verse 20. These brethren after the death of their father Jacob were terrified again. They thought that after the old man had gone, Joseph would now probably turn on them, but he puts it like this: 'But as for you, ye thought evil against me: but God meant it unto good, to bring to pass, as it is this day, to save much people alive.' There is a perfect statement, it seems to me, of this whole doctrine.

Consider, too, Psalm 105. Here we find the Psalmist reviewing the story of the children of Israel, and in verse 23 he says, 'Israel also came into Egypt; and Jacob sojourned in the land of Ham. And he increased his people greatly; and made them stronger than their enemies.' Then verse 25 says, 'He turned their heart to hate his people, to deal subtilly with his servants.' It was God who turned the heart of the Egyptians to hate His own people, the children of Israel.

Then there are other such statements in the New Testament; here are some of the most important and crucial. In John 12 verses 37 to 41 we read, 'But though he had done so many miracles before them, yet they believed not on him: that the saying of Esaias the prophet might be fulfilled, which he spake, Lord, who hath believed our report? and to whom hath the arm of the Lord been revealed? Therefore they could not believe, because that Esaias said again, He hath blinded their eyes, and hardened their heart; that they should not see with their eyes, nor understand with their heart, and be converted, and I should heal them. These things said Esaias, when he saw his glory, and spake of him.' Verse 39 is especially important there.

But then in Acts 2 : 22–23 there is a remarkable statement in the sermon preached by Peter on the day of Pentecost: 'Ye men of Israel, hear these words; Jesus of Nazareth, a man approved of God among you by miracles and wonders and signs, which God did by him in the midst of you, as ye yourselves also know:' – notice this – 'him, being delivered by the determinate counsel and foreknowledge of God, ye have taken, and by wicked hands have crucified and slain.' Peter is referring to the crucifixion and he shows how they had done something, yes, but it was God who was behind it all and brought it to pass. 'The determinate counsel and foreknowledge of God' led to this action that was done, first by the Jews taking Him and then handing Him over to these wicked men, these pagan Romans, to do the deed.

[173]

You will find the same thought in the prayer offered by the church as recorded in Acts 4. Peter and John had been tried and set free on condition that they stop preaching and teaching in the name of this Jesus. And 'they went to their own company, and reported all that the chief priests and elders had said unto them. And when they heard that, they lifted up their voice to God with one accord'; they began to pray, and we read, in verses 27 and 28, 'For of a truth against thy holy child Jesus, whom thou hast anointed, both Herod and Pontius Pilate, with the Gentiles, and the people of Israel, were gathered together, for to do whatsoever thy hand and thy counsel determined before to be done.' Again they refer to the death of our Lord upon the cross, and what we are told is that Herod and Pontius Pilate and all the others were simply doing whatsoever God's hand and counsel determined before to be done. The death of Christ was accomplished by men, yes, but still more important is this: it was God who brought it to pass. It was His action. He used men actually to do it, the physical part of it, but it is by 'the determinate counsel and foreknowledge of God'.

The death on the cross is God's way of giving us salvation. Never think of the cross of Christ in terms of the action of men only. If you do, you have got it wrong. It is God who was 'in Christ, reconciling the world unto himself' [2 *Corinthians* 5 : 19]. It is God who 'hath laid on him the iniquity of us all' [*Isaiah* 53 : 6]. It is God who 'hath made him to be sin for us, who knew no sin; that we might be made the righteousness of God in him' [2 *Corinthians* 5 : 21]. Here it is preached on the day of Pentecost and ever afterwards. It is God's action, though men come into it in this extraordinary manner.

So you will find that in Romans 11 : 8, as Dr Dodd has reminded us, there is a further statement of the same thing. Here, we are dealing with this blindness in Israel: 'According as it is written, God hath given them the spirit of slumber, eyes that they should not see, and ears that they should not hear.' Now Dr Dodd does not pay any attention to the fact that the Apostle is quoting Scripture there again. He attributes it to a lapse on the part of Paul. But it is not Paul's idea; it is God who said it; it is the Scripture that said it.

Then you find it once more in 2 Thessalonians 2 : 11–12. Now we are looking forward: 'And for this cause God shall send them strong delusion, that they should believe a lie: that they all might be damned who believed not the truth, but had pleasure in unrighteousness.' You have the same doctrine taught in I Peter 2 : 8. Here he is describing our Lord as 'a stone of stumbling, and a rock of offence, even to them which stumble at the word, being disobedient: whereunto also they were appointed'. And my last quotation is in the Epistle of Jude in the fourth verse: 'For there are certain men crept in unawares, who were before of old ordained to this condemnation, ungodly men, turning the grace of our God into lasciviousness, and denying the only Lord God, and our Lord Jesus Christ.'

There, then, are these parallel statements which we have in the Scripture. You see the way to approach the problem? Here is a statement, here are parallel statements. Clearly, this is not some temporary lapse or failure on the part of the great Apostle, this clever debater who stoops just to win a debating point. No, it is plain teaching in the Scripture, and it is by no means confined to the Apostle Paul.

So having seen that, what is the teaching? It is this: It does not mean that God creates sin, neither does it mean that God creates an evil disposition in the heart, as, for example, Dr Dodd suggests. God does not, or cannot, do that. We have a statement by the Apostle James that ought to put us right on this once and for ever, where he says in chapter I verse 13, 'Let no man say when he is tempted, I am tempted of God: for God cannot be tempted with evil, neither tempteth he any man.' God is not the author of evil, God cannot be tempted by evil and He never tempts anyone.

So, then, the teaching is this: God does not create evil or put it there, but He aggravates what is there for His own great purpose. God never made Pharaoh an unbeliever, but because he was an unbeliever God aggravated his unbelief in order to bring to pass His own great purpose of showing His power and His glory. He did not create the evil disposition in Pharaoh. We are not told that. All we are told is that Pharaoh being the man he was, God used him for His own purpose. And not only that; God saw to it that he was there at that particular point and juncture in order that He might do this through him.

How is it that God hardens the heart in this way? We are told that He hardened the heart of Pharaoh, and, as we have seen, Pharaoh hardened his own heart also. Pharaoh was opposed to

God and all that God was doing, and God makes that even worse. Now that is the teaching and it is the explanation of the various passages of Scripture which we have considered.

But how does God do this? Well, already in the Epistle to the Romans in chapter 1 verses 24, 26 and 28, we have been told one of the ways in which He does it. Verse 24: 'Wherefore God also gave them up to uncleanness through the lusts of their own hearts, to dishonour their own bodies between themselves.' Verse 26: 'For this cause God gave them up unto vile affections: for even their women did change the natural use into that which is against nature.' Verse 28: 'And even as they did not like to retain God in their knowledge, God gave them over to a reprobate mind, to do those things which are not convenient.'

What do these verses mean? Well, one of God's ways of hardening is that He withdraws His restraining influences. The world fell into sin but God put a limit, a restraint upon it, and this world would be complete chaos and hell if He did not do so. But the moment He draws back His restraining influence there is hardening. When the sun is withdrawn, the ground is hard and frozen, but when the sun comes out it will melt. The withdrawal of the sun produces hardening. So that is one of the ways in which God produces hardening. He hands people over to a reprobate heart; He leaves them to themselves, and takes away everything that tends to produce the softening.

But secondly, in chapter 7 of Romans, we see another way in which God causes hardening, and that is, by emphasizing His justice and His righteousness in the law: 'For when we were in the flesh, the motions of sins, which were by the law, did work in our members to bring forth fruit unto death' [*Romans* 7 : 5]. Or again in further verses of that same chapter, verses 8, 9 and 10: 'But sin, taking occasion by the commandment, wrought in me all manner of concupiscence. For without the law sin was dead. For I was alive without the law once: but when the commandment came, sin revived, and I died. And the commandment, which was ordained to life, I found to be unto death.' And in verse 13 he sums it all up: 'Was then that which is good made death unto me? God forbid. But sin, that it might appear sin, working death in me by that which is good; that sin by the commandment might become exceeding sinful.'

We can put it like this. Here is a man who is a sinner; the law comes to him and begins to speak to him about his sin and to denounce it, and it infuriates him and he becomes a still greater sinner. The law that tells him not to sin, incites him do it all the more. Not only that, it even inflames his passions and his desires. Now as I have pointed out,[1] this shows the whole danger of this moral teaching, and the teaching about sex at the present time. It is said, 'Let us teach these people about these things and they will not do them.' Will they not? It will merely stimulate their appetite to do them. In telling them not to do a thing you are introducing them to the thing. By prohibiting it, by telling them it is wrong, you are making them worse than they were. And so you have the same doctrine exactly taught in Titus 1 : 15: 'Unto the pure all things are pure: but unto them that are defiled and unbelieving is nothing pure; but even their mind and conscience is defiled.' You will find people reading books on sex and morality ostensibly to do themselves good, and they will tell you afterwards that they were much worse after they had read them than they were before. That is because of the evil that is already there. When the law comes and righteousness and justice speak, it aggravates the evil in the evil man.

But then there is a third way in which God effects this hardening of the hearts of men. It is by the display of His mercy. Was there anything that infuriated the Pharisees and scribes more than the sight of our blessed Lord and Saviour sitting down with publicans and sinners? There He was showing His interest in them and His love to them, and it made the Pharisees and the scribes ten times worse than they were before! It was just this element of mercy and of grace and of compassion in our Lord's teaching and life that finally made those people crucify Him and put Him to death.

The fourth way in which God hardens the heart is this: He even provokes desires in people. Now we must be clear about this. What do you make of that case of Joseph's brethren? They plotted against their brother and they took that terrible action, yet Joseph says, and says rightly, that God did it. Now I remember hearing a man preaching on that once, a man who

[1]See *Romans: An Exposition of Chapters 7:1–8:4: The Law, its Functions and Limits*, 1973

until a few years ago was regarded as a great and popular evangelical. He read out his text, Genesis 50 : 20, and his first remark was 'Of course Joseph was quite wrong'. Well, again, we see how people sit in judgment upon Joseph as they also do on the Apostle Paul himself. But Joseph was not wrong, he was absolutely right! You see, what that preacher was trying to say was that though these men had really done it – and it was a terrible thing – that God overruled it and turned it in the right way. But that is not what Joseph says, and that is not what happened. It was God who sent Joseph down to Egypt. He knew about the famine that was coming. It was He who did it and He did it through Joseph's brethren. He will even provoke a desire, He can provoke thoughts. 'But', someone will say, 'is not that creating evil?' no! They were already evil, unjust men; He simply used the evil that was already there to bring about His own purpose. He did not make them sinners; they already were. All God does is to take such men and to use them to bring His own great purpose to pass. He has not created evil at all, but the general stimulus of His influence can thus work upon the evil mind to do something very wrong. But ultimately it is to bring to pass God's purpose.

So the fifth and last explanation is that we are actually taught that at times God even uses Satan. He used him in the case of Job. Now there is a very interesting statement in 1 Corinthians 5 : 5 which must have perplexed many Christians. Paul there talks about handing a man over to Satan for the punishment of the flesh, in order that the spirit might be saved. What does that mean? It means this: 'When a man will not listen to scriptural teaching,' says the Apostle '– that man of yours who is guilty of incest and so on – then, I have handed him over to Satan. Let Satan handle him and that will bring him to his senses.'

Now here in Romans 9 we are dealing with the obverse, as it were, of that: that God sometimes hardens a man by taking away all His restraints and simply handing him over to Satan. I believe that we are living in such an age. I think it is the explanation of the times in which we live, that God is handing over evil people to a reprobate mind. This is the explanation of all this filth and mockery on our television sets. God is, as it were, withdrawing the restraints, handing over to Satan, hardening for His own great and glorious purpose.

We do not see the purpose yet but we know that God does have one. He has done this many times in the long history of the human race. He allows this hardening to take place until everything is absolutely hopeless, and then He comes in in the power of His might. Why does He do it like that? we may ask. And the answer is that if He did it in another way, then we would be ready to say that we had done it, that it is our evangelism or our prayers that have done it. But God allows everything to become so hard that it is obvious to all that nobody could do it but He Himself.

But that is only a partial explanation. There is the central statement, that God produced Pharaoh at that point and hardened his heart, in order that His great power might be shown through him. We will go on to draw this out and to expand it still further in the next study and see the great and grand conclusion at which the Apostle arrives.

Fifteen

*

*Therefore hath he mercy on whom he will have mercy, and whom
he will he hardeneth. Thou wilt say then unto me, Why doth he
yet find fault? For who hath resisted his will? Nay but, O man,
who art thou that repliest against God? Shall the thing formed say
to him that formed it, Why hast thou made me thus? Hath not the
potter power over the clay, of the same lump to make one vessel
unto honour, and another unto dishonour? What if God, willing to
shew his wrath, and to make his power known, endured with
much longsuffering the vessels of wrath fitted to destruction: and
that he might make known the riches of his glory on the vessels of
mercy, which he had afore prepared unto glory, even us, whom he
hath called, not of the Jews only, but also of the Gentiles.*

Romans 9 : 18–24

We saw in the previous chapter that Paul is showing in verse 17
that God had produced Pharaoh, or caused him to stand in
history at that particular point and juncture, in order that He
might use him to His own honour and glory. We explained that
it does not mean that God had created Pharaoh in order that He
might do that, but God, taking Pharaoh as he was, a sinner and
an unbeliever, hardened his heart for His own eternal purpose.

Then, having said that, the Apostle sums it all up in verse 18;
he sums up his two cases – Jacob and Esau, and Pharaoh – the
case for saying that God can have mercy on whom He will have
mercy, and, secondly, that He will harden whom He will. In
other words, Paul is showing that God is free to carry out His
own sovereign will in His own way and whenever He pleases
and chooses.

But the teaching can be put like this; it is really there
implicitly in that seventeenth verse. God is over all, and, being

[180]

almighty and all-powerful and sovereign, He can even use evil to display His own glory; and what the Apostle is really saying in that seventeenth verse is that God used Pharaoh in that way. As we have seen, it is not that He merely allowed Pharaoh to harden his own heart; nor is Paul saying that God made Pharaoh a sinner. God took Pharaoh as he was, and aggravated and accentuated what he was; He hardened his heart, in order to serve His own purpose.

And that purpose was, says the Apostle, that He might show forth His power and He told Pharaoh that He was doing that.

It happened in this way. Let us imagine that the first time Moses and Aaron appeared before Pharaoh, asking him to allow the children of Israel to leave Egypt so that they might go back to their own land – let us imagine that, the very first time they made the request, Pharaoh had given in and had allowed them to go. Well, it probably would be something that would just be recorded in history as something that had taken place, but no more. But that is not the way in which it happened. What happened was that Pharaoh refused, and because he refused God worked a miracle in order to humble him. He refused again, and there was another miracle. And he refused again, and there was another miracle. You can read for yourselves the account of all these in the book of Exodus, and it is important that you should do so.

So what the Apostle is saying here is that God did that, and He did it in that way. He increased this obduracy and resistance and evil in Pharaoh in order that through that He might give this tremendous, signal demonstration of His power and of His lordship. Pharaoh, of course, was a great dictator, a mighty emperor, with great armies, one of the world's conquerors of that time. But he was utterly humbled – humbled to such an extent that at last, against his will entirely, he had to give in and to allow the children of Israel to go. So what the Apostle is saying is that God hardened the heart of Pharaoh in order that through that and in that way He might do this thing: '. . . for this same purpose have I raised thee up, that I might shew my power in thee.'

And he did show it. You remember how up to a point the magicians of Egypt could reproduce the miracles that were worked by Moses and Aaron and their rod. But the moment came when they could not. Thus all human greatness and human self-confidence was humbled to the dust, even the might and power of Pharaoh himself, '. . . that my name might be declared throughout all the earth'. And it was, of course. You read these historical books and you will find that when the children of Israel were passing through various countries, and when they arrived in the land of Canaan, the people there began to tremble. They said, 'These people have come amongst us who were delivered by their God out of the bondage and the captivity of Egypt; this is the mighty God who crushed Pharaoh and his hosts and his chariots in the Red Sea' – and they were full of fear. So by hardening Pharaoh's heart, by increasing his resistance, God was able to give this tremendous display of His almighty power. It became known 'throughout all the earth'. And here it is in the Scripture, and it has been known ever since throughout the world wherever this history is known.

Then, having said that, in verse 19 Paul raises an objection. Now in our subdivision of this matter, earlier, we saw that verses 19 to 24 constitute a new section, a subsection of the main argument. It is a general argument, and we must carry all this in our minds. The general argument of this whole chapter and of chapters 10 and 11 is this: Because the Apostle has stated so clearly in chapter 8 that God has a great eternal purpose and that nothing can frustrate it, then the assurance which every Christian should have about his ultimate glorification is absolute. Nothing – 'neither death, nor life, nor angels, nor principalities, nor powers, nor things present, nor things to come, nor height, nor depth, nor any other creature, shall be able to separate us from the love of God, which is in Christ Jesus our Lord'. It is absolute!

'But wait a minute,' says somebody, 'what about the case of the Jews? God gave promises to them, but look at them; they are outside the kingdom; they are rejecting the gospel. Has not God's word fallen down?' And we saw how, in answer to that, Paul's fundamental proposition is, 'They are not all Israel which are of Israel.' Israel is a special spiritual people inside the visible Israel; these are the seed: not the Ishmaels, but the Isaacs; not the Esaus, but the Jacobs. And all this is something that God works out by His great process of election – '. . . that the purpose of God according to election might stand'. And it will stand; it will never fail; the purpose of God is sure.

And then, we have seen how he puts up the objection in verse 14 and deals with it in the two cases. But having dealt with it in that way, here again another objection arises, and it is this that introduces a further subsection in this main general argument. 'Why doth he yet find fault? For who hath resisted his will?' In other words, who can resist or stand up against and continue to stand up against the will of God? The answer is, nobody! So then, why does God save some and punish others? Is it fair, is it right? As God ultimately cannot be resisted, is it just on God's part to punish unbelief and to give salvation to those who do believe?

Now here, of course, we are face to face with the argument which is most frequently brought against the whole doctrine of election and predestination, and that is what Paul deals with now. So let us notice some general points, as we come to look at this most important matter. The first is that this objection proves to the hilt that our exposition of the previous passages is the right one, and that Paul is teaching in the previous passages that God, and God alone, determines the salvation of every man. A man is saved because God has chosen him; He shows mercy to whom He will show mercy, and whom He will He hardeneth. I emphasize this again because, as I have reminded you, there are people who try to get out of this difficulty by saying that because God is omniscient He knows that certain people are going to believe when they hear the gospel, so He chooses them because of that. He knows, too, that the others are not going to believe and therefore He hardens them.

But it cannot mean that, because nobody would take any objection to that; everybody would say that that was quite just and fair. But people do object to the teaching of the Apostle; they say, 'Why doth he yet find fault? For who hath resisted his will?' So you see this objection surely proves beyond any doubt whatsoever that the Apostle has been teaching that salvation is entirely the result of the sovereign will and election of God and nothing to do with us at all.

The second point is that there is nothing new in this objection to this doctrine. People were objecting to it in the first century and they have been objecting to it ever since. It has nothing to do with modern learning, modern knowledge, modern science – nothing at all. Let us get rid of that idea. We are not being clever nor modern when we argue against this; people have always done it.

Thirdly, we cannot but comment on the honesty and the thoroughness of the great Apostle. He raises the problem, and he puts it before us. Before you ever thought of this objection, he has put it into your mouth. I say this in order that we may thank God for the Scriptures. There is nothing that man can ever think of but it has already been dealt with and answered here. The trouble with people who argue against Christian doctrine is that they do not know their Bible. If they did they would talk much less. Indeed, all of what they say has already been answered; the Apostle has already dealt with it. His honesty, his thoroughness! The Scriptures are truly marvellous. This is the word of God!

Then the fourth general point is that to reject this doctrine of his is not only to reject the teaching of the Apostle Paul; it is to reject what is plainly and clearly taught in the Scriptures, which is a most solemn and serious matter. We saw in our last study that people are so liable to say, 'Ah, but that is only Paul's opinion.' But you must not say that. This man is an inspired Apostle. You must accept all his teaching if you really believe in the inspiration of the word of God. If you feel with Peter that many things in what Paul writes are hard to be understood, then I agree. But remember that Peter calls it the Scriptures [2 *Peter* 3 : 16]. Let us be careful; we are not just disagreeing with the Apostle Paul.

Those then are some general comments, so now what is the problem that the Apostle raises here? A common way of putting it is this: How can we reconcile the sovereignty of God and the responsibility of man? Does not this teaching of the Apostle seem to be doing away with man's responsibility? Others have put this in a very blunt and bold way by saying that this teaching of the Apostle is nothing but sheer fatalism; he is teaching nothing but a doctrine of necessity. He is saying that people are just machines, as it were, or that they are so bound by some rigid deterministic fate that what happens to them happens of necessity. There, then, is the problem. Let us see how the great Apostle deals with it.

Now this is most important. There is no need for me to emphasize that the passage we are looking at is a most important one. It is a classic statement – and one about which men have argued and debated throughout the centuries, but it is important for this reason. It seems to me that it clears up many peculiar popular misconceptions and prejudices, if we only pay attention to what it says. This passage shows us how far we can go in this matter of understanding God's ways; it shows us the sign which says, 'No further', and we need to be shown that. And, at the same time, I think I shall be able to show you that it teaches us the relationship of God's sovereignty and man's responsibility, giving equal weight to both. As we go to the end of the chapter and come on to chapter 10, we shall see that the emphasis is mainly on man's responsibility. But here in this section, the great emphasis is on God's sovereignty. Paul emphasizes both.

What, then, is his actual reply? Here again in order to clarify our thinking let us make a subdivision of verses 20 to 24. It is quite simple. The first subdivision is in the first part of verse 20: 'Nay but, O man, who art thou that repliest against God?' That is a rebuke to the questioner. Then the second half of verse 20 and the whole of verse 21 are given to an explanation of the Apostle's assertion of God's sovereignty and entire freedom in what He does with fallen humanity. Then, to help us, verses 22 to 24 give us an explanation of God's object and purpose in doing this. Verse 22 shows His object and purpose in the manifestation of His wrath, and verses 23 and 24 show it in the manifestation of His mercy.

So having done that we can proceed to a detailed consideration of the passage; and here the main thing we find is the absolute importance of observing the terms which the Apostle uses. Half the trouble with this passage arises because people take the terms or the words at their face value without examining them, or discovering what they are really saying, and then go off at a tangent. So let us watch what the Apostle says and pay great attention.

How then does he deal with the objection? Well, the first thing he does is to rebuke the questioner and refute the question. Before he deals with the argument he says, 'Nay but, O man, who art thou that repliest against God?' This is a most important point. What is he rebuking here? He is surely rebuking the spirit in which the question is put. And this is something that is always vital. We need to be reminded that in discussing a subject such as this, we are not just looking at a subject of abstract academic or theoretical philosophy; we are not just looking here into some human opinions or human argumentation. You do not approach a subject like this as you approach the subject of the Common Market, which is purely a matter of human opinion. We are in a different realm.

That, then, is virtually what Paul is saying. But watch the way in which he says it; let us see how he brings out this element of rebuke. 'Nay but', he says – which means, 'Surely!' 'Nay surely!' He expresses his surprise, his astonishment. And then notice the word, 'repliest' against God. Now that word 'repliest' is a most interesting one. The word Paul uses means 'to answer by contradicting' or 'replying against'. There is a prefix to the word which introduces this notion of 'against', and the authorities say that the word is used in order to indicate a spirit of contention.

Now that is the whole point. What the Apostle is rebuking here is that spirit of contention. He is not rebuking a man who is in a genuine difficulty and who really wants light and help and understanding. The Bible never rebukes that. What it is so very concerned about is the enquiry and the form in which it is made. You see, this is an objector who confronts God, as it were, and who contradicts. This is a man who is displaying a wrong spirit, somebody who is immediately suggesting that God is unjust. 'Why doth he yet find fault?' You see it in the question and hear it in the accent, do you not? The questioner says, 'This is all wrong! As nobody can stand up against God finally, what right then has God to punish anybody? What right has God to harden any heart or to hate anybody or to send him to hell? The thing is unjust.'

Now that is what the Apostle is rebuking. And as we have seen in all the past studies nothing is more important here than our spirit. That is what Paul starts with, and it is absolutely vital. We have no right to go on considering this matter at all unless our spirits are right. If we take up this attitude towards God of contradicting Him or imputing unrighteousness to Him or suggesting that He is unjust, already our spirit is wrong and we cannot hope to be right anywhere in our understanding of the teaching.

Then, we must notice the way in which the Apostle administers the rebuke. It is most dramatic, and striking. 'Nay but, O man, who art thou that repliest against God?' You see this tremendous and terrible contrast: man – God! Wait a moment, says the Apostle. Before I begin to consider what you have just said, and the point of view which you have adopted, let me just for a moment remind you who you are. 'Who art thou?' Man! And you are standing up against and replying against and contradicting not me, nor another man, but God!

And this is always the cause of our trouble with the biblical truth, is it not? We begin to speak before we stop to consider who we are and our right to speak. We take up the cudgels and we take up our position and we speak with feeling. God have mercy upon us! We do not realize what we are doing. The trouble with man, the self-confident man who stands up full of his twentieth-century knowledge, the great philosopher who is examining God and His ways, the trouble with such a man when he objects with violence to any teaching in the Scripture is that he does not realize the truth about himself. 'Who art thou?' Realize your smallness, realize your insignificance, realize your finite character, your mortality, your sinfulness, your perversity, and realize the smallness of your mind and understanding. Try to inculcate and develop in yourself the spirit of the Psalmist in the eighth Psalm, the humble believer who looks up into the heavens, the work of God's hands and then looks at himself and says, 'What is man, that thou art mindful of him?' That is the contrast: 'Who art thou?' On the other hand, 'what is man?'

And then, of course, the second thing we are ignorant of is the truth about God. 'O man, who art thou that repliest against God?' – His greatness and His glory and His eternity and His majesty. Now all this is something that is emphasized everywhere in the Bible. Let me just give you some examples of it. There is no point in proceeding to the detailed argument, as the Apostle says, until we are right about this. Until your spirit is right you cannot discuss this, and it would be wrong to discuss it with you. We must start where the Apostle starts, so let me give you some illustrations. Take what we have already seen about the glory of God. We had it in the list of things here in Romans 9 : 4, the things that characterized the children of Israel: 'who are Israelites; to whom pertaineth the adoption, and the glory, and the covenants, and the giving of the law'. In Exodus 19, you remember, God gave a manifestation of Himself to the people. Why? In order to put them in the right place and in the right position. It is as if He were saying, 'Now I gave you great signs before I brought you out of Egypt, but I know you, and how ready you are to forget them and to think of yourselves as a nation, self-contained. I want you to realize who you are, and who I am, who has called you out of Egypt and who is taking you into Canaan.' So He gave them a manifestation of His glory, the mount burning with fire and so on. And the object of that was to humble these people that they might walk obediently and quietly with their God.

But that is only one manifestation. Before God did that to the whole nation, He had done it to Moses himself personally and particularly. Even Moses had to be put right on this. In Exodus 3 : 1–6 we read, 'Now Moses kept the flock of Jethro his father in law, the priest of Midian: and he led the flock to the backside of the desert, and came to the mountain of God, even to Horeb. And the angel of the Lord appeared unto him in a flame of fire out of the midst of a bush: and he looked, and, behold, the bush burned with fire, and the bush was not consumed.' Now notice this: 'And Moses said, I will now turn aside, and see this great sight, why the bush is not burnt.' The intellectual modern scientist going to investigate the phenomenon! 'And when the Lord saw that he turned aside to see, God called unto him out of the midst of the bush, and said, Moses, Moses. And he said, Here am I. And he said, Draw not nigh hither: put off thy shoes from off thy feet, for the place whereon thou standest is holy ground. Moreover he said, I am the God of thy father, the God of Abraham, the God of Isaac, and the God of Jacob. And Moses hid his face; for he was afraid to look upon God.' You see the contrast, the readiness to investigate! But he is prohibited, 'Put off thy shoes . . .' Stand back! You do not investigate this as a man; I, the Lord am speaking to you, 'I am the God of thy father . . .'

The same thing also had to be done with Joshua. Here is Joshua at a critical moment: 'It came to pass, when Joshua was by Jericho, that he lifted up his eyes and looked, and, behold, there stood a man over against him with his sword drawn in his hand: and Joshua went unto him, and said unto him, Art thou for us, or for our adversaries? And he said, Nay; but as captain of the host of the Lord am I now come. And Joshua fell on his face to the earth, and did worship, and said unto him, What saith my lord unto his servant? And the captain of the Lord's host said unto Joshua, Loose thy shoe from off thy foot; for the place whereon thou standest is holy. And Joshua did so' [*Joshua* 5 : 13–15]. He is in the presence of the Lord, so he must humble himself and take off his shoes. The ground is holy; the whole approach has got to be different. No longer an investigation – 'Art thou for us, or for our adversaries?' – but humility, worship and reverence! Here it is even with such men.

Then in the book of Job the matter is again put before us very clearly and this, of course, is particularly appropriate. Poor Job! He was tried by terrible difficulties and he could not understand it. He was a good man, he was a godly man, yet he suffered all these calamities, and the great book of Job tells us about his complaints, his arguments and disputations. 'Oh that I might be able to state my case to Him', says Job, 'He does not give me a chance, He is terrorizing me. If only I could stand up and state my case.' And he does that frequently. But now we come to the end of the story in chapter 42 : 1–6 and God has spoken to Job in the previous chapters. Read them for yourself and see how God gives a manifestation of Himself and His being and His glory to Job. He addresses him and says, I want you to realize the One to whom you have been speaking, against whom you have been bringing your complaint and trying to marshal your arguments.

'Then Job answered the Lord, and said, I know that thou canst do every thing, and that no thought can be withholden from thee. Who is he that hideth counsel without knowledge? therefore have I uttered that I understood not; things too wonderful for me, which I knew not. Hear, I beseech thee, and I will speak: I will demand of thee, and declare thou unto me. I have heard of thee by the hearing of the ear: but now mine eye seeth thee. Wherefore I abhor myself, and repent in dust and ashes.' Poor Job! How he regrets what he had said in the heat of the moment and in the pain and the agony of his tribulation: his questioning of God, his beginning to feel that God was not righteous and that God was not just. Oh, what a fool I have been! he says. I was talking without realizing what I was saying; I was speaking in ignorance. That is what a man says when he realizes that he is addressing God! 'O man, who art thou that repliest against God?'

But the Bible is full of this kind of teaching. You find the same thing exactly in Isaiah 6 – you see, we have not yet started to deal with the argument, have we? Are you disappointed about this? Did you hope that at long last I was coming to it? No, not until your spirit is right, not until you are fit to hear the argument, not until you have got rid of all self-opinion and self-reliance – everything that can be regarded as opinionatedness. It has got to be banished. We are not fit to consider the doctrine until we get rid of that.

There it is at the beginning of Isaiah 6 again, in the vision that was given to him. 'In the year that king Uzziah died I saw also the Lord sitting upon a throne, high and lifted up, and his train filled the temple. Above it stood the seraphims: each one had six wings; with twain he covered his face, and with twain he covered his feet, and with twain he did fly. And one cried unto another, and said, Holy, holy, holy, is the Lord of hosts: the whole earth is full of his glory. And the posts of the door moved at the voice of him that cried, and the house was filled with smoke. Then said I, Woe is me! for I am undone; because I am a man of unclean lips . . . for mine eyes have seen the King, the Lord of hosts.' That is the attitude. That is the right condition.

Or go to Ecclesiastes chapter 5 verse 2, and this is what you will read: '. . . God is in heaven, and thou upon earth.' And you find it too, of course, in the Lord's Prayer. Before you begin to make any requests of God, you start by realizing who He is; before you begin to indulge in your sentimental, sloppy, modern notions about the love of God, you say, 'Our Father, which art in heaven, Hallowed be thy name.' And then, and only then, are you entitled to go on.

Yes, says the author of the Epistle to the Hebrews, 'let us have grace, whereby we may serve God acceptably with reverence and godly fear: for our God is a consuming fire' [*Hebrews* 12 : 28–29]. What is being rebuked is that which the Apostle Paul describes in the Epistle to the Colossians: 'Let no man beguile you of your reward in a voluntary humility and worshipping of angels, intruding into those things which he hath not seen, vainly puffed up by his fleshly mind, and not holding the Head, from which all the body by joints and bands having nourishment ministered, and knit together, increaseth with the increase of God' [*Colossians* 2 : 18–19]. And here in

Romans 9 the Apostle is rebuking this sort of man who intrudes into things which he has not seen, 'vainly puffed up by his fleshly mind' – 'Why doth he yet find fault', seeing that nobody can resist him? The fleshly mind brings its arguments and the Apostle rebukes it immediately – 'O man, who art thou that repliest against God?'

At this point we must look at something which he says in the next sub-section, but I must bring it in here because it is a part of the rebuke; he goes on repeating it. 'Shall the thing formed' – that is what you are – 'say to him that formed it . . .' There again is the contrast: man – God! 'The thing formed' is an interesting word. It is the word from which we get our present word 'plastic': 'the thing formed' – plasma! And this is what you are, says the Apostle, you with your objection. You are only the thing formed, the plastic material, and God is the one who handles and forms and models it. Then to bring it right home to us he goes on and uses another comparison: 'Hath not the potter power over the clay, of the same lump to make . . .?' The contrast is between man and God, the thing formed and the one who forms – a lump of clay and the potter. So it is that the Apostle rebukes the evil spirit in which this question is put, this man who arrogantly gets up and says, 'Well, then, in that case God is not fair; this is unjust. How can He do the two things at the same time?'

But someone may still feel that the Apostle's argument is unfair here. Do you feel that he is just browbeating you or trying to bludgeon you, that instead of dealing with your objection and your argument he attacks you personally, as it were, and talks about your spirit? Is it fair? But it is not unfair for this reason: the Apostle, in what he has been saying in the previous verses, has not just been putting forward his own opinion. What he has been saying is this: 'The scripture saith to Pharaoh'; 'God saith to Pharaoh'. It is God whom he has been quoting.

So he points out to this clever objector and says in effect, 'Look here, you are not arguing against me, you are arguing against God. I have not been putting before you my own personal theories. In each instance I have given you quotations from the Scripture. I have quoted to you that God said, "Jacob have I loved, but Esau have I hated." *I* have not said that about God; it is God who says it about Himself; and in all my other illustrations I have been giving you the word of Scripture, which is the word of God. So then', says the Apostle, 'when you stand up like that and say, "Why doth he yet find fault?" I just want you to realize that you are not criticizing me; you are not querying a human opinion or the teaching of some great theologian; you are criticizing the Almighty God.'

Here then we have the plain teaching of this Apostle; he is quoting the Scriptures, the word of God, and in addition to that, he is divinely inspired. So that if you object to this teaching you are objecting to the teaching of God Himself concerning Himself.

Therefore, all the Apostle wants us to realize is that we must be very careful in what we say. We must not start to speak about this subject until our attitude is right, and until our spirit is right. So we need to be told at the very outset, 'O man, who art thou?' – realize the truth about yourself. You are a bit of plastic material, you are nothing else, and you are standing up against this great Artificer; you are nothing but a man and He is God; you are on earth, He is in heaven. Realize this truth about yourself before you go any further. Remember that you are nothing but a bit of clay in comparison to God, and that He is the Potter.

Do we always approach the Scriptures in that way? Do we always enter into discussions on this doctrine or any doctrine in that way? So then let us henceforth, whenever we come across anything in the Scripture that is difficult, before we begin to express our opinion, remember the word of the Apostle to us: Who are you? There is only one way to approach the Scripture. It is to listen to the injunction that God gave to Moses and to Joshua: 'Put off thy shoes from off thy feet, for the place whereon thou standest is holy ground.'

So when you discuss this or any item in the whole of the Bible, always remember that you are discussing the word of God, the revelation of God, and therefore God Himself. You must not discuss this as you discuss anything else. You have your right to your opinion in every other respect, in every other matter – not here. Here you take off your shoes, you must become as a little child, you must humble yourself, and if you do not do so you must of necessity be wrong in your opinion. It is only to the humble that God reveals the truth. Our Lord said, 'I thank thee,

O Father, Lord of heaven and earth, because thou hast hid these things from the wise and prudent, and hast revealed them unto babes. Even so, Father: for so it seemed good in thy sight' [*Matthew* 11 : 25–26].

'O man, who art thou that repliest against God?' Let us make certain that our spirits are right and then we can go on to consider the detailed argument as the Apostle puts it before us.

Sixteen

*

*Thou wilt say then unto me, Why doth he yet find fault? For who
hath resisted his will? Nay but, O man, who art thou that repliest
against God? Shall the thing formed say to him that formed it,
Why hast thou made me thus? Hath not the potter power over the
clay, of the same lump to make one vessel unto honour, and
another unto dishonour? What if God, willing to shew his wrath,
and to make his power known, endured with much longsuffering
the vessels of wrath fitted to destruction: and that he might make
known the riches of his glory on the vessels of mercy, which he
had afore prepared unto glory, even us, whom he hath called, not
of the Jews only, but also of the Gentiles?*

Romans 9 : 19–24

In our last study, we dealt with the first part of Paul's reply to the
objection in verse 19, and that was the rebuke to the questioner:
'Nay but, O man, who art thou that repliest against God?' We
brought out the tremendous sarcasm that is involved there, the
contrast between man and God; and that is what, of course, the
Apostle was anxious to do. We worked that out together and we
justified the Apostle in answering in that way. What he is really
saying is, not that we should never ask any questions at all, but
that we should never contend with the plain teaching of God's
word. We can express our difficulties, and if we do so in the right
spirit, we shall be helped. But what we must never do is argue
with God, and especially in this spirit that suggests that God is
unrighteous or unfair or unjust. That is what Paul condemns
and the Scripture, of course, always, everywhere, does the same
thing.

Now having done that, we can proceed to the next step in the
Apostle's reply – namely the portion which is found in the

second half of verse 20 and the whole of verse 21. Here the Apostle asserts God's sovereign right to show mercy or to harden as He wills and as He pleases. Let us follow him as he does so and take first of all the second half of verse 20. Having rebuked the questioner he says, 'Shall the thing formed say to him that formed it, Why hast thou made me thus?' Here, you notice, he is carrying on, in a sense, the rebuke which he has given, and he does so in a manner which shows the utter absurdity of our attempting to question or to query what God has done.

But at the same time he also defines yet more clearly what he has already hinted at as to the relationship that exists between God and man. Now this, of course, is something which is absolutely vital. In the first half of verse 20, instead of the words 'O man', the New English Bible uses the word 'Sir', but that is not right, because in the original the words used by the Apostle were 'O man' – to show the creatureliness of man who thus pits himself against Almighty God. And the Apostle is so concerned about this that he really repeats it in this further section, and it is vital to this whole position with which we are dealing. Let me remind you again that this is not only the statement of the Apostle Paul. He has been quoting Scripture! And if you disagree with this doctrine you are not disagreeing with the Apostle Paul, still less with me; you are disagreeing with God!

In other words, let me also remind you that when you come to any part of the Scripture, you realize that this is not Shakespeare; this is not Euclid; this is not a textbook of philosophy! This is God's Word, and you approach this in an entirely different manner; you take your shoes off your feet! You realize that all your learning and all your ability is of no help to you at all. When you come here you must become as a little child; you need the enlightenment of the Holy Spirit.

In other words, people who tell us openly that they sit in judgment on any part of the Bible are those whom I would never expect to understand doctrine. They cannot possibly do so. Those are the people who deny the doctrines of the Christian faith and do not even see the need of them. As they themselves are the authorities, with their own ideas and not the word of God, one does not expect them to understand, and so one expects from them the blasphemies that they emit so confidently. But we, I say, must come here in the spirit that the Apostle teaches us: 'O man, who art thou . . .?' Remember who you are and what you are, your finite, limited, sinful condition, and remember that you are dealing with something that God Himself, the Almighty, has revealed.

So here he presses that home upon us still further. Having reminded us of our creatureliness as mere men he now says, 'Shall the thing formed say to him that formed it, Why hast thou made me thus?' This is a further putting of us in our place. Remember, he says, that you are nothing but 'the thing formed', which means, as we saw, plastic material.

Now it is important to observe that Paul here does not say 'the thing created', but 'the thing formed'. You will see the significance of that later. He is here describing man as something that has already been created – plastic material. He is not talking about the bringing into being out of nothing: that is creation. No, he says, here is a mass of plastic material which is going to be formed and which has been formed. And that, he says, does not turn to the one who has put it into shape, and say, 'Why hast thou formed me thus?'

And then, of course, what he is saying is that as man's relationship to God is that of this lump of plastic material to the artificer who shapes it, is there anything in the world that is more ridiculous and more absurd than for this helpless mass of substance to try to question and to query the one who has put it into shape and to ask the question, 'Why hast thou made me thus?' And his point is that that is exactly the position of anybody who, coming across this doctrine which says, 'Jacob have I loved, but Esau have I hated', asks God, 'What right have You to do that? On what grounds can You justly do this thing? On what grounds do You condemn anybody to damnation? On what grounds do You choose anybody to mercy and to salvation?' Paul says it is as ridiculous and as monstrous as that.

But even there the Apostle is not merely putting forth his own ideas; he is once more quoting Scripture. So, you see, Scripture answers the questions all along, but Paul just puts it there in the form of a question to show how utterly ridiculous and absurd the thing is. 'Shall the thing formed . . .?' He ridicules the idea; it is entirely absurd!

But in verse 21 Paul takes this idea a bit further. He elaborates it and works it out still more clearly and explicitly; and, of course, he has only one object in doing this. People coming to this passage, as we have seen, are always trying to explain it away. They try to get rid of the notion that we are taught here that God chooses some to salvation and rejects others. This is impossible, they say, it is unjust – and they try to say that the passage does not say that; that it simply means that God in His foreknowledge knew that one man was going to believe and not the other. And we have shown that if it were that, then there would be no objection to it at all. But it is not that. And these terms which Paul uses here – 'the thing formed' and 'him that formed it', and what he is coming on to now in verse 21 – make any such attempt to get out of the difficulty altogether futile.

So here, then, he puts it still more explicitly: 'Hath not the potter power over the clay, of the same lump to make one vessel unto honour, and another unto dishonour?' Now surely that is plain enough? The relationship that he is describing between God and mankind is the relationship between a potter and a lump of clay. In other words, this is so clear that there is no way of dismissing what the Apostle is saying – and there is our contrast once more. Man – God! The thing formed – One who formed it! Clay, lump – Potter, the Great Artificer!

Once more it is very important that we should be clear that the Apostle still is not putting forward his own opinion, he is again quoting from the Scripture. In Isaiah 45 verses 9 to 11 we read, 'Woe unto him that striveth with his Maker!' God forbid that that 'woe' should come upon anybody who hears these words. Do not strive with your Maker, my friend!

The passage continues, 'Let the potsherd strive with the potsherds of the earth.' Then, notice this: 'Shall the clay say to him that fashioneth it, What makest thou? or thy work, He hath no hands? Woe unto him that saith unto his father, What begettest thou? or to the woman, What hast thou brought forth?' – that is the question at the end of verse 20 in Romans 9 – 'Thus saith the Lord, the Holy One of Israel, and his Maker, Ask me of things to come concerning my sons, and concerning the work of my hands command ye me.' Clearly, the Apostle has that passage in his mind.

Surely, also, he has equally in his mind Isaiah 64 verse 8. This is the cry that came up out of the heart of Isaiah when he was pleading for revival: 'But now, O Lord, thou art our father; we are the clay, and thou our potter; and we all are the work of thy hand.' It is the same idea. And then you find it in Jeremiah also, in chapter 18 verses 1 to 6: 'The word which came to Jeremiah from the Lord, saying, Arise, and go down to the potter's house, and there I will cause thee to hear my words. Then I went down to the potter's house, and, behold, he wrought a work on the wheels. And the vessel that he made of clay was marred in the hand of the potter: so he made it again another vessel, as seemed good to the potter to make it. Then the word of the Lord came to me, saying, O house of Israel, cannot I do with you as this potter? saith the Lord. Behold, as the clay is in the potter's hand, so are ye in my hand, O house of Israel.' So, the Apostle here is not speaking as a brilliant philosopher or debater or arguer, trying to prove his doctrine of election. No, he is quoting Scripture; he is quoting what God Himself has said upon this matter.

Of course, the passage is a statement about which people have argued and contended throughout the centuries. They have lost their tempers and become bitter and violent, and they have entered into a party spirit and have refused to speak to one another. What a terrible thing! What a terrible thing to do with any statement in God's Word! I am much more concerned about our attitude to this than about anything else. Let us remind ourselves again that if we cannot discuss a passage like this in a calm, collected, reasonable, humble spirit, we have no right to look at it at all, and we will certainly never understand it. Our spirit is absolutely essential and vital.

So what does the passage mean? Let us first look at the terms: 'Hath not the potter power over the clay . . .?' Now when Paul speaks of 'power' here, he chooses a word which means 'authority' or 'right'. Let me prove that to you. In verse 22 we read, 'What if God, willing to shew his wrath, and to make his power known . . .' Now in the Authorized Version we have the word 'power' in both instances, but in the Greek there are two different words, and whereas the word in verse 21 is the word that generally stands for 'authority', the word in verse 22 means 'dynamic'. It literally means 'force' – physical power as it were. But not here. Here the word means authority and right.

Paul's picture is that of a potter making various utensils and implements for household use and so on; some of them are put to very honourable use; the others are equally necessary but they are not quite so honourable, these Paul calls 'dishonourable'. There are things which have to be used in everyday life; some you put onto the table and they are shown, others are kept out of sight, but they are very necessary. It is the same sort of distinction as you find in 1 Corinthians 12 where the Apostle, in dealing with the various members of the body, says that some are less comely than others, but they are all in the body. They are not all like the face or the eyes and the hands. There are other functions in the body; we do not talk about them and they are out of sight but they are absolutely essential. 'Some to honour, some to dishonour'; some comely, some less comely. So all Paul is saying is this: 'Surely the master potter has the right and the authority to do as he wills and as he chooses with that mass, that lump of clay, to make one vessel unto honour, and another to dishonour.'

Now this is, of course, where we come to the crux of the whole matter. Paul does not say that God has created some people to honour, and some to dishonour. He is not, let me remind you, talking about creation and saying here that God Almighty created some people in order that they might sin and go to damnation. The very terms that are used not only entitle us to say that, they compel us to do so. They are perfectly clear, as we have already seen when Paul uses this term 'plastic material', not 'the thing created'.

But here we go still further. He talks about 'clay', a 'lump' of clay. In other words, the figure that the Apostle is using is not the figure of creation; he is talking about something that is done with material that has already been created. Now that is absolutely vital to the whole case. 'Creation', we have seen, means 'creating out of nothing', but here we are starting with plastic material, with a lump of clay, and what the Apostle is arguing through his figure is that God in His relationship to man in salvation is in the same position as the potter to a lump or a mass of clay. The potter does not create the clay; he starts with it, it is there in front of him on the bench, and he is now going to do something with it.

Now, I emphasize this because it teaches us that the Apostle is not dealing here at all with God's purpose in the original creation of man, or with what God does with human nature as such. He is dealing with God's relationship to fallen humanity. He is concerned here only about salvation, not about creation, and he puts it in this kind of picture. Fallen humanity is like a lump of clay which is already there and what Paul is discussing is what God does with this lump. Look at the sentence again: 'Hath not the potter power over the clay, of the same lump to make one vessel unto honour, and another unto dishonour?' – and that is an interpretation, remember, of 'Jacob have I loved, but Esau have I hated'; or of what God did with the children of Israel and what He did to Pharaoh and his hosts, which we have already considered.

Now this is essentially different from the original creation, because in the original creation it was not only creation from nothing, but, still more important, God created man 'in his own image and likeness'. That is the opposite of 'dishonour'. He looked upon man, as He looked upon the whole of creation, and we are told that He saw that 'it was good'. God never created anything unto dishonour, but here we are dealing with a potter who makes one vessel unto dishonour. And that proves that it cannot be dealing with human nature as such, still less with man as he was made at the beginning. It is an account of what God does with fallen humanity.

So there is the key to the whole explanation of this statement that has mystified so many people. They get hold of the idea that God deliberately made some people that they might go to hell. That is a lie! It is not taught anywhere in the Scripture. What the Apostle is dealing with here is what God does with fallen men and women, and that is true of the whole of humanity. The lump of clay is not 'humanity'; it is 'fallen humanity', it is humanity as the result of the original sin of Adam and Eve. Charles Hodge puts this very well when he says: 'We are dealing here with God as moral Governor, not as Creator.'

And, of course, in putting it like this, the Apostle is simply stating in other terms what he has already been saying all the way from verse 6. There we were introduced to this whole question of the two sons of Abraham, Ishmael and Isaac, and you remember how we interpreted that. They were both children of Abraham, they both came out of the same 'lump' as it were, out of the same stock – that is Abraham. But then we saw that out of that same lump God formed one to dishonour, Ishmael, and formed another to honour, Isaac. Both were inheritors of fallen humanity through Abraham, both were in the same position, they were in the same lump. Fallen humanity – that is the thing right the way through. It is the same with Jacob and Esau, and with them it is still even more obvious because they were twins. But one is formed to salvation – that is Jacob, and the other to damnation. It is the same argument throughout, and all he is saying here is that God has a right to do this.

Furthermore, this is the only subject under consideration here. The Apostle is asserting that the whole of humanity, everybody born into this world from Adam, is already lost and under condemnation – everybody. But God chooses some to salvation, and others He hardens and consigns to perdition. And as the potter has the right to make one vessel to honour and another to dishonour out of the lump of clay that is in front of him, God has an equal right to choose some to honour and to consign the others to dishonour.

On what grounds do I say that? Here is the answer: All deserve damnation as the result of the sin of Adam. That is proved in chapter 5 verse 12: 'Wherefore, as by one man sin entered into the world, and death by sin; and so death passed upon all men, for that all have sinned.'[1] There it is! We all sinned in Adam, the sin of Adam is on us all, and we all receive the condemnation. We are all born in sin and we deserve damnation as the result of the sin of Adam. And not only that; we deserve it also as the result of our own deliberate choice, as the result of our own deliberate sins and disobedience.

But I want to go further. Nobody deserves mercy, not one! We have no claim whatsoever upon the love of God. 'All we like sheep have gone astray'; we have all 'sinned, and come short of the glory of God'; 'There is none righteous, no, not one'; 'the world . . . guilty before God'. And nobody can dispute it! So there is our position. We not only deserve no mercy; we have no claim upon God to give us mercy. That is the lump of clay.

And all the Apostle is saying is that God, surely, has a right, therefore, to do what He likes with this. If He condemned the whole to perdition nobody would be able to voice a single complaint; but if He chooses to make some unto honour and

[1]See *Romans: An Exposition of Chapter 5: Assurance*, 1971.

some unto dishonour, why shouldn't He? Has He not a right to do what He likes with His own grace and mercy and compassion? Nobody has a claim, nobody can bring any complaint. We all deserve hell. If God chooses to show favour to some, why shouldn't He?

Of course, to argue against this is so monstrous, because we ourselves are constantly doing this very thing. If somebody tries to take from us the right to do what we like with our own we become furious. That is why many people dislike Communism; they say it takes everything from you, you can no longer do what you like with your own, and they think this is most unjust and iniquitous. But they are not willing for God to have that position. You see how utterly illogical we are. God the almighty Creator, says the Apostle, has a right as Creator, as Judge, as Sovereign Lord; He has complete freedom and right to do as He wills and as He likes. And that is precisely what He does with this lump of fallen, sinful humanity. From the very beginning, according to this principle of His – God's purpose 'according to election' in verse 11 – He has decided to choose some to honour and some to dishonour. Hence Isaac, Jacob, and the children of Israel. So that is Paul's statement.

Now I do want to make this quite clear; no one is created evil. It is inconceivable. God created all things good. No one has ever been forced to sin. 'God cannot be tempted with evil, neither tempteth he any man' [*James* 1 : 13]. Mankind in its representative and its head, Adam, who was perfect and sinless and who had complete free will and complete freedom of choice, rebelled against God and sinned, and so we have all fallen and sinned with him because we all by nature are in Adam. And what the Apostle is dealing with here is what God does with humanity in the light of that, and he says that He has an absolute right to do as He wills in His own sovereign will and Lordship. With such a hopeless mass, which could be all consigned to perdition, He has nevertheless, because of His grace and glory and His purpose, chosen and elected and formed some out of that mass unto glory and honour and others to perdition and to dishonour.

Now that, and that alone, is what the Apostle tells us here. He does not go any further because he cannot; he does not know. You see, what we all want to ask at this point is: *Why* did God decide to do this? *How* does God decide to make one unto

honour and one unto dishonour? There is only one answer to that
– I do not know! Nobody else does.

But we must add to that. You have no right to ask your
question. That is the ultimate mystery. I cannot go beyond the
Scripture, and all the Scripture tells me is that God does that and
that He has a right to do it, and that if I raise the question as to
whether He has a right to do it I am not only being a fool, I am
calling upon my head woes from God, for I am trying to contend
with my Maker. That is all I know, I cannot go further. We must
not even enquire.

So let me put the teaching to you like this: If any man is saved it
is entirely because of the mercy and the choice of God: 'Therefore
hath he mercy on whom he will have mercy, and whom he will he
hardeneth.' So that whenever a person is saved, that person is a
Christian for one reason only. It is because of the election and the
mercy of God. You were in that lump, that mass of perdition, and
if you are now out of it, it is entirely because of the mercy of God.
But I add this: If people are lost, it is entirely their own responsibility. How is that? Well, because it is a part of their inheritance
from Adam. They are responsible in Adam, as we are responsible
for things that our Governments did, perhaps, a hundred years
ago. We cannot dissociate ourselves. We are responsible for the
sins of our forefathers, for the actions of our country. We are
responsible in that way.

But on top of that we are responsible because we have confirmed what Adam did, we have done it ourselves also. Adam sinned as our representative but we, in turn, have all sinned. Everyone deliberately chooses to sin. We have not been forced to sin;
we have wanted to do it. We went against conscience; we went
against law. When we sinned, we sinned deliberately. But, even
further, everyone who does not believe the gospel is deliberately
rejecting it and its offer of salvation. So let me sum it up like this:
If people are saved, it is entirely of the mercy of God; if they are
damned, it is their own responsibility. That is obviously what the
Apostle is teaching here. It came out in the teaching concerning
Pharaoh. God hardened Pharaoh's heart, Pharaoh hardened his
own heart, and we saw that there was no contradiction there.

So that is the teaching of the Scripture at this point – that God
has this complete right and freedom to do as He wills with this
mass of humanity that has sinned against Him. He chooses to

save some – that is the marvellous thing – and He chooses not to save others. And for His own purposes He sometimes 'hardened' those others in order to display His glory and His power through them. That really does not come in; it does not make any difference at all. The vital thing is that He chooses to save some, and to send the others to the perdition and the damnation that we all so richly deserve.

Finally, then, let me put it like this. Perhaps I should not do this, but I am trying to help. This is a great mystery, the mystery of God's eternal will. The principle on which He does this, we do not know. All He tells us is, 'Jacob have I loved, but Esau have I hated', and He did that while they were both still unborn in the womb of their mother. Now this is a mystery and natural man objects to it and feels it is wrong. People say that they do not believe that, and some of them foolishly say that they are looking forward to going to heaven and that they would like to have half an hour with the Apostle Paul and put him right on some things. That is an exact quotation! A quotation of what a man said in a Christian pulpit in London a few years ago. People do not understand this teaching and so they express these blasphemous opinions.

But I want to show you how utterly inconsistent they are with themselves and with what they really believe themselves. They object to this teaching and say, 'Where is free will? Where is man? Where is man's responsibility?' Well, I have already shown you where man's responsibility is; he is responsible for his damnation; he is not responsible for his salvation.

But what is it that these people really believe about man, these scoffers against the Bible, these scoffers against Christian doctrine? What are their answers to the questions: Why does man act as he does? How do you explain man? Well, there are only three ultimate explanations. One is called *contingency* – that there is no rhyme or reason in anything; it is all accidental and haphazard. The second is the doctrine of necessity which sometimes goes under the name of *fate*. 'Ah', they say, 'there it is, you cannot help it, you are fated to do it; you are like that and it is necessity.' That is a very common belief in the world. Determinism! That everything is determined and that man is not free at all.

Now I am quoting what non-Christians believe, and there are many subdivisions of this doctrine of necessity or determinism.

Take the Communists for instance, the followers of Karl Marx. How do they explain man? Well, they say that man is to be explained in terms of what they call 'dialectical materialism'. They say that the whole of history can be explained in terms of capital and labour, demand and supply.

That is the supposed discovery of Karl Marx – that he discovered this dialectic, that you can explain the whole of human history, and therefore the lives of individuals, in terms of this conflict. There is the master, here is the servant. Capital–labour, demand–supply, and so on; and this has determined the whole course of history. They believe that; they are determinists. They do not believe that man is free; they say that man is a slave of this process which they are trying, of course, to help along, and they say that it is happening inevitably, and that ultimately the whole world will have evolved through this process until you have a perfect state, which will be classless and there will be no capital and labour, there will be no masters. We will all be masters. That is one view of this determinism.

But there is another, the biological view. Now I do hope you are getting the force of this argument. These are the arguments, these are the things that are believed by people who object to this teaching of the Apostle Paul here, because, they say, it means that man cannot do anything about it – where is man's free will? But that is what they really believe of man at the same time. Some of them believe it, though, in terms of this biological view. These are very scientific. They say that what a man is, is determined by various glands in his body. They are quite serious about this; they say that the relative proportions of the thyroid gland, the pituitary gland, the suprarenal glands, and so on, determine what we are. They have no difficulty in explaining Hitler; he had too much suprarenal gland, where our adrenalin and power comes from. And so they explain Shakespeare, Beethoven and everybody else. Man is nothing but the result of the interplay of these biological forces that are within him.

But there is one other, an interesting one – the explanation given by Freud, the father of psychoanalysis, whose teaching has been given from Christian pulpits. Freud teaches – and here I quote from the Reith Lectures that were delivered in 1962 by Professor Carstairs, the man who criticizes the Christian church for putting 'Chastity before Charity'. He is a Freudian, as so many people are, and what he actually said is a great statement about Freud and his teaching. He said, 'The confusion which prevails in popular thinking about the concepts of determinism and personal responsibility contributes to this partial eclipse of moral values . . .' He had just been giving figures to show the appalling increase in the number of people in our prisons; it has gone up to three times what it was before the war, indeed three times what it was in the hundred years before the war. He then gave figures about juvenile delinquency and so on, and he was trying to explain this. He then continued, '. . . by showing how often our apparently deliberate actions are in fact determined by motives of which we are unaware. Psychoanalysis has under-mined our confidence in the reality of free-will.'

And he is quite right; it has. If you follow the teaching of Freud and these psychoanalysts you cannot possibly believe in free will; because Freud says that what people do, what people think, and their reactions and behaviour, are determined not only by the characteristics of their father and mother and grandfather and grandmother on both sides, but also by what happened to them when they were in the womb, and by what happened to them when they were brought up as children. Professor Carstairs mentioned some of these things in his lecture: that it depends partly whether people were breast-fed or bottle-fed; it depends also upon the way they were treated in the matter of hygiene by their mothers. Was she one of these people who was over-concerned about the cleanliness of her baby or was she not? Those are the sort of things which are going to determine how people will behave. And then, of course, there are these experiences in early childhood when they are yet unconscious, these dawning sex impulses and so on – those are the things that determine behaviour.

That is the teaching of psychoanalysis. One man seriously suggested that the only hope for the future of this world is that children should be brought up by parents and school-teachers who themselves had undergone a process of psychoanalysis and who had been rid of these things that have been hampering the forward march of the human race and liberated into a new way of living. It was the only hope, he said, and it must happen to them while they were children because 'the child is father of the man'.

So there it is. That is the alternative to the teaching of the Apostle Paul. Do not talk to me about 'free will'; there is no such thing. There is no such thing as free will in fallen man. The Bible teaches that, Freud teaches that, even all these people teach that. You see, what we have here is the biblical doctrine of *certainty*. This is the third explanation; not contingency, not necessity, but certainty, the certainty of that which is produced by God.

There is one final argument. People seem to think that if you reject this doctrine of Paul, then you are in a happy position. You say, 'I do not believe that it is God who elects and that whom He wills He saves, and whom He wills He hardens. A man must be free, it must depend upon man's own choice, upon man's decision.' But wait a minute, let us look at it like this. Let me show you where you are if you reject the doctrine of Paul as taught here. Take Acts 28 : 24. Here is the Apostle Paul; he has gathered the Jews together into his private lodging in Rome, and he preaches the gospel to them, and this verse says, 'And some believed the things which were spoken, and some believed not.' That is the problem, is it not? Why do some believe, and some not? Those people were Jews, all of them the same: same background, same everything, but some believed, some did not believe. How often has this happened in a family! Two brothers, with the same father and mother, the same home, the same upbringing, who went to the same school, the same chapel and the same Sunday-school, and heard the same gospel – everything the same. One believes, the other does not. What decides it, what determines it?

'Ah,' says somebody, 'it is quite simple. Free will!' Very well, one chooses to believe, the other chooses not to believe – and you think you have finished when you have said that, but you have not. This is the problem that you leave with me, and with all the psychologists: why is it that one chose to believe, and the other chose not to believe? I want to know that – why? Why did some believe Paul's preaching, while others did not? But what is it that makes some want to believe and others not?

'Oh well,' you say, 'one saw things in one way, and the other saw them in a different way.' Yes, but you still have not helped me. *Why* does one of them see it like this, and the other one like that? You see, you must ask these questions. 'Well,' I am told, 'I don't know, one of them was like that, and the other was different.' All right! But tell me, why was one like this, and the other different? Let us go further back. 'Well,' you say 'he must have been born like this, and the other was born different.' All right! Are we responsible for the way in which we are born? Are you responsible for the nature with which you were born? Are you responsible for the ability with which you were born? Of course you are not. But, if you reject this teaching that we have here in Romans 9, that is where you are left – it is utterly accidental. One man believes – well, because he happens to be born like that; the other disbelieves because he happens to be born like that; he does not control it.

The vital question is this: What is it that determines a man's will? And the moment you ask that question it comes back to one of two things: it is either God's purpose, or else it is pure accident, a matter of glands, a matter of upbringing, a thousand and one factors entirely beyond our own control. In no case have you got free will. There has been no such thing since man fell. The only man who has ever had free will was Adam, and we know what he did with it. Since then, we have all been born in sin, we are 'shapen in iniquity'. And what makes any man a Christian is the purpose and the will and the choice of God.

So you see if you reject the teaching of the Apostle here you are not only rejecting his teaching, you are rejecting the teaching of God Himself! And it is not surprising that the alternative is complete chaos, utter contingency, sheer hopelessness, though it may masquerade at times in terms of some blind fate or some mechanical deterministic necessity.

May God give us His Spirit, and give us the grace to look into these marvellous and mysterious things.

Seventeen

*

Thou wilt say then unto me, Why doth he yet find fault? For who hath resisted his will? Nay but, O man, who art thou that repliest against God? Shall the thing formed say to him that formed it, Why hast thou made me thus? Hath not the potter power over the clay, of the same lump to make one vessel unto honour, and another unto dishonour? What if God, willing to shew his wrath, and to make his power known, endured with much longsuffering the vessels of wrath fitted to destruction: and that he might make known the riches of his glory on the vessels of mercy, which he had afore prepared unto glory, even us, whom he hath called, not of the Jews only, but also of the Gentiles?

Romans 9 : 19–24

We saw in the last chapter how Paul teaches that the relationship between God and fallen humanity is this: 'Hath not the potter power over the clay, of the same lump to make one vessel unto honour and another unto dishonour?' We emphasized, too, that this is not referring to creation at the beginning. Here is this mass of perdition, this lump of fallen humanity and the Apostle says that God has a right to do as He likes with it. It all deserves to be damned, but God has chosen to save some and out of it to make some vessels unto honour, and of the rest to make vessels to dishonour. Why should He not? He has a right because He is God, because the whole world lies guilty before Him. And we ended by showing why modern man in particular is the very last who should cavil at this kind of teaching because he is generally a fatalist or a determinist, a Freudian or something like that. However, in many ways I need not have given those arguments because this passage is more than sufficient in and of itself.

So now we proceed with Paul's argument because he goes on

in verses 22 and 23 to bring in something further. In verses 20b and 21 he has been asserting God's *right* to do this, but in verses 22 and 23 he gives us God's *reason* for doing so. Now there was no need for this. We have no right to ask for reasons. We have no claim upon God at all; we deserve nothing but punishment and hell. If you think that you deserve anything else, then you do not know God and you do not know yourself either. The attitude taken up by all who have had any glimpse of God, as we read in the Bible, is that of Isaiah. They feel that they are people of unclean lips and they fall down in utter hopelessness and helplessness. We have no right to ask for any reason, but God in His infinite kindness and condescension stoops to our weakness and gives us reasons, and here the Apostle does that very thing.

Now he puts it in rather an odd way. There is a little difficulty about these two verses, because the Apostle does something which he does now and again, and I could almost say, Thank God that he does! He starts off a sentence and does not finish it. There is nothing wrong in that as long as the meaning is plain. You notice he starts off with a condition, which reads in the Authorized Version, 'What if God . . .' However, there is no 'what' in the original; Paul says, 'If God, willing . . .' In other words he starts with a condition and you expect that there will be a sort of conclusion – but he never gives us the conclusion. 'What if . . .', well then, you say, there is a reply to that, but he does not give us the reply. The reply is conveyed, as it were, by the very form in which he puts the question. So it could be taken something like this: 'If God has done this, what can man reply against it?' That is what he is really saying, and sometimes you can make a question like that more dramatic by not supplying the answer. You start with your condition but you do not supply the conclusion. So what Paul is saying is, 'What objection can there be to that?'

Let us look, then, carefully at his statement and at what he is saying. Taking the two verses together, we see that Paul says that the reason for God's action in hardening some and punishing them, and in showing mercy and compassion to others and saving them, is that His own glory and His own being might be made known and might be manifested. Both aspects of God's action do that, says Paul, and they both do it at the same time. There is the general statement, but then he divides it up into two. In verse 22 we have the manifestation of God's wrath and in verse 23 we have the manifestation of God's mercy.

This, again, is a most important statement. He starts verse 22 by saying, 'What if God, willing to shew his wrath . . .' Now this word 'willing' is not a good translation; it really means 'wishing', and it is even stronger than that; it could be translated 'What if God inclined to . . .'. And then even that is not strong enough because it means 'a deep and a strong desire'. A German commentator of the last century has, I think, put it very well: 'Notwithstanding that His holy will disposes Him not to leave unmanifested His wrath and His power.' That is a very good way of putting it. It is a paraphrase but it does bring out the meaning: 'Notwithstanding that His holy will *disposes* Him.' And it disposes Him very strongly. God, with this whole disposition of His nature to do this, nevertheless . . . Let us bear that in mind.

Now the Apostle is asserting, therefore, that everything in God, because He is God, because of His holy nature, because of His just and righteous character, hates sin. Sin and God are eternal opposites, and with all the intensity of His being God abhors sin and desires to punish it. That is something that is of necessity true about God. And the Apostle says that in punishing sin, therefore, God shows forth these aspects of His own glorious being and character. It is in punishing sin, in bringing destruction upon those who are sinners, that God has made known, and does make known the power of His wrath.

This is something, of course, that we see constantly as we read the Bible; it is in the Old Testament and in the New. The Apostle has already given us one very striking example of that in the case of Pharaoh which he quoted in the seventeenth verse, and here he is saying that same thing once more. He is saying that God's reason for doing this is that He might display and give this clear demonstration, not only of His wrath against sin and His utter abhorrence of it, but also of the power of His wrath, of His might and of His greatness. Of course, that is only one illustration of it, and the Apostle says that in every manifestation of His wrath upon sin, God is making known His attitude towards sin, His power to punish it, and thereby this fuller manifestation of the glory and the majesty of His person.

Now what we sometimes tend to forget is that this aspect of the character and the being of God would never have been known if He did not punish sin – 'What if God, willing to shew his wrath, and to make his power known . . .' – so this is very important. You see, the Apostle is facing this whole problem from the standpoint of the being and the attributes of God. Half our trouble arises as we consider this kind of doctrine, from the fact that we start and end with ourselves. Consider God!

The truth is that because God is God and because He is what He is – I say it with reverence – there are certain things that He must do, and one of them is that He must punish sin. God would not be God if He did not do so. His very nature is such that He must. And what the Apostle says, therefore, is that God in punishing sin lets us know this about His nature. The wrath of God against sin, as Paul has reminded us in verse 18 of Romans 1, is something that has already been revealed. 'For the wrath of God is revealed from heaven against all ungodliness and unrighteousness of men, who hold [down] the truth in unrighteousness.'

The ultimate trouble with people who do not believe in the doctrine of the wrath of God is that they do not believe the biblical revelation of God. They have got a God of their own creating. Generally, people who reject the biblical doctrine of the wrath of God also reject the biblical doctrine of redemption and of salvation. They are quite consistent. If you do not believe in God's wrath there is no real need for the sacrifice on Calvary's hill. So it is important that we should view all these things in the light of the great doctrine of God Himself.

Now, furthermore, you notice that he puts it like this: 'God, willing to shew his wrath, and to make his power known, endured with much longsuffering the vessels of wrath fitted to destruction.' The wrath of God, he says, is shown to 'the vessels of wrath', and that is a term which is used very commonly in Scripture. It means an instrument or utensil, as it were, through which God shows His wrath. Sometimes the expression 'children of wrath' is used. The Apostle says to the Ephesians, 'Among whom also we all had our conversation in times past in the lusts of our flesh, fulfilling the desires of the flesh and of the mind; and were by nature the children of wrath, even as others' [*Ephesians* 2 : 3]. It is the same kind of idea.

But the really interesting and significant word is the word 'fitted'. The right translation here again, or at least the full translation, is 'the vessels of wrath having been fitted', or, 'the vessels of wrath ripe for destruction'. Or, still more loosely, it could be rendered 'the vessels of wrath being ready for destruction'. The significance of the word is that the Apostle does not say that it is God who has fitted them for this; all he says is that they 'have been' fitted for destruction. He does not tell us who has so fitted them.

Why is this so important? For this reason: in the twenty-third verse, when we come to 'vessels of mercy', what we read is, 'which he had afore prepared unto glory'. In other words God has not prepared the vessels of wrath to destruction but He has prepared the vessels of mercy unto glory which, of course, puts this absolutely into line with what we have seen in our previous exposition. God never created a sinner. He did not create this 'lump' of fallen humanity. God created man perfect in His own image and likeness, as He created the whole world perfect. It is man who fits himself for destruction, not God.

And it is most interesting how the Apostle brings that out here: 'the vessels of wrath fitted, having been fitted to'. What has done this? Well, what has fitted them to it is their own sin first of all in the fall of man, their own sin and their own disobedience. Then there is also the hardening process which we have already considered in the case of Pharaoh – man's failure to react to the light and the grace of God's love, and thereby becoming still more sinful – and that fits him still more for destruction than he was already fitted. But the serious and the important thing is that it is made quite clear that they are not fitted for destruction by God.

And you notice that what they are fitted for is nothing short of destruction, what Paul calls in 2 Thessalonians 1–9, 'everlasting destruction from the presence of the Lord'. That means perdition; it means eternal punishment out of the presence of God and His glory and out of the enjoyment of His being for ever. 'Destruction'! So then Paul says that God has shown and has manifested this aspect of His character in connection with these vessels of wrath that have become fit for nothing but that destruction.

But then he goes on to say another most interesting thing here

– that though God would have been fully justified in consigning to that destruction the whole of fallen humanity, and though He would have been justified in doing it immediately, actually He has not done that. What has He done? He has 'endured', Paul says, 'with much longsuffering' these 'vessels of wrath fitted to destruction'. Now this means, I believe, that Paul is again carrying in his mind the case of Pharaoh which he has already considered in verse 17. God knew beforehand exactly what Pharaoh was going to do and announced to Moses that He was going to harden his heart. But God did not immediately destroy Pharaoh; no, He endured him; He endured his rebellion, his arrogance, his disobedience. He endured it for some time; He sent Moses and Aaron back to him to plead with him and so on, and it was only after a period that He finally destroyed him and his hosts in the Red Sea.

Now the Apostle says that this is a general principle in God's dealing with the whole of fallen humanity, and this raises a question that we have all often considered. The question can be put like this: Why does God tolerate the world at all? Why did He not destroy the whole of humanity the moment Adam sinned? Why does God tolerate so much evil and godlessness in this present world? Christian people have often felt like asking that question. You will often find the Psalmist asking it; he cannot understand God. Why does He tolerate this? Why does He not arise and destroy His enemies?

Well now, that is the very question that the Apostle, I think, is putting before us here and it is very good that we should consider it, not only because Christians often ask it, but also, as 2 Peter 3 reminds us, because scoffers and unbelievers are very fond of putting this question also. They come forward and they say, 'Ah, you people preach that there is a great God who is over all, and that He is a Judge, who will judge the world in righteousness. You say that He judged it once at the Flood and that He is going to judge it again, but "Where is the promise of his coming? for since the fathers fell asleep, all things continue as they were from the beginning of the creation"' [2 *Peter* 3 : 4]. They say, 'You Christian preachers, you have been saying that this Jesus of yours has risen from the dead, that He has ascended into heaven and is seated at the right hand of God, and that He is only waiting until His enemies shall be made His footstool. You say that He will come back and judge the world in righteousness, and destroy His enemies, the devil and hell included, and set up His glorious kingdom; but', they say, 'when is it going to happen? You have been saying that for years now and nothing is happening.' They were saying that in the first century and we are in the twentieth century, and there are many people whose faith is shaken by this kind of question.

Now that is the question that Peter answers there in that third chapter of his Second Epistle and I always feel that it is a very interesting commentary on this verse in Romans 9 that we are looking at together. Peter says, 'Beloved, be not ignorant of this one thing, that one day is with the Lord as a thousand years, and a thousand years as one day.' That is important – but notice, 'The Lord is not slack concerning his promise, as some men count slackness; but is longsuffering to us-ward [or to you-ward], not willing that any should perish, but that all should come to repentance' [2 *Peter* 3 : 8–9]. So then bear that in your minds and the statement in Romans 2 : 4, which reads like this: 'Or despisest thou the riches of his goodness and forbearance and longsuffering; not knowing that the goodness of God leadeth thee to repentance?'

We have considered that very thoroughly, and it is important that we should bear in mind the conclusions we arrived at at that point.[1] The question is: Why does God tolerate evil men for so long? Why does He not – if He is holy as you say – destroy them immediately?

These are the answers: First, it is because of His longsuffering, His compassion. This is a doctrine that perplexes some people so let us look at the evidence. Go back to the book of Ezekiel, chapter 18. Verse 23 reads, 'Have I any pleasure at all that the wicked should die? saith the Lord God: and not that he should return from his ways, and live?' Then verse 32: 'For I have no pleasure in the death of him that dieth, saith the Lord God: wherefore turn yourselves, and live ye.' And then in chapter 33 : 11 we find, 'Say unto them, As I live, saith the Lord God, I have no pleasure in the death of the wicked; but that the wicked turn from his way and live: turn ye, turn ye from your evil ways; for why will ye die, O house of Israel?'

[1] See *Romans: An Exposition of Chapters 2:1–3:20 The Righteous Judgment of God*, 1989.

Now take those statements with that in Romans 2 : 4, the statement we have before us, and the statement in 2 Peter 3 : 9. What do they mean? They mean that God has compassion, that He is longsuffering, that He has no pleasure in the death of the ungodly. That is perfectly plain and clear.

'But how do you reconcile that', asks somebody, 'with the teaching which we have here in Romans 9?' The answer must surely be this. Those other verses concentrate on what God *desires* or what gives God pleasure, but here, in Romans 9, we are dealing with what God has willed in the sense of *decreeing*. God, as God, cannot have any pleasure in the death of a sinner; He cannot have pleasure in a sinner at all. The whole notion of sin is displeasing to Him. God has no pleasure in that or desire for it. So it is not the desire of God that any should perish; indeed it is the desire of God that all should come to repentance.

But it is not God's will that all should come to repentance. Because it is His desire that all should come to repentance, He has ordained that the gospel should be preached to all, and that all men everywhere should be commanded to repent and to believe the gospel. The free offer of salvation is to be made to everybody. That is the expression of God's 'desire'. But here in Romans 9 what we are being told is this: why does anybody believe at all? God's desire that men should be saved does not save anybody. It is God's will and determination that saves, and what we are told about that is that God has willed and determined to save only some.

This is most important. God, in His longsuffering and enduring, as we are told, shows that He has no pleasure in what unbelievers are, and no pleasure in destroying them. He is allowing them to go on, as it were, in order that they might listen to the gospel. That is God's desire and pleasure, but it does not save them. His longsuffering and patience with Pharaoh did not change him. Our Lord's patience and longsuffering with Judas did not change him. God's longsuffering with this world in which we live with the whole human race is not bringing it to belief in the Lord Jesus Christ. But what a demonstration it is of the longsuffering and the patience of God! We would never know anything about them if He did not withhold His wrath.

You see, the verse is really saying that God, whose whole being urges Him to punish sin, held back that urge, as it were, in order that He might show this longsuffering, this patience with sinful man. So that is His first reason for enduring 'with much longsuffering' the evil that is in the world, and he is doing that with the whole of humanity until this present hour.

But then there are further reasons, and the second is this: By enduring like this, with longsuffering, these vessels of wrath, God is at the same time rendering them quite inexcusable. This to me is a most important argument. They are inexcusable, of course, because of the offer of His grace. Have you ever contemplated this question? Why was the Old Testament, or the old dispensation period, such a long one? Whatever your figures may be, whether you accept those of Archbishop Ussher or not, it seems to have been at least 4,000 years. Why were there so many years after the Fall before the birth of our Lord and Saviour? Why that long interval? What is your answer to that question? Why do you think that God endured all that we read of in the Old Testament, and that we can also read of partly in the secular history of the nations of the world?

It seems to me that there is only one answer: Mankind from the beginning has always been self-confident; that is one of the first results of the Fall. Man's pride! – pride of intellect, pride of understanding, pride in his own power, pride in what he can achieve! And man has always taken the view, as he does now, that he can save himself. There are these modern people who say that if a man reads the New Testament, likes the teaching of Jesus, and decides he is going to follow Him, then that makes him a Christian and all is well. But that is just man's self-confidence, and that has always been his trouble. Man has always said that he could save himself if only he were told what to do.

So God told him what to do. He gave the law to the children of Israel; there it is in perfection; others copied it. Not only that, He gave the Greeks a full opportunity of producing their great philosophers, elaborating their great teachings and drawing their blueprints of their utopias by which they were going to put themselves and the whole world right. And God gave them a thorough opportunity to do it. If He had stopped it at the beginning, they would have said, 'Ah, but you did not give us a chance, you only gave us a year. If you had given us ten years we would have done it.' And if He had given them ten years they would have said, 'If you had given us 100.' What is 100 years? Then it would have been 1,000 ... Well, He gave them at least 4,000! You see, they have no excuse left. God gave the ancient world a full opportunity. As Paul puts it in 1 Corinthians 1, it was when 'the world by wisdom knew not God, [that] it pleased God [through] the foolishness of preaching to save them that believe' [verse 21]. Greece and Rome and every other civilization had exhausted itself and had ended in failure, and then God sent His Son.

And now it is exactly the same in explanation of the new dispensation in which we live. Why all this long interval? There is still only one answer: God is going to render condemned humanity utterly speechless at the end. They will say, 'If only we had heard about ...' But, He says, you have heard about it; the gospel has been preached now for nearly 2,000 years. The world is without excuse. Such people go to hell because they have rejected the way of salvation that is offered to them. 'Every mouth [shall] be stopped'; nobody will be able to say a word. God's 'longsuffering' in giving an opportunity for every man and woman to hear the message, renders them finally, completely and totally inexcusable.

Do not argue with unbelievers about election and predestination; argue with them about this: Why do they not believe the gospel? That is the problem for them. Why do they continue in sin? Why do they not know that their sins are forgiven? Why have they not been born again? Why not? Here is the answer, hold them face to face with that, render them inexcusable.

And thirdly, God's reason for enduring with much longsuffering these vessels of wrath that are already ripe for destruction is that when the time of their punishment does come, it is made yet more striking. We have already seen this in the case of Pharaoh in verse 17: 'Even for this same purpose have I raised thee up, that I might shew my power in thee, and that my name might be declared throughout all the earth.' We interpreted that, let me remind you, like this: that if God had destroyed Pharaoh and his hosts at the first refusal, we would not have had those great miracles, and it is through them that God showed His power – this overwhelming power that the whole world spoke about then and has been speaking about ever since. And it was only when finally Pharaoh and his chariots and his hosts were drowned and consumed in the Red Sea that the greatness of God's might and glory were really shown; how He brought out this mere handful, as it were, of defenceless people and destroyed this mighty dictator's army and all his hosts. When God does act, it is unmistakable because He has allowed these scoffers to say, 'Where is the promise of his coming?'

And that is the sort of thing they are saying at the present time. They say, 'There is not a God at all. If there were, He would not endure all this; if He could stop it, He would; if He could punish, then He would do so. No,' they say, 'there is no God!' And God allows them to say it all, but then, when they seem to have proved their case to the hilt, and when the whole world is becoming godless and irreligious, when it is as it was in the time when our Lord came on this earth, steeped in iniquity and in foulness, then God will arise and the coming will be still more wonderful and glorious. When He is revealed, as Paul tells us in 2 Thessalonians 2 : 8, with all 'the brightness of his coming', it will be still more wonderful and glorious for the very reason that it has been delayed. And when He comes, the destruction will be correspondingly more awful than ever, when kings and others, as we are told in Revelation 6, shall cry to the rocks and the mountains, 'Fall on us, and hide us from the face of him that sitteth on the throne, and from the wrath of the Lamb.'

But finally let me quote a passage from 2 Thessalonians in full, so that we may keep this thought in our minds. Paul says, 'We ourselves glory in you in the churches of God for your patience and faith in all your persecutions and tribulations that ye endure: which is a manifest token of the righteous judgment of God, that ye may be counted worthy of the kingdom of God, for which ye also suffer: seeing it is a righteous thing with God to recompense tribulation to them that trouble you; and to you who are troubled rest with us, when the Lord Jesus shall be revealed from heaven with his mighty angels, in flaming fire taking vengeance on them that know not God, and that obey not the gospel of our Lord Jesus Christ: who shall be

punished with everlasting destruction from the presence of the
Lord, and from the glory of his power; when he shall come to
be glorified in his saints, and to be admired in all them that
believe . . . in that day' [2 *Thessalonians* 1 : 4–10].

Eighteen

*

Thou wilt say then unto me, Why doth he yet find fault? For who hath resisted his will: Nay but, O man, who art thou that repliest against God? Shall the thing formed say to him that formed it, Why hast thou made me thus? Hath not the potter power over the clay, of the same lump to make one vessel unto honour, and another unto dishonour? What if God, willing to shew his wrath, and to make his power known, endured with much longsuffering the vessels of wrath fitted to destruction: and that he might make known the riches of his glory on the vessels of mercy, which he had afore prepared unto glory, even us, whom he hath called, not of the Jews only, but also of the Gentiles.

Romans 9 : 19–24

We saw in our last study that in verse 22 the Apostle gives us God's reason for punishing the ungodly, and particularly His reason for punishing the ungodly in the way that He does. We saw that in doing this, God seems to put a restraint upon everything that is in Him that urges Him to punish them; with His own being desiring, urging Him to manifest His wrath upon the children of disobedience, God, as it were, holds it back; He 'endures with much longsuffering'. We have seen a particular example of it in the case of Pharaoh, but it is also to be seen so clearly in His dealings with the children of Israel over this long story, too, and in His dealings with individual characters that are put before us in the pages of the Old Testament.

This is a great mystery, but it is something that is taught very frequently and in many places in Scripture. There is, for instance, the statement in Genesis chapter 15 verse 16 – '. . . for the iniquity of the Amorites is not yet full'. But our Lord Himself made a remarkable statement about all this and it is recorded in Matthew 23 : 34–36 where He is addressing the Pharisees: 'Wherefore, behold, I send unto you prophets, and wise men, and scribes: and some of them ye shall kill and crucify; and some of them shall ye scourge in your synagogues, and persecute them from city to city' – then – 'that upon you may come all the righteous blood shed upon the earth, from the blood of righteous Abel unto the blood of Zacharias son of Barachias, whom ye slew between the temple and the altar. Verily I say unto you, All these things shall come upon this generation.' As if to say – and it is of course the teaching – that God did not visit the full and the final punishment upon the children of Israel at the very moment when they committed their sin or their crime; there was only a kind of temporary punishment, a kind of instalment of punishment; that God as it were has been treasuring it all up, holding it back. But now He says, 'Upon you it is finally to be poured out.'

Now that is a prophecy, of course, concerning what was going to happen to the children of Israel in A.D. 70. And it did! Their city was destroyed and they were thrown out, cast out, amongst the nations. At last the wrath of God had been revealed, the period of longsuffering had come to an end. So, you see, the teaching is there in our Lord's words to the authorities quite as plainly and as explicitly as it is in this statement in Romans 9, indeed more so.

And so we saw earlier that God has chosen to do this in order that certain things might be revealed. One is compassion, that He does not take any 'pleasure' in punishing the ungodly; secondly, in order that He might render them utterly inexcusable because of the opportunities He has given them; and thirdly, to make their punishment still more striking when it comes. The Jews had laughed at their prophets, they had ridiculed them, and they had gone on sinning. Prophets had been addressing them for at least eight centuries, but they paid no attention. Calamities came; still it made no difference. But at last it came, and the destruction of Jerusalem and what accompanied it in A.D. 70 is one of the most amazing and astonishing phenomena that the human race has ever witnessed.

Those, then are three reasons why God delays and shows this longsuffering, but there is also a further reason which we find in verse 23. Now there is a good deal of dispute among the authorities as to the precise relation between verses 22 and 23. Are they two separate but parallel statements, or are they two parts of one statement? Is the Apostle saying that on the one hand God does something in the manifestation of His wrath and He does something else in the manifestation of His mercy? Or is verse 23 a further explanation of verse 22 – that God 'endured with much longsuffering the vessels of wrath fitted to destruction' in order 'that he might make known the riches of his glory on the vessels of mercy, which he had afore prepared unto glory'?

Well, it is a question that cannot be decided, and in a sense it really does not matter very much, because the meaning is much the same in both cases. Both things, of course, are true, and we can, therefore, take it in both ways. I do think that one of the reasons for the longsuffering which is manifested towards the vessels of wrath is that there might be this prolonged period of grace during which those who are to be saved shall be saved. There is a suggestion to that effect also in 2 Peter 3 : 18, as we saw in the previous exposition, and the Apostle Paul, I suggest, is partly saying that here. The same period contains the two things and the two elements.

But is is also good and right that we should take them as separate statements. So the Apostle is putting two questions. First, what if God did restrain for a while the manifestation of His wrath and the manifestation of His power? – and that, of course, is two questions in one. What if God does manifest His wrath and His power to these people in that way, exercising longsuffering before He does so? Then comes the next question in verse 23: What if God does 'make known the riches of his glory on the vessels of mercy, which he had afore prepared unto glory'? And therefore the ultimate question is this: What is your objection to that, where is the injustice involved in it? And, of course, in putting it in the form of a question like that, Paul is really supplying the answer.

The answer is this, and it is common to the two questions: Everything that God does is a revelation of some aspect or other of His being and of His character. In punishing the ungodly, God manifests His wrath and His power, and at the same time His compassion, because of the way in which He shows it; but in showing mercy towards them who are to be saved He shows 'the riches of his glory'.

Now here, it seems to me, is the Apostle's great argument, that God manifests His character, both in the wrath and in the mercy. You notice the phrase that Paul keeps on repeating – that He *shows* this. Verse 22: 'What if God, willing to *shew* his wrath?' And in verse 23: 'That he might *make known* the riches of his glory'. God is all along making it known to us, making it plain. Indeed we have already had this whole idea in verse 17 and what he is dealing with here is the objection to what he taught in that verse. 'For the scripture saith unto Pharaoh, Even for this same purpose have I raised thee up, that I might shew my power in thee, and that my name might be declared throughout all the earth.' That is the overriding object, that God is declaring, manifesting, certain aspects of His own eternal and glorious being. And what the Apostle is asking is, Why should He not? Where is the injustice of God showing His power and His wrath upon those who so richly deserve it – 'fitted to destruction'? What is wrong about God showing, if He chooses, mercy to certain people, when none of them at all deserves it? That is Paul's answer. But now we must look in detail at verse 23 – the manifestation of 'the riches of God's glory on the vessels of mercy' – because it is indeed a wonderful and a glorious statement. And the phrase, of course, that must arrest us at once is 'the riches of his glory'! The theme, in other words, of verse 23 is that God's main purpose in salvation is to show and to make known the riches of His glory.

Now the ultimate truth about God, His ultimate attribute, if we may so speak, is glory. We talk about the power of God, His omnipotence, His omniscience and His omnipresence, and all these various other attributes, but of course ultimately what makes God God is His glory! You cannot describe it; you cannot define it! All the Bible itself does is to give us some kind of description of men and women who have had a glimpse of the glory of God; they fall to the ground and they feel utterly unworthy. Glory! What is it? Well, all I know is that it is perfect light, perfect love; it baffles description. So that everything that God does is in some shape or form the manifestation of His glory. And yet we must notice this most interesting thing: the Apostle does not put the manifestation of God's power and His wrath in terms of glory. He keeps that only to what He does in the manifestation of His mercy. And I emphasize this because though the glory of God is manifested in His power and in His wrath, yet the Apostle is anxious that we should realize that if we really want to know something about the glory of God, then we must look at Him as He manifests and shows His mercy to those upon whom He will show mercy!

This is something that has astounded the saints and has stimulated them throughout the centuries to express their wonder and amazement. Listen to Samuel Davies, for instance, putting it in his well-known hymn:

> *Great God of wonders! all Thy ways*
> *Are matchless, godlike, and divine;*
> *But the fair glories of Thy grace,*
> *More godlike and unrivalled shine.*

Or again it has been put like this:

> *For the grandeur of Thy nature,*
> *Grand beyond a seraph's thought;*
> *For created works of power,*
> *Works with skill and kindness wrought;*
> *For Thy providence that governs*
> *Through Thine empire's wide domain,*
> *Wings an angel, guides a sparrow,*
> *Blessèd be Thy gentle reign.*
>
> *But Thy rich, Thy free redemption,*
> *Dark through brightness all along, –*
> *Thought is poor, and poor expression, –*
> *Who dare sing that wondrous song?*
>   Robert Robinson

Then the same idea is found also in Isaac Watts' hymn:

> *Now to the Lord a noble song!*
> *Awake, my soul! awake, my tongue!*
> *Hosanna to the eternal Name,*
> *And all His boundless love proclaim.*
>
> *See where it shines in Jesus' face,*
> *The brightest image of His grace;*
> *God, in the Person of His Son,*
> *Has all His mightiest works outdone.*

The spacious earth and spreading flood
Proclaim the wise and powerful God;
And Thy rich glories from afar
Sparkle in every rolling star.

It is magnificent poetry apart from its being truth, is it not?

But in His looks a glory stands,
The noblest labour of Thy hands;
The radiant lustre of His eyes
Outshines the wonders of the skies.

And that is just what the Apostle is saying here. What it means, in other words, is that the salvation of a single soul is the most wonderful thing that God has ever done. He has surpassed and eclipsed everything. All His ways are matchless, godlike and divine; the creation, providence, the manifestation of His power over Pharaoh and his hosts, the manifestation of His wrath – all these things are manifestations of the glory of God. But they are nothing when you put them beside what God has done in the redemption of man. Even creation becomes nothing when you put it beside this; providence is nothing, punishment is nothing; everything is eclipsed here. This, the Bible teaches us, is indeed the very wonder of heaven itself.

Now that is expressed so wonderfully in Ephesians 2, where the Apostle says that He has quickened us, and raised us up together with Christ, and made us sit together in heavenly places, in order 'that in the ages to come he might shew the exceeding riches of his grace in his kindness toward us through Christ Jesus' [verse 7]. That is how He is going to show this 'in the ages to come'. God is going to show all succeeding generations and ages 'the exceeding riches of his grace in his kindness toward us'. You see – 'the riches of his glory'! And all future generations will look at this and be filled with amazement.

But not only that, says the Apostle, He goes further than that. It is not only all generations of men that will be filled with amazement at God's glory in the redemption of men; this is something that even astonishes the principalities and powers in the heavenly places. We read in Ephesians 3 : 10, 'To the intent that now unto the principalities and powers in heavenly places might be known by the church the manifold wisdom of God.'

Now 'the principalities and powers in heavenly places' is a reference, of course, to the good angels and the archangels. God made them and they have spent all their lives in His presence. They have been there praising Him and looking on; they have spent their time in the glory of heaven. But according to the Apostle, God is going to show even them something of His 'manifold wisdom' which they had never seen before, in and through the church, in and through these people who are called here 'vessels of mercy, which God had afore prepared unto glory'. In us! The members of the body of Christ! Those who are given salvation and redemption.

So this is what the Apostle is telling us here in Romans 9 : 23. He speaks of '*the riches* of his glory' – and he means by that, that there is no end to it, it cannot be measured. 'Thought is poor, and poor expression', says Robert Robinson quite rightly. You cannot express it. The Apostle cannot. He has to talk about 'the exceeding riches of his grace' or about 'the unsearchable riches of Christ'. He has to talk about 'the breadth, and length, and depth, and height; and to know the love of Christ, which passeth knowledge'. 'The riches of his glory'!

Now this, says the Apostle, is what God has manifested in showing mercy to those whom He saves, and here are some miserable creatures objecting to it, saying, 'This is not fair; it is not just that some should be saved and others should not.' Oh, how blind they are to the riches of His glory! If they had only had a glimpse of it they would be so filled with astonishment that they would not be able to say anything else.

So let us follow him, then, as he leads us into this. It is in redeeming those who are the vessels of mercy that God really shows the ultimate truth about Himself. Take, for instance, how the Apostle puts it in 1 Corinthians 1. The Corinthians thought they were very clever, and wanted to have more philosophy. Dear me, says the Apostle, can you not see? 'Where is the wise? where is the scribe? where is the disputer of this world? hath not God made foolish the wisdom of this world?' Then he goes on to say, 'The Jews require a sign, and the Greeks seek after wisdom: but we preach Christ crucified, unto the Jews a stumblingblock, and unto the Greeks foolishness.' 'Always that cross'! they say, 'there is nothing in it, it is a failure, it is nonsense – a carpenter dying on a cross! You say that is salvation? Utter foolishness!' – 'But unto them which are called, both Jews and Greeks, Christ the power of God, and the wisdom of God' [1 *Corinthians* 1 : 20, 22–24]. It is there He shows His power and His wisdom. But above everything else, in salvation and redemption He shows His love and His grace. 'The riches of his glory'!

How does he show it? How can Paul say that God shows and makes known the riches of His glory in His dealings with these vessels of mercy? The answer to that question is not difficult. The first answer is that He shows the riches of His glory in saving us – in the mere fact that He has anything at all to do with us, for we are all 'by nature the children of wrath, even as others' [*Ephesians* 2 : 3]. We are all by nature a part of that lump of clay, fallen humanity. When Adam sinned we all sinned – 'for that all have sinned'. Death came upon all because of sin in Adam. There we are, all deserving of wrath, all hell-deserving sinners, every one of us. Of course if we do not believe that, we will know nothing about grace or the riches of God's glory. We cannot hope to begin to understand, let alone to measure them, unless we know something about the depth of sin!

In other words, the measure of the riches of God's glory is His grace! What is grace? Grace is favour shown to those who are utterly and completely undeserving. Grace is kindness shown to people who deserve nothing but punishment. They deserve nothing good at all, and yet in spite of that they are shown great favour. That is the meaning of the word 'grace'. And the riches of God's glory are shown in His grace toward us.

Now, of course, the Apostle has already told us that in this same Epistle in chapter 5. 'For when we were yet without strength, in due time Christ died for the ungodly. For scarcely for a righteous man will one die: yet peradventure for a good man some would even dare to die. But God commendeth his love toward us, in that, while we were yet sinners, Christ died for us. Much more then, being now justified by his blood, we shall be saved from wrath through him. For if, when we were enemies, we were reconciled to God by the death of his Son, much more, being reconciled, we shall be saved by his life' [*Romans* 5 : 6–10]. There it is: 'God commendeth his love toward us'! God makes His love known to us, God manifests His grace to us, in that while we were yet sinners, while we were enemies, Christ died for us.

So that is one beginning of our attempt to measure the riches of God's glory. But let us go on and take the steps in their logical order. The riches of His glory are shown then in this: there is God in heaven, here is creation and man as the lord of creation. Man sinned and forfeited every claim upon God; he had been warned beforehand and if he had been immediately destroyed for ever and for ever there would have been no ground of complaint. But God looked upon these vessels of mercy in mercy and in grace. That is the first step, and the first manifestation of the riches of His glory.

But then, having done that, He now prepares a plan. He conceives a great purpose of saving, out of this mass of fallen humanity, a people for Himself; and here again we are looking at the glory of God. It is not possible for us, because of our dullness and because of our slowness, to apprehend these things. And yet this is the very thing that we are told in the Scripture everywhere, that though God is in no way obligated to us, though He had lived, existed, in and of Himself, the three Persons of the blessed Holy Trinity from eternity, without man, without creation at all, and though He was able to do so for ever and for ever had He so chosen – yet the almighty, holy, Trinity of Persons became concerned about this fallen mass of humanity and in their eternal glory they had a council to conceive a plan whereby some should be saved. And what we are told is that God did not depute this matter to some angels or archangels. This is the plan of God Himself, the everlasting and eternal God. Infinite in all His attributes, beyond measure of our understanding, He stoops even to consider this matter!

But He did more than that; He evolved His great purpose – the thing we read about in the previous chapter of Romans in verse 28: '. . . who are the called according to his purpose'. He took it up Himself and He evolved His plan. The three Persons in the blessed Holy Trinity were involved and this was all done, as we are told, 'before the foundation of the world'. This is 'the mystery, which from the beginning of the world hath been hid in God', and we see the three blessed Persons dividing this work and this plan up amongst themselves. It was the Father's plan but it had to be carried out, and the Son volunteered to be the executive agent. But then after the work had been done it needed to be applied, and the Holy Spirit volunteered to do the applying.

So this is the division of the work of salvation among the three Persons in the Trinity, sometimes called 'the economic Trinity'. What it means – and this is the astounding thing – is that the second Person in the Trinity humbles Himself and makes Himself subordinate to the Father. The three Persons in the Trinity are co-equal and co-eternal. 'In the beginning was the Word, and the Word was with God, and the Word was God' [*John* 1 : 1]. 'I and the Father are One.' The three Persons in the Trinity are equal, but for the sake of your salvation and mine (that is what the Apostle is talking about) the Son subordinates Himself to the Father. He says, 'Here am I: send Me.' So He came in the form of a servant and He was dependent upon His Father.

But then in turn the Holy Spirit subordinates Himself to the Son and to the Father. The Spirit 'shall not speak of himself' – which does not mean that He will not say things about Himself so much as that He is not going to originate things Himself – 'He shall glorify me', and 'He will bring to your remembrance all that ever I have said unto you.' The Spirit, co-equal with the Son and the Father, subordinates Himself to that task.

Now what the Apostle is trying here to tell us is that in the salvation of those who are redeemed, God is 'making known the riches of his glory', and there is something of it. The three Persons in the Trinity have gone to this trouble to make this plan, to have this purpose; that they have thus divided the labour among themselves and the Son and the Holy Spirit have subordinated themselves to the Father. What for? In order that a single soul may be saved! This is 'the riches of his glory' and we would know nothing about this if these vessels of mercy were not saved. It is when we know about salvation that we begin to know something about this.

This can be worked out in all sorts of details. It is interesting to see how the Apostle put it in Ephesians 3 about himself and the bringing in of the Gentiles. He says that this is a further manifestation of the plan – 'How that by revelation he made known unto me the mystery; (as I wrote afore in few words, whereby, when you read, ye may understand my knowledge in the mystery of Christ) which in other ages was not made known unto the sons of men, as it is now revealed unto his holy apostles and prophets by the Spirit; that the Gentiles should be fellow-heirs, and of the same body, and partakers of his promise in

Christ by the gospel' [*Ephesians* 3 : 3–6]. So that in every part and aspect of it God is making known something further of the riches of His glory.

Then the next step that I think we come to logically is the Old Testament preparation for all this. The Bible is the history of redemption. That is what it really amounts to. And all the history, all that you have about other nations, comes in simply because it throws some light upon the history of redemption. Some foolish people would have us believe that the Old Testament is the history of man's search for God. It is not! It is always the history of God searching for lost man. When God, as it were, came down from heaven into the garden of Eden after Adam and Eve had fallen, that is the beginning of that history, and all the rest just has reference to that. That is all!

You see, the Bible is not really a book primarily about this world and this life; it is a book about God's people, about these vessels of mercy and what God is doing about them and His object and His purpose. And so the history of this world is only incidental. This world is going to be destroyed, but there will be a new world for these people. You have, therefore, references to this world simply because it comes into the history of redemption and the history of the people whom God is preparing for Himself, and all this is a manifestation and a making known of the riches of God's glory. So it is there in the Old Testament.

And what you find there, in essence, is this: God makes that announcement in the garden of Eden about His purpose, and what you find in the Old Testament is just the outworking of that one great purpose – the seed of the woman shall bruise the serpent's head. That is the purpose; it is going to happen. And then you see this as a line running right through the Old Testament story; sometimes you have almost lost it, but back it comes. It is always there, and it goes right the way through. You see it, for instance, in Abel rather than Cain; you see it in Seth the son of Adam and Eve; then all sorts of things happen, but you see it in Noah, and then in one of the sons of Noah – Shem – this line being worked out and pursued. And as you see it you are amazed at the glory of God and the wonder of His ways and how He keeps His purpose going.

And next you come to Abraham, of course; and then, as we have seen, to Isaac rather than Ishmael, and then Jacob rather than Esau – and on and on it goes. Judah – and then it seems to be lost almost entirely at times, but there it is all along. And where you see the special glory of it, of course, is in this respect: that in spite of the folly and the sin and the recalcitrance of these very people whom God has chosen, in spite of their idolatry and their backsliding, in spite of everything that is true of them, God keeps the purpose going. And in doing this He shows us the glory and the wonder of His ways.

Perhaps this is seen most clearly of all in the case of certain particular individuals. Let us look at two of them. Look at a man like Jacob; who of us would ever have thought that Jacob was the man to be chosen? You would have chosen Esau, would you not? He seems a much nicer man, much kinder, generous; the other man, scheming, underhand, sly, and all the rest of it. But Jacob is God's man, and God makes something of him. You see, it is not affability that matters in the sight of God; it is not a mere bucolic, animal kind of stolidity and niceness that matters. It is character, it is understanding, it is a knowledge of the purpose of God and putting that into the first position. So God shows His glory in taking a man like Jacob and making of him His man through whom the promise is to be sent on and continued.

And you get much the same thing as you read the life story of a man like David. David fell into terrible and most grievous sin, but he is the man after God's heart. And in all this, and in other individuals in exactly the same way, God in that Old Testament preparation is showing us something of the riches of His glory.

Now I cannot refrain from asking certain questions before we move on to the next study. Does anybody object to this? Does anybody still feel that this is unjust? Is it wrong that God should show the riches of His glory in this way? Are you still troubled with your little questions, 'I cannot see this, I cannot understand . . .' – are you still saying things like that? Well, not only have I failed completely in my exposition if you still are feeling like that, I wonder whether you know anything at all about the grace of God in the Lord Jesus Christ.

'The riches of his glory'!

Nineteen

*

Thou wilt say then unto me, Why doth he yet find fault? For who hath resisted his will? Nay but, O man, who art thou that repliest against God? Shall the thing formed say to him that formed it, Why hast thou made me thus? Hath not the potter power over the clay, of the same lump to make one vessel unto honour, and another unto dishonour? What if God, willing to shew his wrath, and to make his power known, endured with much longsuffering the vessels of wrath fitted to destruction: and that he might make known the riches of his glory on the vessels of mercy, which he had afore prepared unto glory, even us, whom he hath called, not of the Jews only, but also of the Gentiles?

Romans 9 : 19–24

We have now reached the end of this great argument. The Apostle is replying to the suggestion that he puts before us in the nineteenth verse. People have asked, Why does God find fault with anybody if it is a question of His choice – if salvation is entirely and only and solely His action? The Apostle proceeds to answer that question and we have been following him step by step. We are now dealing with the latter part of the argument, the part that he develops in verses 22 to 24, and what he says in verse 23, as we have seen, is that everything that God does is a manifestation of Himself. Back in the first chapter the Apostle has told us in verse 19 and following, how God in creation had made something of Himself known. 'Because', he says, 'that which may be known of God is manifest in them; for God hath shewed it unto them. For the invisible things of him from the creation of the world are clearly seen, being understood by the things that are made, even his eternal power and Godhead; so that they are without excuse.' In other words, the creation reveals and manifests to us God's eternal power and Godhead. You look at creation and, if you have eyes to see, you will see God the Creator, and all the wisdom and the power that He displays in that way. So everything that God does is a manifestation of some aspect or other of His character and of His being. And what the Apostle is saying here is that in the manifestation of His wrath God is making something known about Himself. And in exactly the same way in the manifestation of mercy He is making known another aspect of His great and glorious being – the riches of His glory.

This is a very wonderful thing. I do not know what you have been feeling about all this as you have thought about it and meditated about it. Has it not come to you as a bit of a surprise to find such a statement, such a phrase in such a context? How foolish we are as we read the Scriptures! So many people say, 'Oh, I don't read the ninth of Romans; that is that difficult passage, nothing there but predestination and the sovereignty of God and so on – hard and dry doctrine'! So many people regard this chapter as a kind of wilderness. And yet here, you see, suddenly we come across one of the brightest nuggets in the whole of the Bible: 'the riches of [God's] glory'! Have you heard anybody, when they are talking about Romans 9, referring to this phrase? Is it not rather odd, is there not something wrong with us that we can ever refer to Romans 9 without saying, 'Ah, that is the chapter in which we read about "the riches of his glory"'? I wonder how many of us, if we were quite honest, would have to admit that we never knew that that phrase was to be found there at all, and that we thought there was nothing there but this argumentation and statement about the sovereignty of God. But here it is! I refer to that in passing, but we must never read the Scriptures casually; we must always be ready for something unexpected and surprising, something glorious, something wonderful. In the middle of a great argument suddenly you find a priceless gem!

So now we are trying to look at different aspects of these 'riches'. You see, we are like people who having been in some sort of desert, burrowing our way along, following a track, find ourselves suddenly discovering some great palace with golden doors, and we have gone in and we are going from chamber to chamber and room to room looking at this amazing wealth, 'the unsearchable riches of Christ', 'the exceeding riches of God's grace'. That is what we are doing.

Well, we have been through some of the rooms; we have seen that the riches of God's glory are shown in the fact that He has anything to do with us at all. Secondly, we looked at the glory of the plan itself, and then we looked at the working out of this in the Old Testament dispensation. It is all marvellous! The wisdom and the power and the love of God! The irresistibility of the grace of God!

But now we come to what is in many ways the central chamber of all in this palace of riches, the riches of God's glory and grace – the Lord Jesus Christ! Look again at those words of Isaac Watts which we quoted in the previous exposition, because I think he has put this so perfectly. Let me give you one of the verses once more:

> But in His looks a glory stands,
> The noblest labour of Thy hands;
> The radiant lustre of His eyes
> Outshines the wonders of the skies.

And so it does! 'God, who commanded the light to shine out of darkness, hath shined in our hearts, to give the light of the knowledge of the glory of God in the face of Jesus Christ' [2 *Corinthians* 4 : 6]. The riches of His glory are ultimately to be seen all concentrated together in the face of Jesus Christ.

Of course, this is something that no man can describe. We can but look at it and glimpse it. You see something of this glory of God in the face of Jesus Christ even in the Old Testament. Every time the Angel of the Covenant appears that is who He is, this special servant of the Lord. He is the Lord Jesus Christ coming down in that particular form as a theophany in order to prepare for His eventual coming in Bethlehem. You can find it, then, in the Old Testament.

But, of course, it is when you come to the New Testament that you really begin to see it. This is how Paul himself puts it elsewhere. He is never tired of saying this. He never comes across it but that he goes off into some sort of apostrophe; he cannot contain himself. Here is one of them: 'And without controversy great is the mystery of godliness: God was manifest in the flesh, justified in the Spirit, seen of angels, preached unto

the Gentiles, believed on in the world, received up into glory'
[*1 Timothy* 3 : 16]. The riches of His glory!

We find it also in John 1 : 14: '. . . and we beheld his glory, the
glory as of the only begotten of the Father, full of grace and
truth.' Or again, in the first two verses of the First Epistle of
John: 'That which was from the beginning, which we have
heard, which we have seen with our eyes, which we have looked
upon, and our hands have handled, of the Word of life; (for the
life was manifested, and we have seen it, and bear witness, and
shew unto you that eternal life, which was with the Father, and
was manifested unto us.' And then there are those wonderful
pictures of it in the book of Revelation.

This, then, is what we are talking about. The riches of God's
glory are to be seen supremely in the person of His Son. Think of
the incarnation, how God sent forth His Son from heaven to be
'made of a woman, made under the law'. Why did He ever come?
He came for us! To save us! That mercy might be shown to us!
And that is just what the Apostle is talking about. God, he says,
is making known the riches of His glory in and through us, 'the
vessels of mercy'. So it is there in the incarnation – the whole
coming, the virgin birth, how the eternal Son of God, the
eternal Word, was indeed 'made flesh, and dwelt among us', was
born as a helpless babe in that stable and put into the manger –
this is the riches of God's glory.

Look at His love, look at the poverty that He knew, look at the
suffering that He endured, look at the temptations to which He
was subjected. He 'was in all points tempted like as we are, yet
without sin'. Why? Well, the answer given is this: in order that
He might be a faithful and a sympathetic High Priest – for us! He
went through all that, His Father sent Him through all that, for
our sakes. You see the riches of God's glory in all this.

And then of course supremely you see it in His death upon the
cross on Calvary's hill.

> *When I survey the wondrous cross,*
> *On which the Prince of glory died,*
> *My richest gain I count but loss,*
> *And pour contempt on all my pride.*
>
> *See from His head, His hands, His feet,*
> *Sorrow and love flow mingled down;*

Did e'er such love and sorrow meet,
Or thorns compose so rich a crown?
Isaac Watts

Look at the cross – what is it? Well, this is the most wonderful of all the wonderful manifestations of the riches of God's glory. That is where you see the love of God! – in that He has made His only begotten, dearly beloved Son 'to be sin for us' and in smiting Him. For us! The vessels of mercy! That we might not share the fate of the vessels of wrath! He tasted death for us! He 'was made a little lower than the angels for the suffering of death' [*Hebrews* 2 : 9]. The riches of His glory!

And then you go on. You see Him dying and you see them taking down His body and burying Him in a grave; the One through whom and by whom all things were made, and without whom was nothing made that is made – buried in a grave! And then the mighty resurrection! Here is the glory of God – the Master over everything, the devil and hell and death, everything, everything is under His power. And He raised Him again! Why? Well, we have already had the answer at the end of the fourth chapter of this great Epistle: 'Who was delivered for our offences, and was raised again for our justification'. And it is God who has done it all! God in all this is displaying the riches of His glory.

And then the ascension! Oh, the Apostle is reminding us of what he has already said at the end of chapter 8. 'Who shall lay any thing to the charge of God's elect? It is God that justifieth. Who is he that condemneth? It is Christ that died, yea rather, that is risen again, who is even at the right hand of God, who also maketh intercession for us.' And He is there, waiting until 'his enemies be made his footstool'. But that is not the end. He will come again, and receive us unto Himself, and wind up the whole process. The glory of God is seen supremely in the face of Jesus Christ.

But the thing, of course, that the Apostle is emphasizing, and that I must therefore emphasize, is that the object and the purpose of all this was to 'make known the riches of his glory on the vessels of mercy . . . even us, whom he hath called, not of the Jews only, but also of the Gentiles'. And if we are not thrilled to the very depth of our being at the contemplation of that, I wonder whether we are Christians! The riches of His glory are seen in and through us! All this has happened for us!

But we must go on. We now turn and look at these riches as seen in the work and the person of the Holy Spirit in this connection. And here, of course, there is that great crucial event of His coming on the day of Pentecost and the dispensation which has followed ever since then. Again, something of the glory of God through the Holy Spirit is seen in the Old Testament – how He came upon certain men and gave them certain abilities, architectural and other abilities; how He gave the ability to the prophets to prophesy. He revealed truth to them and enabled them to record it and to write it. This, too, is something of the riches of God's glory because it was all done for us; it is all a part of this process. We would never have had anything of this at all if God had not decided to show His mercy upon these vessels of mercy. So even in the preparation we see something of the glory of God in the person and the work of the Holy Spirit.

You see it even before that in His work of creation and so on, but it is, again, only as you come to the New Testament that you begin to see this at all plainly and clearly. In John's Gospel, chapters 14 to 16, all this is revealed in a special way. Our Lord says that He is going to send this other 'Comforter' and tells us what He is going to do, what He will be like and what He will do; and it is all a part of this great purpose, this plan, this scheme of God for our salvation, seen, then, in the person and the work of the Holy Spirit.

But, further, let us look at the riches of God's glory as they are to be seen in us. We are the vessels of mercy and, as we have seen, the Apostle's argument in writing to the Ephesians is that it is in and through *us* and what He does with *us* that God shows this aspect of His glory even to the principalities and powers in the heavenly places. And the 'ages to come' likewise are going to see it 'in his kindness toward us through Christ Jesus'. So then we must concentrate on this and the Apostle helps us to do so. Notice the way in which he puts it: 'And that he might make known the riches of his glory on the vessels of mercy, which he had afore prepared unto glory, even us . . .'

Now this phrase, 'afore prepared' – which means prepared beforehand – is a wonderful phrase. You remember that in dealing with the expression 'fitted to destruction' in verse 22 I indicated that we would have to emphasize the difference between that and this phrase in verse 23. With regard to 'the vessels of wrath', all we are told about them is that they are 'fitted to destruction'. We are not told that God has fitted them, but that they are fitted, by the fall of Adam, but they have equally fitted themselves; and here they are ripe for the wrath of God and destruction. 'Fitted' – but not by God! But when it comes to us, 'the vessels of mercy', what we are told is 'which he [God Himself] had prepared beforehand unto glory'.

Now, once more, of course, this is nothing but a kind of recapitulation, the Apostle's summing up of what he has already told us in great detail in chapter 8 and especially in verses 28 to 30. What does he mean by saying that God has prepared us beforehand for glory? Well, partly he means this: 'We know that all things work together for good to them that love God, to them who are the called according to his purpose. For whom he did foreknow . . .' What the Apostle is saying is that you and I who are Christians have been prepared beforehand by God Himself for that ultimate glory.

How has He done this? What is this preparation? The first thing is this 'foreknowing', knowing beforehand, knowing before we were ever born, knowing us before He had even created the world.[1] That is always the first step, that God sets His heart, His affection upon these vessels of mercy who are to be delivered and who are to be saved, and He does that away back in eternity. And there are ample Scriptures to prove that.

Then, of course, having thus known us in this special manner He 'predestinates' us. This involves choosing and deciding what He is going to do with us. Now this to me is the most wonderful thing in the whole of Scripture, the thing that moves one to the depths of one's being – that the almighty and everlasting God, who might very well have consigned us all to eternal destruction, thought about us individually, we who are Christians, before the foundation of the world, and decided what He was going to make of us. Can you take in that thought, that the eternal God has known you in that way?

And then He has worked out this great purpose, this predestinating. But I must again emphasize what we had cause to emphasize in the earlier part of this chapter, because it seems to

[1] See *Romans: An Exposition of Chapter 8:17–39: The Final Perseverance of the Saints,* 1975.

me to be a very wonderful part of this whole process of preparation. We saw when we were considering verse 6 that there was a direct intervention of God in the births of both Isaac and Jacob, and my argument now is that He does precisely the same with every one of us who is a Christian. We are 'separated from our mother's womb' as the Apostle Paul himself was, as Jeremiah was. All this is something that God planned before time, and He has brought it into being.

We must not get confused about this. Our becoming Christians in an experiential sense happens in time, but the whole teaching of this entire Epistle, and particularly this chapter, is that God is bringing it to pass. So, then, this is a part of the preparation. We were prepared even before we were born. It is a great mystery. Yes, but we are dealing with the riches of God's glory! Who can explain His mind, who can understand His workings? One of our hymn writers has said,

> Earth from afar has heard Thy fame,
> And babes have learnt to lisp Thy name;
> But O the glories of Thy mind
> Leave all our soaring thoughts behind.
>
> Isaac Watts

So entirely and utterly and absolutely beyond us and our highest comprehension and imagination! But that is what we are taught, that God has been preparing us; He is preparing a people, this new humanity in Christ, and these are steps in this great process. The time came that you and I should be born, and God saw to it that we were born, and in that particular way.

But then we come to our actual calling in time. We have been prepared from eternity, but in particular we are called in time. You are born and you seem to be like everybody else, and you live a life of sin, and you may argue against the gospel, and you may reject it, and you may utter your blasphemous thoughts. But God's purpose is carried out. A time comes when you are convicted by the Holy Spirit; you do not know why it happened, and you do not understand how. You realize that what our Lord said to Nicodemus is the truth: 'The wind bloweth where it listeth, and thou hearest the sound thereof, but canst not tell whence it cometh, and whither it goeth: so is every one that is born of the Spirit' [*John* 3 : 8]; it is at a given point in time, but it was known to God before the foundation of the world.

You are convicted of sin, and it can happen in many ways. It may happen in a meeting; it may happen when you are on your own; it may happen when you are reading the Bible – it can happen in endless ways. But it is God who does it! He had planned to do it. He brought you into this world in order that it might happen. That is the teaching of this chapter. And so you are brought to repentance; you are converted and turned round; and you are aware that you are a 'new man in Christ Jesus', that you have got a new nature inside you, and you are amazed at yourself. Of course! Because you have not done it.

If you are not amazed at yourself you are not a Christian, my friend! All Christians are miracles and they should be amazed at themselves. They have this new life within them, this life from God, they are 'partakers of the divine nature'. What am I talking about? The riches of God's glory! This is what God does to us, the vessels of mercy, and it is in this way He shows this thought of His, this mind, this power, this love, grace and compassion. And here it shines in and through us!

But then it goes on. He puts His Spirit within us, and the Spirit incorporates us into Christ. We are 'in Christ'. He is the Head, we are members of the body, and we have participated in Him: crucified with Him, dead with Him, buried with Him, risen with Him, seated in the heavenly places in Him. It is true of you! This is not some theory; I am telling you what is true of you as a Christian. You are one of God's vessels of mercy, and He is showing what He is in doing all this to you!

And, of course, He goes on working in us. The Spirit brings us into an increasing conformity to the image of God's Son. It was all there in the eighth chapter, you remember: 'Whom he did foreknow, he also did predestinate to be conformed to the image of his Son, that he might be the firstborn among many brethren.'

Then you go on to consider how He puts us all into the church, which is the body of Christ. The universe as such – creation – pales into insignificance by the side of this 'new creation.' 'She is His new creation by water and the Word.' The church! The body of Christ! What a conception! Read these epistles as they unfold the doctrine concerning the church, in particular the first four chapters of Ephesians; how He breaks down the middle wall of partition bringing Jews and Gentiles together. What a work! Is anything more difficult than to reconcile irreconcilables? Was anything harder than to bring together a Jew and a Gentile? Not only to reconcile men unto God but unto one another. But He has done it! He has made 'of twain one new man, so making peace', and you and I are parts of that church.

But, to go further, we see something of the riches of God's glory even in the way in which He chastises us. 'All things', remember, 'work together for good to them that love God' [*Romans* 8 : 28]. Even when you are having a hard and a difficult time, it may be a part of this glory, because God is going to bring you to that perfection, to that conformity to the image of His Son, and He seems to be working against His own purpose. But He is not. He knows us and He reveals His love to us. 'Whom the Lord loveth he chasteneth.' Have you ever seen the glory of God in your chastisements? We must learn to look for these things; that is what the Scriptures are here for. They are to make us look, to give us these openings, and you follow the openings. And the next time you are chastised because of your sin, you stand back in amazement and marvel at the glory of God, that, though He is so great and so almighty, He knows you and He is chastening you in particular because you are His child. And there He gives you a glimpse into something of His Fatherly heart that you had never seen before. So all this, you see, is a part of the way in which God shows the riches of His glory in what He does in us. That is the argument. In us! The vessels of mercy!

And then the final word, of course, is this: 'which he had afore prepared unto *glory*'. This is the thing that leaves us speechless, as it were! That this is true of us, we who deserve nothing but the punishment of hell and everlasting destruction; we who are sinful and who can say truthfully about ourselves in the words of Charles Wesley, 'Foul and full of sin I am' – for we all are – we who can say with the Apostle Paul, 'In me (that is, in my flesh,) dwelleth no good thing' [*Romans* 7 : 18]; we who also can say with him, in the Epistle to Titus, that we were 'hateful, and hating one another'. What miserable, wretched creatures we all were in sin!

Yes, but this is how Paul puts it there in Titus: 'We ourselves also were sometimes foolish, disobedient, deceived, serving divers lusts and pleasures, living in malice and envy, hateful, and hating one another. But after that the kindness and love of God our Saviour toward man appeared, not by works of righteousness which we have done, but according to his mercy he saved us, by the washing of regeneration, and renewing of the Holy Ghost; which he shed on us abundantly through Jesus Christ our Saviour; that being justified by his grace, we should be made heirs according to the hope of eternal life' [*Titus* 3 : 3–7].

Now that is just another way of putting what he says in this verse that is before us. That is what He is preparing us for. He takes us from that sinful position and He is going to raise us to the glory. And consider this extraordinary way in which He does it: He justified us by faith alone without our works, without even our desire, with nothing. He gives us the very faith itself; He gives us everything. And thus, in a manner entirely opposite to what man would ever have imagined, we are saved. We are 'the vessels of mercy, which he had prepared afore unto glory'.

I like repeating this; I like to talk about this glory to which we are going – don't you? Can you ever hear of this too frequently? That you and I are going to be glorified in our very bodies! We shall see Christ and be like Him and we shall reign with Him. We shall reign over angels; we shall reign over the world; we shall be partakers of the inheritance with Him. We are 'joint-heirs' with Him now, and we are going to be joint-sharers in the inheritance with Him. That is the glory! – perfectly redeemed, body, mind and spirit, with not a trace of evil or sin anywhere near us, but without spot, or wrinkle, or any such thing – whole, entire, glorified, even as He is glorified!

So then, says the Apostle – and here is his argument, you see, let me draw it out now – What would we really know of God and His glory were it not for all this? In other words, it is in His mercy to us that the riches of His glory have become known. So I summarize his argument like this: God in His righteous, holy character hates sin and is filled with wrath against it. Is there anything wrong in that? Is there any injustice in that? Have you any objection to the fact that He, who is holy, who is light and in Him is no darkness at all, hates sin with the whole intensity of His divine nature? Is there anyone in the whole universe who has ever lived amongst men who does not deserve to be punished and to be punished eternally? Not one! Is there any ground of complaint against the manifestation, the making known of the wrath and the justice of God? There is none! God is free to punish all if He so chooses, and if all were punished no one would be able to lift a finger or to open a mouth.

But what if, on the other hand, He chooses and wills to spare some and to save some, do you object to the riches of God's glory, do you feel that that is unjust? Has not the God, who has a right to damn us all, an equal right to save some if He so chooses? Why not? Where is the injustice? Who has been wronged? No one, because no one has any claim whatsoever. Do you want to ask, 'But why are only some saved?' The answer to that is that none deserve it; all should be damned, and therefore God is free to show and manifest His mercy when He wills, when He chooses, and where and when and in whom He pleases and He chooses.

But I cannot leave it at this. Why do we always look at one side only of this matter? Why is it that anybody can ever read the ninth chapter of Romans and not be lost in wonder, love and praise when he comes to this phrase 'the riches of his glory'? – because that is the effect that this chapter should have upon us. The surprising thing, the astounding thing is not that anybody is damned but that anybody is saved! Nothing but the riches of God's glory could ever have done that. Nothing but this eternal character of God that we have been looking at could ever have brought it to being.

What is the difficulty? It is that man in sin has always had a desire to know what he is not meant to know, so people ask the question, 'Why are only some saved; on what principle and on what grounds does God do that?' Let us be clear about this. I do not know! I will go further, I am not meant to know! I will go further still, I should not even desire to know! Sufficient for me is that any one individual is ever saved. It is the riches of God's glory alone that can ever do that. And having seen that, I have seen more than enough. What fills me with amazement is that I am in this and that God has ever had mercy upon me, and that in His grace He has ever made me a vessel of mercy and brought me to the position in which I am. I do not want to know any more, for the desire to know any more is a desire to comprehend the incomprehensible, to understand that which is God Himself and which one never can.

I imagine that in eternity we shall have the full explanation, but here on earth it is not God's will that we should have it. All we are told is that God has a right to condemn all and therefore He has a right to do as He wills with all. And we are told that it is His will that some should receive mercy and be prepared for that everlasting and eternal glory which He has made possible for us because of the riches of His glory. If you still want to ask questions, my friend, then, I can only tell you that they cannot be answered and that I am amazed that you still want to ask them. If you are not overwhelmed by this thought that He sent His only Son from heaven into this sinful, evil world and even to the death of the cross, and a grave for you – if that does not make you just fall before Him in worship and adoration, then I think you had better go back to the beginning and ask Him to have mercy upon you and to open the eyes of your understanding by His Holy Spirit.

If you are still anxious to cavil and to ask your questions and bring your objections, it is because you do not know about the riches of His glory, and that is what you need to know. Once you have seen that, you will not ask any questions; you will just praise and thank Him and express your amazement and astonishment; you will say:

And can it be, that I should gain
An interest in the Saviour's blood?
Died He for me, who caused His pain?
For me, who Him to death pursued?
Amazing love! how can it be
That Thou, my God, shouldst die for me?

Charles Wesley

That is the attitude of the man who has seen this blessed glorious truth and seen himself as a vessel of mercy.

And so, in verse 24, the Apostle finishes the whole argument: 'Even us, whom he hath called, not of the Jews only, but also of the Gentiles'. 'Now then,' says Paul in effect, 'in the light of what I have been telling you, are you still in trouble over this question of Jew and Gentile? Well, you should not be. The whole of humanity was lost; it was God's will to take hold of a man amongst those in that mass of perdition, a man called Abram, and to pull him out and to turn him into a nation and call him

Abraham. It was God who did that. But that does not mean that everybody born of him is now automatically saved and going to be a Christian. Not at all! The God who chose him is at equal liberty to choose anybody He likes, and He does; sometimes Jew, sometimes Gentile. Why not?'

That is his answer, finally, to the Jews. 'Do not imagine', he says, 'that there is anything special about you as such, or anything to recommend you to God, or any claim that you have upon God and His mercy; not at all.' A man is never saved by heredity – never! You are not saved because your parents were Christians or because you belong to the Jewish nation or any other nation. Heredity does not come in at all. That has been demolished by this chapter.

It is God who saves every one of us and that is where you see the riches of His glory. He who made the stars and the constellations and the whole of creation and who handles history and providence and everything else, who knows us one by one, every one of us – it is He alone, and nothing else – not ancestry, not upbringing, not good works, not righteousness, nothing in us at all; it is altogether the action of God. He can do it to a Jew; He can do it to a Gentile. He has made the whole world; He made man at the beginning, and these distinctions are to Him meaningless and irrelevant. And so He does it to us: some of us are Jews, some of us are Gentiles. But that is not the thing that matters. It is the God who always does it to each individual and who is free in His sovereign Lordship to show mercy to whom He will show mercy, and to show wrath upon whom He will show wrath.

Blessed be the name of God! Oh, the riches of the glory of God revealed and manifested unto us – even us – in this glorious plan and purpose of salvation, and supremely in the face of Jesus Christ!

Twenty

*

As he saith also in Osee, I will call them my people, which were not my people; and her beloved, which was not beloved. And it shall come to pass, that in the place where it was said unto them, Ye are not my people; there shall they be called the children of the living God.

Romans 9 : 25–26

We come now to a new subsection in the argument of this ninth chapter of Romans. It is continuing the theme that has occupied the whole length of the chapter, and that is, as we must constantly bear in our minds, the whole question of the position of the Jews with regard to the Christian church and therefore with regard to the kingdom of God. Now the Apostle has concluded his argument in verse 24 by saying, 'Even us, whom he hath called, not of the Jews only, but also of the Gentiles'. The point of his argument has been to show that salvation is always the immediate result of the action of God Himself. Man does not save himself, nor does he determine his own salvation. It is entirely and altogether of God, the God who has said, 'I will have mercy on whom I will have mercy, and I will have compassion on whom I will have compassion.'

Furthermore, he has been proving that God chooses 'out of Israel', but also equally out of the Gentiles; salvation is not confined to the Jews by any means whatsoever. And the mere fact therefore that people may happen to be physical descendants of Abraham, Isaac and Jacob does not automatically save them. There is no such thing as an automatic salvation because of our birth or nation or anything else.

And the Apostle has had to go into all this because it was so clear in those days that the majority of the Jews as a nation were refusing the gospel of Jesus Christ, and that the largest number of people in the church consisted of Gentiles. That fact, of course, was the very thing that was troubling the Jews so much and caused them to stagger. This admission of the Gentiles into the church, and the statement and the preaching that they were 'fellow heirs' with the Jews, was to the Jew nothing but sheer blasphemy. And that is the very position with which the great Apostle is dealing.

That, then, is the point at which we have arrived and now he goes on to show that not only is all that true, but nobody should be surprised at it; and nobody should be surprised at it because there is nothing new in this. 'Why', he says, 'do the Jews stumble at this, or why does anybody stumble at it, because all this teaching is not some personal argument of mine? God Himself clearly revealed to the prophets, hundreds of years before these things happened, precisely this very thing which has actually taken place.' So now the Apostle is going to give his evidence to show that this is so.

Before we come to look at it, however, is it not interesting to observe once more the Apostle's method? There is, as we have already seen, nothing so entrancing as to watch the working of a great mind, and that is the privilege we have when we read Paul's Epistles. He did not just say things anyhow, somehow; he did not say the next thing that came into his mind. He has a plan, a scheme; he is always orderly. And this is something that those who preach should learn from him. Do not imagine that you are giving a manifestation of spirituality by not having order in your sermons or your addresses or your Sunday-school lessons. It is not a hallmark of spirituality not to have order. It is the exact opposite. Here is this mighty man filled with the Spirit of God, and yet observe the order, observe the arrangement, observe the logic and the sequence, observe how he marshals his evidence and presents his case. Nothing is more important for us than to know how to present our case whether in public or in private; and here, Paul's method is this: he does not just quote verses; he uses his verse to support the argument he has already developed.

Now there are some people who seem to think that it is just enough to read a string of verses and just make a little comment. That is not preaching. That is not really presenting the case. No,

Paul here has worked out his great theological principle, but he knows his Old Testament so well that he has taken out of it this great central principle about the election of grace – as he has called it in the eleventh verse, 'the purpose of God according to election'. He sees it running through the whole of the Old Testament so he works out his great argument, giving little illustrations as he passes. Then, having developed the great argument, having arrived at his principle, he is now going to support it and confirm it by the evidence which is provided by Scripture itself. That is how he does it, and it seems to me to be incomparably the best method that one can ever think of. You just bring in your Scripture to underline or buttress your argument, and to establish it beyond any doubt or peradventure.

And Paul does this lest anybody might say that he, clever man as he was, was foisting his own ideas upon them. People are always ready to say that. They say, 'Ah, here is this man; he says he has read the Scriptures but he is just giving his own views and theories.' Now Paul demolishes any such argument or objection simply by producing the Scriptures which say plainly and explicitly the very thing that he already has been demonstrating to them.

Turning, then, to this interesting subsection, I think it may help if I can give a kind of general analysis of the remainder of the chapter from verse 25 to the end. This is what Paul does. In verses 25 and 26 he produces the scriptural evidence to prove that God through the prophets had foretold that the Gentiles would come in and be fellow-heirs with the Jews. In verses 27 and 28 he brings his scriptural proof of the fact that the rejection of the bulk of the nation of Israel was prophesied, and that only a 'remnant' of them would be members and citizens of the kingdom of God in the form of the church. Then, in verse 29 he shows how, according to the Prophet Isaiah, this remnant, even, had been brought in. It is an astonishing thing, but they have.

And, finally, when he comes to verses 30 and 31, Paul does something which is so characteristic of him; he sums up the argument of the whole chapter with his formula, 'What shall we say then?' That is always his way of summing up: 'What are we going to say in the light of all this?' And in the two verses he tells us what he has to say; he states the position as it is, which is that in general it is the Gentiles who are in the kingdom and the Jews who are out. And then in the last two verses – verses 32 and 33 – he explains the tragedy of the rejection of the Jews, the reason why they are out rather than in. And that in turn, of course, provides a kind of introduction to chapter 10 in which he works this out in great detail.

That, then, is the analysis and so now we start with verses 25 and 26, in which the Apostle shows and proves that the admission of the Gentiles into the kingdom of God was something that had long ago been prophesied. You see, he must demonstrate this, because verse 24 insists upon it: 'Even us, whom he hath called, not of the Jews only, but also of the Gentiles'. He must do two things: he must prove that the Scriptures have prophesied the admission of the Gentiles and, also, the rejection of the bulk of the Jews. In verses 25 and 26, then, he starts with the Scriptures which prove the first of these facts.

Here again it is interesting to watch the mind of this man. You notice that he reverses the order of what he says in verse 24 – '. . . us, . . . not of the Jews only, but also of the Gentiles'; and yet when he takes up his quotations he starts with the Gentiles. He deals with the admission of the Gentiles first and puts the rejection of the Jews second in verses 27 and 28. Why does he do this? Well, to me there is only one adequate answer and explanation. The great Apostle was not out primarily just to demonstrate his case, but to win his fellow-countrymen the Jews. You remember how he began the chapter? 'I say the truth in Christ, I lie not, my conscience also bearing me witness in the Holy Ghost, that I have great heaviness and continual sorrow in my heart. For I could wish that myself were accursed from Christ for my brethren, my kinsmen according to the flesh.' That is his object. He grieves at the fact that they are outside. And what he is trying to do in this whole argument is to persuade them, to make them see it, so that they will come in.

So Paul does his best for the Jews in every way. He does not start off here, when he comes to the quotations, by giving the Scriptures which show that they are going to be pushed out and punished and so on. No, he leaves that as long as he can, so he takes up the admission of the Gentiles first. He is sparing his fellow-countrymen; he does not rush at any condemnation; he is trying to win them, trying to persuade them. He enjoys being positive. He has got to prove his case with regard to the Jews, but he seems to postpone it as long as he can. From which I deduce that the Apostle was not only a great man and a great debater, a great logician and teacher, but also a very great gentleman.

I make this point partly because of Professor Carstairs, who, in delivering his Reith Lectures,[1] said more or less that the Apostle Paul was a bully, a domineering sort of man who liked his own way always. How ignorant these people are of the Scriptures! No, the Apostle Paul was a true gentleman, and he is constantly giving us evidence of it in matters like this which seem to be comparatively trivial and unimportant. 'What does it matter which he puts first?' asks someone. Well, it does matter, and here we must learn another lesson. If we want to win people, as we should, then let us keep our denunciation back as long as we can. We have seen that our Lord tolerated the Pharisees and scribes almost to the end of His ministry. Take the Gospel according to Matthew – He does not really attack them and denounce them until you come to chapter 23. Some of us start with denunciation and then think we can win people after-wards. No, we must give people a chance, give them an opportunity. They are blinded by the devil; we must not be in too much of a hurry to be negative and denunciatory. We should put the positive, and make it as attractive as we can. We must do everything we can to win people. And the more certain we are that they are wrong, the more we should go out of our way to try to win them to the truth. Let us all decide to emulate Paul's example in this. There is something even more important than proving that you are right in what you say, and that is to have a heart of love and a desire for the salvation of men and women. So here, again, we see that we cannot afford to rush over the Scriptures. We must watch everything and we shall find some remarkable things where we least expect them.

Now then let us look at the actual quotation. Verse 25: 'As he saith also in Osee [Hosea], I will call them my people, which were not my people; and her beloved, which was not beloved.' And a further quotation from Hosea: 'It shall come to pass, that in the place where it was said unto them, Ye are not my people; there shall they be called the children of the living God.' Now

[1]In 1962. See pp.205–206.

the first quotation in verse 25 is from Hosea 2 : 23, but it is interesting to observe that what the Apostle says here is not an exact quotation either from the Hebrew Bible, or from the Septuagint translation of the Old Testament, which was the Old Testament that was used, of course, in the Roman world at the time when Paul and our Lord lived. The Apostle was very familiar with it, and quite often he does quote directly from the Septuagint version. But here he does not quote exactly either from it or from the original Hebrew itself. How do we explain that? Was the Apostle feeling tired when he wrote? Was he being careless? Was he making an actual mistake?

Many people have stumbled over this. The so-called higher critics, who do not believe in the inerrancy of Scripture, and who really do not believe in the divine inspiration of the New Testament writers, are very fond of using this as an argument for their case. 'There you are,' they say, 'you people are literalists and you insist upon every word, but the great Apostle did not; look how loosely he quotes! He is not punctilious about every single word being in at the right point and in the right place and so on. No, he was interested only in the general sense, and, therefore', they say, 'when you talk about "verbal inspiration" you are doing something that obviously the apostles themselves did not believe in.'

So what is the answer to this? It is that the great Apostle was a man who was deeply versed in the Scriptures; he knew his Scriptures probably as no man has ever known them. He was the last man in the world to be careless or to allow himself to make mistakes. 'If that is so,' says somebody, 'what is the explanation?' Well, the explanation, surely, is this, and it is a most important point: it was the same Holy Spirit who led and guided the Prophet Hosea in what he wrote, as led and guided the Apostle Paul in what he writes here. It is the same Author of the Scriptures in the Old Testament and in the New. Remember Peter's statement with respect to that: 'No prophecy of the scripture is of any private interpretation. For the prophecy came not in old time by the will of man: but holy men of God spake as they were moved by the Holy Ghost' [2 *Peter* 1 : 21]. That is the Old Testament. That is the prophecy.

And exactly the same thing is true of the Apostle Paul himself. He is being led by the same Spirit. The only person who has any right, therefore, to vary the exact form of the expression is the

Holy Spirit Himself and it is He who does so in the case of the Apostle Paul. He states the same essential truth as He stated through Hosea, but He states it in this slightly different form, and my argument is that He alone is entitled to do so. So that this, far from being an argument against the inspiration of the Apostle Paul, is, to me, one of the final proofs of his inspiration.

I say that for this reason: none of these men played with the Scripture or handled it loosely. Quite the reverse. Paul has called the Scriptures 'the oracles of God', and he was like all Jews in the reverence which they paid to these Scriptures, in the way they had guarded them, and in the way they had copied them. It was one of the most outstanding characteristics of these men, and especially the Pharisees, among whom the Apostle Paul had been brought up. You do not get any carelessness among such people. So that if the Apostle were just writing in and of himself and not under the influence of the Spirit, he would most certainly have had his documents with him and he would have copied out his quotation exactly and accurately. But he clearly did not do that; he was being led and guided and inspired by the Spirit, and the Spirit Himself introduced this slight and utterly immaterial variation. We have seen exactly the same thing before in the seventeenth verse of the first chapter.[2]

But I draw a second conclusion also from this point which is a practical one for us. The fact that the Holy Spirit varies it like this does not entitle us to do the same thing, and we must be careful to be accurate. We have no right, because we are not inspired as the Apostle was, to vary the words. I say this, of course, because we are familiar with the fact that many people even in expounding this paragraph, and indeed the whole of this great chapter, do the very thing which I am saying we should not do. In order to make it fit in with their own ideas they do not hesitate to leave out words or sections of verses, or they do not hesitate to take a piece from another place. You may be familiar with the methods of the higher critics; you can see it in some modern translations. They vary the actual documents in the Greek in order to make them fit in with their own preconceived notions. But we are not entitled to do that. If there is a variation

[2]See *Romans: An Exposition of Chapter 1: The Gospel of God*, 1985.

it is the Holy Spirit's variation through the inspired Apostle. It does not give us any right to play fast and loose with the Scriptures or to chop and change in order to substantiate our own particular views.

There is also a further point which we must make about this quotation. Hosea, in chapter 2 : 23, as indeed in the whole of his prophecy, is quite plainly and clearly dealing with the ten tribes of Israel. There was a division in Israel; ten of the tribes went off in rebellion and were separated from Judah and Benjamin, and they formed a kingdom of their own which is referred to as the northern kingdom, or else as Israel, in contrast to the southern kingdom, or Judah. Now Hosea was one of the prophets that addressed the northern kingdom, these ten tribes, and he wrote to them just after the first year of the Assyrian captivity to which they were subjected.

But here we have the Apostle Paul taking these writings of Hosea and applying them to the Gentiles, who did not belong either to the northern or the southern kingdom. Has he a right to do a thing like that? And he is not alone; the Apostle Peter does exactly the same thing. In 1 Peter 2 : 10, he says, 'Which in time past were not a people, but are now the people of God: which had not obtained mercy, but now have obtained mercy.' So on what grounds do they do this? What right has Paul to take this prophecy addressed to a particular people, the ten tribes, and say that this is the truth about the Gentiles?

This is a very important question. The Pharisees and those known as the Rabbinical writers were very fond of using Scripture to serve their own ends. It is not confined to them; every heretic has done the same thing and it is still being done. It is something about which we should all always be careful. People very often hold a wrong view, and then they say, 'Scripture says this'; but they are quoting a Scripture which really does not apply to the case. So is the Apostle guilty of doing that very thing? Now this is a vital point in the whole matter of the interpretation of prophecy. It does not only apply to this passage, it applies to many others in the New Testament. In other words, it is important for us to know exactly how the New Testament writers use the Old Testament and how they handle the prophecies.

Firstly, then, it is not, of course, a misuse of Scripture. No man inspired by the Holy Ghost misuses Scripture. No, the explanation is simple: the prophecies of the Old Testament generally have more than one application. The first applies to the immediate situation of the Jews, to whom they were writing. But prophecy generally has another, a remoter application. In addition to dealing with a particular situation that then obtained, it uses that as a prophecy of something that is going to happen under the New Testament or the gospel dispensation.

And that is precisely what we have here in this particular example. God's method is always the same. It is the same God who was operating in the Old Testament as in the New, and one of the great functions of the Old is to be a prophecy and a picture of the New. The classic illustration of this is the history of the children of Israel being delivered from the bondage and captivity of Egypt; how they were brought out, and how they had to kill the lamb and paint its blood over the lintels and the door-posts, and eat the unleavened bread, how they were brought out and taken through the Red Sea by a miracle while their enemies were destroyed behind them and how they were led through the wilderness, crossed the Jordan and went into Canaan. Now that is all history. God did that to them, He saved His earthly human people in that actual manner. That is the first meaning.

But Scripture everywhere keeps on telling us that that has a second application also; that it is a wonderful picture of the spiritual salvation of the soul that has come in and through our Lord and Saviour Jesus Christ. He is a second Moses, a second Joshua; He is our Passover Lamb, and so on. All these things, which actually happened, are used by the New Testament in such a way as to tell us this: 'Now all this has long since been foretold and has been prophesied.' This double application in prophecy is a very important principle. Very often the prophets and the people themselves did not understand this; sometimes they did.

Peter tells us something which is very significant in this whole connection: 'Of which salvation the prophets have enquired and searched diligently, who prophesied of the grace that should come unto you: searching what, or what manner of time the Spirit of Christ which was in them did signify, when it testified beforehand the sufferings of Christ, and the glory that should follow. Unto whom it was revealed, that not unto themselves, but unto us they did minister the things, which are now reported unto you by them that have preached the gospel unto you with the Holy Ghost sent down from heaven' [*1 Peter* 1 : 10–12]. There it is. First and foremost the Prophet was speaking to the immediate situation, but he was aware that there was something more than that in it; there was a prophecy of something that was to happen in a yet bigger manner in a spiritual sense. So we must always bear in mind this possibility of the two applications – the immediate and the remote.

Now this passage is an illustration of that very thing. The ten tribes were, of course, a part of Israel originally, but they had rebelled under Jeroboam and they had gone off and had formed that northern kingdom, and the result was that they were cut off from the commonwealth of Israel; they had virtually become pagan. You remember how Jeroboam had set up that worship at Dan; they were certainly no longer the people of God. So the Prophet addresses them as such.

And what the Apostle is saying here under divine inspiration is that while that was the first and the immediate application, it also had this other one. And he says, in a wonderful way, that we are now actually seeing the fulfilment of the remoter meaning that was in that old prophecy of Hosea so long ago. He was not only writing about the northern kingdom; he was also writing about what was going to happen to the actual pagans, those who are altogether and entirely outside the commonwealth of Israel. So when Hosea says that these people are to be brought back, these rebellious ten tribes of the northern kingdom, he is saying at the same time, 'If they can be brought back, so can Gentiles; if they who have made themselves pagans can be brought back, so can actual pagans be brought back.' The two applications blend together and so both become true. So that what Hosea actually said, in the ultimate sense, is that Gentiles are to be saved and are to be citizens of the kingdom of God in addition to the Jews.

Then verse 26 really says almost exactly the same thing: 'And it shall come to pass, that in the place where it was said unto them, Ye are not my people; there shall they be called the children of the living God.' Now there is no need to stumble over that expression 'in the place where . . . there . . .' Some people understand it as meaning that this is a prophecy of all the Jews going back to Palestine. But it does not mean that at all.

What it means is that in that hopeless place where they are, even there they can be saved. You do not have to go back to Palestine to be saved; you are saved where you are. It is just a very dramatic way of saying, 'Even in that hopelessness, even there . . .' Let me put it in its New Testament form: He 'came and preached peace to you which were afar off, and to them that were nigh'. There, in that far off position, the Word comes to them and they are saved and delivered by it.

Finally, then, let me draw your attention to the wonderful description which is given in these two verses of the difference that salvation makes. What are we, what is all mankind by nature? Here is the answer: We are not God's people. 'I will call them my people, which were not my people.' That is the terrible thing about being in sin, and about not being a Christian – you are not God's people! You are 'without God', you are 'in the world'. What a terrible thing! There is no teaching in the Scripture about the universal Fatherhood of God, and the universal brotherhood of man. No, all by nature are out of relationship with God, and in no relation to His covenants or His promises.

Not only that. 'Not beloved'! And that means two things. It means being like a faithless wife. You remember what poor Hosea had to do; he had to marry 'a wife of whoredoms', just to bring out this great picture. Mankind by nature is like that, 'not beloved'. No, quite the reverse. Horrible! A faithless wife, with God not interested, not concerned, and not loving. 'Not beloved'! The Apostle in Ephesians 2 : 12 reminds the pagans of what they were, when he says, 'Ye were . . . aliens from the commonwealth of Israel, and strangers from the covenants of promise, having no hope, and without God in the world.' What a terrible position! That is everybody who is not a Christian! Shut off from the light and the blessing and the life of God.

But notice what we become; this is the wonderful thing. 'I will call them my people, which were not my people.' If you are a Christian that is what you are! Do not think of Christianity merely in terms of forgiveness of sins. It is that, but it is much more than that. You are not only forgiven when you become a Christian; you are changed from not being a people to becoming the people of God, from being an outcast and without God in the world to being 'children of the living God', with all that is meant by the term 'children'. God says to such people, 'I will be your God, and you shall be to Me a people.' But in addition, 'I will call them my people, which were not my people; and her beloved, which was not beloved.'

And this, I remind you, does not merely mean that now God loves us; it goes beyond that. We become betrothed to Him; we become married to Him! That is the picture that is used so frequently in the Bible. The church is 'the bride of Christ', with all that that represents, not only by way of dignity and position, but especially of care and concern and guardianship.

And so in demonstrating and proving and substantiating his case, the Apostle at the same time reminds us of what we are in Christ and of the change that has taken place: 'not a people', now a people! 'Not beloved', now beloved! 'Children of the living God'!

Twenty-one

*

As he saith also in Osee, I will call them my people, which were not my people; and her beloved, which was not beloved. And it shall come to pass, that in the place where it was said unto them, Ye are not my people; there shall they be called the children of the living God. Esaias also crieth concerning Israel, Though the number of the children of Israel be as the sand of the sea, a remnant shall be saved: for he will finish the work, and cut it short in righteousness: because a short work will the Lord make upon the earth. And as Esaias said before, Except the Lord of Sabaoth had left us a seed, we had been as Sodoma, and been made like unto Gomorrha.

Romans 9 : 25–29

In this section of Romans 9, you remember, the Apostle is adducing evidence from the Old Testament to support and to prove the argument which he has been working out in detail from verse 6 to the end of verse 24. He has to prove the following points: first, that the vital, the only really vital element in salvation, is God's absolute, sovereign choice; secondly, God's freedom of choice, so that He may choose Gentiles if He wills to do so, and that He may reject Jews, the bulk of the nation of Israel, if He so wills. Those are the things that the Apostle has been telling us, and now he proceeds to show how there is nothing new about this, that it is not some new idea that he has conjured up but that this is something that had been stated quite plainly in the Scriptures; and, furthermore, that the position with which they were confronted at that very moment was also something that had been prophesied in the Scriptures.

Both these things, of course, were real stumbling-blocks to the Jews. They could not accommodate themselves and their

[259]

thinking to this notion that Gentiles could ever become citizens
of the kingdom of God. And the other stumbling-block was that
they could not accept the notion that any Jew could be rejected;
to them it was utterly impossible that the bulk of the nation of
the Jews should be rejected as a whole and that the Christian
church, which it was claimed was the form now taken by the
kingdom of God, should consist of many more Gentiles than
Jews. Now to the Jews this was something quite unthinkable, so
the Apostle is doing a very wise, as well as a very subtle thing,
when he quotes the Scriptures to them.

We have seen how he dealt with the question of the calling
and the bringing in of the Gentiles, by means of his quotations
from the book of the Prophet Hosea; and now he turns to deal
with this second aspect of the problem. Having shown that it
had been prophesied that the Gentiles would come in, he now
has to establish this other thing, the rejection of the Jews. The
Jews, as we have seen repeatedly through the Epistle, assumed
that all was well with them simply because they were Jews.

This is something, of course, that is prominent also in the
pages of the four Gospels. This is the supreme tragedy of all the
ages, that 'He came unto his own, and his own received him
not'. Our Lord came of the stock of Israel, of the tribe of Judah.
He came to His own people, and yet it was His own people, of
everybody, who refused Him and who rejected Him. And the
Apostle, as we have seen at the beginning of the chapter, is
himself almost overwhelmed by a sense of tragedy as he
considers this. But nevertheless he has got to put the truth to
them, and having stated his great argument he is now showing
that this again, like the coming in of the Gentiles, had been very
plainly and clearly foretold in the writings of the prophets.

Now there is a subsidiary aspect to the tragedy of the Jews.
The Jews prided themselves on having the Scriptures, what the
Apostle has called at the beginning of chapter 3, 'the oracles of
God'. They were tremendously proud of that, and they had every
reason to be so. The Gentiles had had no such revelation; they
had no oracles, they had no teaching from God, they were
'without God in the world', and they were in the darkness of
ignorance. But the Jews had got the Word of God, and they
prided themselves in their knowledge of the Scriptures. And yet,
in these very verses, what the Apostle is really showing them is

that while they prided themselves on their possession and their knowledge of the Scriptures, their whole trouble was due to the fact that they were blind to the message of the Scriptures. And that, of course, is what makes what we are doing now such a solemn and such a serious thing. We are people who claim to be interested in the Scriptures – well, let us watch our spirits before we go any further. Here were men who lived, in a sense, for the Scriptures, and who believed that they were authorities on them, and yet they were absolutely blind to the plain teaching of the Scriptures. God have mercy upon us, and deliver us and save us from misunderstanding the very Word in which we glory together!

In other words, the Apostle here is doing the precise thing that our Lord Himself did so many times with these same Jews, and particularly with the Pharisees and the scribes. For instance, in John 5 verses 39–40, he says, 'Search the scriptures' – or if you prefer the translation, 'You do search the scriptures'; it does not matter which, it is either a command or a statement about them – 'Search the scriptures; for in them ye think ye have eternal life: and they are they which testify of me. And ye will not come to me, that ye might have life.' There it is so plainly stated by our Lord Himself. You are always talking about the Scriptures, He says, well, go to them, search them, and you will find, if you have eyes to see, that they are full of Me, and yet you are rejecting Me.

This is indeed the supreme tragedy of all the ages, that the Jews were so blinded by their prejudices that they were unable to see their own Word and its meaning. They were so blind to the real truth concerning the Messiah. They had their own carnal notion of the Messiah, so that when the true Messiah appeared, they said, 'Impossible! This is a blasphemer!' Their Messiah was to be a great military personage, and when He came as a carpenter the thing to them was ridiculous, and when He died on a tree of weakness it was monstrous. So the cross became a stumbling-block to the Jews in spite of Isaiah 53, in spite of the paschal lamb, and in spite of the lamb offered morning and evening regularly in all the tabernacle and temple ceremonial, and all the other Scriptures. So the Apostle is showing them now, from the very Scriptures of which they boasted so much, how blind and how inexcusable they were.

This, of course, is Paul's favourite method. You find abundantly in the book of Acts that when he was dealing with Jews or speaking in a synagogue, he always based his argument upon the Scriptures. For example, we read in Acts 17 : 1–3, 'Now when they had passed through Amphipolis and Apollonia, they came to Thessalonica, where was a synagogue of the Jews: and Paul, as his manner was, went in unto them, and three sabbath days reasoned with them out of the scriptures, opening and alleging, that Christ must needs have suffered, and risen again from the dead; and that this Jesus, whom I preach unto you, is Christ.'

So Paul proclaimed the message of the kingdom of God, and then he showed it out of the Scriptures, proving and alleging, reasoning with them out of the Scriptures. And when you are dealing with Jews, of course, it is the obvious method of evangelism. You do not make general statements; you take the Scriptures in which they say they believe and you show them Christ there and also every other aspect of the truth. And here, in particular, Paul is showing them this aspect of the truth, that the Scriptures, the prophets, have prophesied the rejection and the punishment of the Jews, speaking generally of them as a nation.

This, then, is what he does. In verses 27 and 28 he quotes Isaiah 10 : 22–23, and this first statement in verse 27 is a very interesting one. You notice how the Apostle puts it. 'Esaias also', he says, 'crieth concerning Israel.' Notice in particular the word 'crieth'. Paul does not just say, 'Esaias says' or 'Esaias prophesies concerning Israel', but 'cries'. We find exactly the same word in the fifteenth verse of the eighth chapter, where we read, 'For ye have not received the spirit of bondage again to fear; but ye have received the Spirit of adoption, whereby we cry, Abba, Father.'[1] It is a word that has a very deep and profound meaning. It means that we do not just *say*, 'Abba, Father'. No, it is an impassioned utterance, an inarticulate cry; it is a loud cry expressing deep emotion. Indeed some of the authorities tell us that the ultimate origin of this word is that of the screeching of a bird under very great stress.

So this is an interesting and important word. When a man really has the Spirit of adoption he knows that God is his Father, and, welling up out of the depths of his being, comes this cry,

[1]For a more detailed discussion of this see *Romans: An Exposition of Chapter 8:5–17: The Sons of God*, 1974.

'Abba, Father!' It is deep emotion, not just some quiet, polite addressing God as Father! It is like a little child who has not seen his father for a long time; the father appears and the child rushes shouting in its glee and in its happiness at seeing him.

So now Paul says here that 'Esaias crieth concerning Israel', and what he is telling us is that when Isaiah uttered that prophecy he did so with a sense of shock and of amazement; he was almost overwhelmed by grief at the terrible and terrifying message God had given him to deliver. It was an impassioned utterance! Isaiah could scarcely control himself when he said it. Why? Because as a Jew, as a member of the 'children of Israel', he could scarcely believe that this thing was possible. And yet God was giving him that message. It is the last kind of thing he would have chosen to say. He did not like saying it any more than Jeremiah or the other prophets liked saying these things, but God gave him the revelation. And when he saw the truth of what was coming Isaiah 'cried, saying. . . '.

And yet, this is the very thing that the Jews had never seen. They were proud that Isaiah was one of their own prophets; they were proud of the scroll of the book of the Prophet Isaiah; they were reading it; they were studying and expounding it, and there was Isaiah actually crying out in anguish, and still they had never understood what he was saying. They said, 'If you are a Jew you are all right, you are not like those "dogs". Every Jew is saved. Of course he is! He is a member of God's family; he is one of the children of God; we have the covenants and the oracles; all is well with us.' They had never seen the truth. There it was staring them in the face with this cry of anguish from the mouth of the Prophet, but they had never seen it, they had never heard it.

That, then, is how the Apostle introduces the statement: 'Esaias also crieth concerning Israel.' But what does the Prophet cry? – 'Though the number of the children of Israel be as the sand of the sea, a remnant shall be saved.' Now as we look at this statement, and the one that follows in verse 28 which is just an amplification of 27, we find ourselves in the same position as we did in the earlier quotation from Hosea. Again the Apostle does not give the exact quotation, and for the same reason. Far from disproving divine inspiration, as we saw, it proves it more than ever. The Spirit who indited the one indites the other and He varies the expression. And the statement is that though the number of individuals in the nation of Israel may be as numerous as the grains of sand on the seashore, it is only a remnant out of them that will be saved.

Now there is no doubt at all but that here the prophet Isaiah was referring to the promise that God made to Abraham, about Isaac: '. . . and in multiplying I will multiply thy seed as the stars of the heaven, and as the sand which is upon the sea shore' [*Genesis* 22 : 17]. Now the Jews had taken hold of that, this great miracle, the birth of their forefather Isaac. When Abraham was ninety-nine and Sarah over ninety the promise was made; yet Abraham did not stagger in unbelief; he believed God, and so he became the father of all the faithful. Yes, but the promise was that he would have this great progeny, and the Jews gloried in this and interpreted it, of course, to mean that every one of them was always right with God and would be to all eternity.

But Isaiah takes up that promise and he says to this nation, 'Though God promised that you were going to be as innumerable as the sand on the seashore, only a remnant is going to be saved among you.' And remnant, of course, just means that which is left! It is another way of saying what Paul said in verse 6 – that 'they are not all Israel, which are of Israel'. It is the quotation to prove this great argument of his, that it is only a small company in this great mass that really belongs to God.

Now verse 27 deals only with this point, that it is but a few of the Jews who will be saved; it is just a statement to that effect. But in verse 28 the Apostle takes the matter still further; he deals with the rejection, the punishment and the destruction of the mass. That aspect also, of course, is equally essential to the Apostle's argument. It is not enough merely that he should establish that it had been prophesied that only a small portion was to be saved; the staggering thing is that God's own people in the main are rejected and will be destroyed.

So verse 28 takes up the second part: 'For he will finish the work, and cut it short in righteousness: because a short work will the Lord make upon the earth.' Now if we have been in difficulties about translation before, we are in still greater difficulty here. Fortunately there is nothing vital, the meaning is perfectly clear and obvious, but once more it is neither the Septuagint nor the Hebrew. It is a variation, as it were, upon the two. The only word to which we must give attention is the word 'work'. 'For he will finish the work', says the Authorized Version translation. That really is a most unfortunate translation, because the word is not 'work', but 'word'. 'For he will finish the word, and cut it short in righteousness.' That means an utterance; it is used for a doctrine or for reckoning; it is used for account; so that you can translate it like this: 'The Lord will execute His word upon the earth, finishing it and cutting it short.'

Charles Hodge suggests this translation: 'For He will execute the judgment and accomplish it speedily, for the judgment determined upon will the Lord execute in the earth.' It is the word of God's announcement, that is what He will execute. God, through the prophets, has made an announcement, a proclamation. God has said that He is going to punish. 'Very well,' says Isaiah, 'what He has said, He will do. What He has promised He will perform.' That is the real meaning of the statement. And you notice that it is put in this very dramatic form – that He will 'finish' it and He will 'cut it short', and 'a short work' will He make of it. All those ideas suggest suddenness, rapidity, and completion – nothing will be left undone. God will suddenly do this, and He will carry it out to the ultimate limit of what He has said beforehand.

We must, then, work this out and realize its significance. Here is a profound statement to the effect that God's word is always true. Everything that God has said, He will do. He will judge, He will punish, He will destroy, and the thoroughness of God's work is something awful, in the true sense of the word, to contemplate. The Apostle says that God's word has two sides to it. There is the word that pronounces wrath and punishment, and there is the word that proclaims salvation to a remnant; and God will carry out the two sides of His great statement. Now we must remember this: that everything that God has ever said is absolute and will most certainly come to pass.

So as we look at this quotation from Isaiah we must bear in mind what we discovered in connection with the quotation from Hosea – that the prophecies of the prophets generally carry two distinct applications, the immediate and the remote. That was true about the prophecy of Hosea and it is still more true of this particular prophecy here. The statement is that the bulk of the nation will be punished under the wrath of God. What is he referring to? What was Isaiah thinking of when he uttered and wrote those words? There is no doubt that in the first instance he was dealing with what was going to happen fairly quickly to the children of Israel. He may very well have had in mind the history of the departure of the ten tribes to form the northern kingdom, leaving only the two tribes in the original southern kingdom. That is part of it. He may also have had in mind what happened in the Assyrian invasion. However, there is no question at all but that Isaiah had very definitely in the forefront of his mind the attack of the Chaldeans, the destruction of Jerusalem and the carrying away of the people to the captivity of Babylon, so that eventually it was only a 'remnant' of the people who came back to their ancestral home in the land of Canaan.

But, as the Apostle shows us here, that was not the only application. For this is also a striking prophecy of what happened in the first century and especially in A.D. 70, when the city of Jerusalem was again destroyed and demolished by the Roman armies, and the Jews were cast out among the nations where they remain until today. Not only that; it was only a very small number of them that believed the gospel (as the Apostle has already reminded us in verse 24), and continued as citizens of the new form of the kingdom of God which we call the Christian church.

So the Apostle's argument is that when Isaiah wrote those words, the ultimate fulfilment of his prophecy was what we are witnessing now. A.D. 70 had not yet come, remember. The Apostle is particularly referring to the condition of the Christian church, and he could also see coming what happened in A.D. 70. So then here is another great lesson which we obviously learn as we go along. The very position that then obtained in the church had been prophesied eight long centuries before by the prophet Isaiah. Throughout the running centuries God had given these warnings and yet nothing seemed to happen. Things did happen but not to fulfil the prophecy; they seemed to be minor fulfilments, but still the great thing itself had not yet happened.

Now, in many ways, the best commentary on this particular quotation is to be found in Matthew 23 verses 34–36: 'Wherefore, behold, I send unto you prophets, and wise men, and scribes: and some of them ye shall kill and crucify; and some of them shall ye scourge in your synagogues, and persecute them from city to city: [notice this] that upon you may come all the righteous blood shed upon the earth, from the blood of righteous Abel unto the blood of Zacharias son of Barachias, whom ye slew between the temple and the altar. Verily I say unto you, All these things shall come upon this generation.' So the meaning of Isaiah's prophecy is this: God makes this pronouncement of judgment, but then He does not seem to do anything, and the unbeliever and the unenlightened and the unintelligent say, 'Ah well, it is just a threat and nothing is going to happen.' 'Where is the promise of his coming?' as Peter puts it in 2 Peter 3.

But the answer is that God does not always carry out immediately what He says He is going to do, and that is where people are so blind. Because He does not act at once they say, 'He is not going to act at all.' That was so in the days before the Flood. God raised up Noah to preach – a 'preacher of righteousness' – and to warn the people about their sinfulness. 'The wrath of God is on this world', says Noah, 'and God will punish it; He will destroy it.' And the people listened at first, but weeks and months and years passed, and nothing happened, and they began to laugh and joke, eating and drinking, marrying and giving in marriage, until the flood came and destroyed them all. And the same was true of Sodom and Gomorrah.

Oh, there is no greater fallacy than that! God makes His statement, and here we are reminded that He will carry it out. I do not know when. He may delay, for His own gracious purpose, and we have already been given an insight into why He does it. He does it partly in order that He may show something of His longsuffering on the vessels of wrath, fitted to destruction. We have gone into that. But the principle is that, whether soon or late, the day will come and He will do it, and upon one generation will come all that God has ever threatened.

And so it was with the Jews, whom He had tolerated for so many long centuries and had 'borne with their evil manners', as the Scriptures themselves put it. Finally the day came when, as our Lord had prophesied, they were put aside. Our Lord said that God had now come to the point at which He was putting them aside and choosing a nation that should 'bring forth the fruits thereof' – that terrible verdict upon the Jews which our

Lord delivered towards the end of His days on earth. And remember again His statement in Matthew 23. The day has come at last, the moment has come, God has been threatening it throughout the centuries. Now He is going to do it and when He does, it will be a terrible act. And A.D. 70 was just that. According to Josephus and other writers it was one of the most terrible things that has ever happened in the whole history of the human race, God finishing the work in righteousness, cutting it short. It all came suddenly upon that generation; '. . . from the blood of righteous Abel unto the blood of Zacharias son of Barachias', all this wrath of God upon the nation suddenly is poured forth. 'The mills of God grind slowly, yet they grind exceeding small.'

There is an anecdote which well illustrates this, about an old preacher in Canada, who had been preaching in an agricultural district for years and had taught his people not to work on Sundays. He had told them that if they want to be blessed of God they must not do that, they must not break God's laws whatever immediate loss they might have. The old man had preached that to them for years and years. Then, one summer when the weather had been particularly bad, suddenly there was a very fine Sunday, and a big farmer in the area decided that he and his men would go out to work and they carried in the crop. Walking down the road one or two days later he suddenly met the old minister, and he accosted the old man and said, 'Hullo, Pastor! you know what I did on Sunday?' 'Yes', said the old man. 'Well,' he said, 'nothing has happened to me, the house has not burnt down, I have not lost all my family, God has done nothing to me, everything is going on exactly as it was before.' 'Ah, my friend,' said the old pastor, 'God keeps long accounts, He does not always settle His accounts in the fall.'

What he meant was this: God does not always strike immediately, but the point is that He does strike. What God has said, God does. God has pronounced these great judgments upon sin. So do not be foolish, says the prophet Isaiah, do not assume that because it has not come, it will never come. It will come! God 'will finish the work, and cut it short in righteousness: because a short work will the Lord make upon the earth'. And so the Apostle tells these contemporaries of his, these Jews who are rejecting Christ in unbelief, 'You know this is exactly what the prophet has prophesied; you are being rejected, and the Gentiles are coming in, and worse is coming to you. The hour of judgment has struck, God's stated word is now coming into operation.'

In other words this quotation from Isaiah is one of the most relevant that the Apostle could ever have chosen. It shows his knowledge of the Scriptures and his spiritual understanding. It proves his case right up to the very hilt. God's promises were never unconditional. They thought they were, but they were not. God's promises never work themselves out automatically! You must not assume that because you are a Christian your children are Christians. You must not assume that because your parents were, you are. You must not make any of these assumptions about nations or anything else.

No, God gave wonderful, exceeding great and precious promises to the children of Israel, but He gave them some of the most awful threats at the same time. Entering into the promised land, they saw Mount Ebal and Mount Gerizim, the mount of cursing and the mount of blessing [*Deuteronomy* 11 : 29]. Both of them were there. And what the prophet is saying, and what Paul is expounding, is that God always carries out both sides of the statement. Not only the promises, equally the threats. And it was the tragedy of the Jews that they had been blinded to the threats and the warnings, but now they were coming visibly upon them. Do not be surprised, says the Apostle, therefore, at the state and the condition of the church, that she is mainly Gentile and that you as Jews are outside. It is the very thing that God gave the prophet to foresee eight hundred long years ago, and far from saying anything new, I am just holding before you the fulfilment of the promises of God.

Then he goes on in verse 29 and takes the argument one step further, 'And as Esaias said before' – which means 'as he said earlier in his book'. The Apostle has been quoting from these verses in Isaiah 10, and now he says that Isaiah had already said the same thing earlier, in chapter 1. Here, once again, the Apostle varies what you will find in the Old Testament. In Isaiah 1 : 9 we read 'a very small remnant'; but here we read, 'Except the Lord of Sabaoth had left us a seed'. Now this time Paul is using the Septuagint translation. And, of course, it makes no difference – 'remnant' and 'seed' mean almost exactly the same thing. Anybody who knows anything about farming will know that. A man grows potatoes and he either sells them or eats them himself with his family, but he keeps back a few as 'seed' to ensure that he will have a crop next year.

Here, Paul is not thinking of a vegetable seed but of an animal seed that can guarantee the perpetuation of the line. He had talked already in verses 7 and 8 about 'the seed' – 'Neither, because they are the seed of Abraham, are they all children: but, In Isaac shall thy seed be called.' You remember how we worked that out. 'That is,' he says in verse 8, 'They which are the children of the flesh, these are not the children of God: but the children of the promise are counted for the seed.' These are the ones through which the line is perpetuated. So he takes the word 'seed' here to make it correspond to that, instead of the word 'remnant', but it is exactly the same.

Why then does Paul quote this? What is the statement in Isaiah 1 : 9? It is that the nation of Israel deserves total punishment and destruction, like Sodom and Gomorrah. A remnant alone is unpunished and saved. On what grounds is it saved? There is only one answer – it is the mercy and the power of the Lord of Hosts. So this is perhaps the most vital question of them all. The Apostle's argument has been that salvation depends upon the sovereign election of God. We saw in verse 11: 'For the children being not yet born, neither having done any good or evil, that the purpose of God according to election might stand, not of works, but of him that calleth.' Here it is. Salvation is entirely God's action. There would be none of us alive, we would be like Sodom and Gomorrah were it not that 'the Lord of Sabaoth had left us a seed'. He has done it. We have not preserved ourselves, it is God who has preserved us.

Now this is a perfect summary of all the long argument we have been working through. Nobody at all deserves to be saved; every one of us merits destruction and condemnation. Every one of us deserves to be overwhelmed with the destruction of Sodom and Gomorrah. No man deserves to be saved. No man can save himself. And the fact that anybody is saved at all is to be attributed to one thing only, and that is the mercy and the grace of God and His almighty power unto salvation.

All the Jews who have been destroyed have richly deserved

it, because of their sinfulness. Did you notice how Isaiah in chapter 1 gives that catalogue of their sins, their rebellion, their folly and all the rest of it? They deserve complete destruction. That is what they should have had, and the fact that there is a remnant, or a seed, left is entirely due to this amazing purpose of God who is forming a people for Himself in and through His only begotten Son, whom He sent into the world to become incarnate, and to take unto Him human nature, that He might be the firstborn among many brethren.

And He is building up a new humanity in Him, some Jews, some Gentiles. Nobody has a word of complaint because all deserve to be damned and destroyed like Sodom and Gomorrah, and God in His sovereign choice is perfectly free. And that is what He has chosen to do, for the time being at any rate. The position is the exclusion of the Jews, apart from a very small remnant, and the bringing in of the Gentiles, the outsiders. And there is only one conclusion to come to, and that is, that it is all the doing of the Lord of Hosts, the Lord of Sabaoth, and has nothing whatsoever to do with us.

So the Apostle's quotation proves his case. The fact that you are a Jew does not save you. The fact that you are a good man does not save you. Nothing saves you. It is God who saves you; the Lord of Sabaoth has left us a seed. And if He had not, there would be nobody saved at all. He does it because of His love, and because of His power. The gospel is the power of God, and the wisdom of God. It is the power that can create anew. A man does not become a Christian by taking a decision. He is made a Christian by God, who had marked him out before the foundation of the world and who sees to it that he is born, and sees to it that he believes. The Apostle has already said it in chapter 1 verse 16: 'I am not ashamed of the gospel of Christ.' Why? 'For it is the power of God unto salvation' – and entirely His power – 'to every one that believeth.' Yes! He goes on in the rest of the chapter to bring that element in. So do not think that it is your believing that is the vital thing. It is the Lord of Sabaoth who leaves the 'remnant'. The work is entirely His. 'By grace are ye saved through faith; and that not of yourselves: it is the gift of God: not of works, lest any man should boast' [*Ephesians* 2 : 8–9].

Give Him the glory, my friend! The amazing thing, I repeat,

God's Sovereign Purpose

is that there is such a thing as a single Christian. And nothing explains the existence of even one Christian but the love and the grace, the mercy and the power of the Lord Almighty. Let us bow before Him.

Twenty-two

*

*What shall we say then? That the Gentiles, which followed not
after righteousness, have attained to righteousness, even the
righteousness which is of faith. But Israel, which followed after
the law of righteousness, hath not attained to the law of
righteousness. Wherefore? Because they sought it not by faith, but
as it were by the works of the law. For they stumbled at that
stumblingstone; as it is written, Behold I lay in Sion a stumbling-
stone and rock of offence: and whosoever believeth on him shall
not be ashamed.*

Romans 9 : 30–33

In these verses, we come to a new subsection in this ninth
chapter of Romans. In our analysis of it at the beginning and in
our subsequent analyses of the various subsections, we have
indicated all along that the main argument comes to a conclusion at the end of verse 29. So what the Apostle does here, in
verses 30–33, is to draw a conclusion, or to give a summary of
the entire argument that he has been working out, and he
introduces that with his familiar formula: 'What shall we say
then?' In other words: In the light of all this, what is the position
at which we have arrived? That is his method. It is very logical
and it is, of course, the outstanding characteristic of the writings
of this particular Apostle.

Now it is important that we should realize that he is here
drawing a conclusion not only with respect to what has
immediately gone before; it is also a conclusion drawn from the
whole of the chapter, and especially from what he has been
arguing so closely and cogently from verse 6. You notice that in
verses 30 and 31 he just makes a statement of the conclusion. He

puts the facts before us. Then in verses 32 and 33 he gives an explanation of those facts. And you can subdivide that further by saying that in verse 32 he gives the explanation, and supports it in verse 33 as is his custom, by a quotation from the Scripture.

First of all, then, we must look at the facts, and the first of them is: 'That the Gentiles, which followed not after right-eousness, have attained to righteousness, even the right-eousness which is of faith.' Of course we have seen that already; he has really put it in verse 24 where he says, 'Even us, whom he hath called, not of the Jews only, but also of the Gentiles'. That itself was, in a sense, a summary and a drawing of a conclusion, but he has supported it by the quotations that we have been considering. So then, having established it from every conceivable standpoint, from the standpoint of argument and logic and then by driving it right home with his quotations, he arrives at his conclusion.

So let us look at the statement. It is unfortunate that the Authorized Version here refers to '*the* Gentiles'. It is not in the original, which simply says 'Gentiles'. Because when you read 'the Gentiles' you might come to the conclusion that all the Gentiles were believers. But they were not, of course. All he is anxious to say in general is that we are confronted by this astounding fact that 'Gentiles' – even if there were but one, it would be an astonishing thing, but there are more than one – they are in the church and Jews are out. Not all Jews, again, of course, because there was a remnant, as he has been telling us. But he is saying in broad terms, that, looking at the church as a whole, what we see is Gentiles rather than Jews.

However, he is not content with merely leaving it at that. He elaborates it and, of course, the elaboration is not only import-ant, it is also extremely interesting. The characteristic of Gentiles, he says, is that they 'followed not after righteous-ness' – and there is no question about that, because in the very first chapter, from verse 18 onwards, he gave us a most terrify-ing description of the kind of life that was being lived by the Gentiles. We went into it in great detail;[1] it is one of the most terrifying and awful passages in the whole of Scripture. Far

[1] See *Romans: An Exposition of Chapter 1: The Gospel of God*, 1985.

[274]

from following after righteousness they were living a life that was godless, vile, polluted, sinful – language almost fails in an endeavour to describe it.

However, here, in Romans 9, of course, he is referring not merely to the kind of life which they were actually living, he is also saying that they were not a bit concerned about their relationship to God; they were not seeking to be right with Him. That is the important point. Over and above the fact that it was a bad life, the terrible thing about the life of those pagans, those Gentiles, was that they were 'without God', as Paul puts it to the Ephesians, 'without God in the world'.

Or, as he puts it so plainly elsewhere, they were 'worshipping idols', they were utterly unconcerned about 'the only true and living God'. They were not aware of His wrath against sin or of the judgment; they were not aware of their precarious position; they were completely unconcerned about the need of being reconciled to God, and they were doing nothing at all about it. They were indeed, as again the Apostle Paul puts it in Ephesians 2 : 1 – 'dead in trespasses and sins'; they had no spiritual life at all. So this whole question of 'How can a man be right and just with God?' had never occurred to them, they were not interested in it. Yet, he says, the astonishing thing is that Gentiles who were in that state and position 'have attained to righteousness'.

This is a most important point, and I am sorry that here again I have to criticize the Authorized Version translators. They should not have translated this as 'attained unto righteousness'. You will notice that in the next verse the same word appears again – at least in the Authorized Version: 'But Israel, which followed after the law of righteousness, hath not attained to the law of righteousness.' But in the original, it is not the same word, and it is important that we should draw the distinction between the two. The word that we have here in verse 30 should really be translated as 'apprehend'. It is even stronger than that. It means to 'take eagerly', to 'seize'. Now it is interesting that the New English Bible, which has noticed that it is not 'the Gentiles' but 'Gentiles', goes on to translate like this: 'That Gentiles, who made no effort after righteousness, nevertheless achieved it' – which, of course, is entirely wrong! It is even worse than 'attained' because it gives us the impression that as the result of their efforts they achieved it. That is the last thing the Apostle wants to say. Indeed he is saying the exact opposite of that. No, the correct translation here is: 'Gentiles, which followed not after righteousness, have apprehended righteousness' – have 'taken eagerly', have 'laid hold upon' this righteousness, which is, as he says, 'even the righteousness which is of faith'.

So then this is Paul's statement with regard to these Gentiles. They had been quite unconcerned, not interested; they were 'aliens from the commonwealth of Israel, and strangers from the covenants of promise, having no hope, and without God in the world' [*Ephesians* 2 : 12], never giving a thought to these things at all, just living that sinful, evil, vile life. And yet, when they heard the presentation and the preaching of this way of salvation in Christ Jesus, they 'eagerly embraced' it. And as we see in the book of Acts, that is precisely what happened as this Apostle and others went round preaching and presenting the gospel. The Jews were rejecting it, but we are told there that the Gentiles were pleased; they were delighted at it and they rejoiced in this very fact. 'When the Gentiles heard this, they were glad, and glorified the word of the Lord' [*Acts* 13 : 48].

There, then, is the first half of this statement which the Apostle puts before us in his conclusion. But then in verse 31 we come to this sad and tragic contrast: 'But Israel, which followed after the law of righteousness, hath not attained to the law of righteousness.' Now this is what the Apostle has been telling us constantly; the thing that was breaking his heart. This is what gave him his 'great heaviness and continual sorrow', that Israel, of all people, should be outside the church. Why? Because, he says, they actually were 'following after the law of righteousness'. Now 'following' is the same word in both verses 30 and 31 and it really means to 'pursue'. 'Following' is not quite strong enough. They were pursuing it, avidly or eagerly.

So the point that Paul is emphasizing is that the characteristic of the Jew was that he was very much concerned about this question of righteousness, and he was pursuing it with great eagerness. But, he says, 'they pursued after the law of righteousness', which means that they were pursuing a righteousness in terms of the law. It seems to me that that is the only meaning which can be easily and rightly attached to this statement. The authorities have argued and differed a great deal about it, but to me it seems quite obvious, especially from the end of the verse and from the whole context, that the Apostle is thinking here of the law of Moses; not of some general law of righteousness.

The Jews were not interested in a general law of righteousness. They were interested in the Mosaic Law, because they believed that observance of the Mosaic Law was not only the high road to righteousness but the only road to it. So when he says that they were 'pursuing the law of righteousness' he means that they were pursuing this goal of righteousness by means of and through the keeping of the law of Moses. And that was the simple truth about Israel, about the Jews. Now Israel and the Jews are the same people; Paul uses the terms interchangeably and he will go on doing so, as we shall see. So that any attempt to differentiate between Israel and the Jews is utterly unscriptural. I make that point simply because there is a popular cult which does that very thing without any scriptural warrant whatsoever.

Here then is the truth about these people; they were 'pursuing eagerly' to be right with God and they were doing so by trying to keep the law of Moses, and by persuading themselves that they were keeping and had kept it. But, says the Apostle, they have not succeeded: 'Israel, which eagerly followed after the law of righteousness, hath not attained to the law of righteousness.' Now that word here may be rightly translated as 'attained' or, perhaps better, 'did not arrive at'.

You see now the importance of showing the difference between these two words. The Apostle deliberately did not use the same word in verse 30 as he did here. What he says, rightly, about the Gentiles in verse 30 is, that when they heard that message about righteousness in Christ they apprehended it and they avidly and eagerly laid hold upon it. The Jews, on the other hand, said, 'There is the goal, the keeping of the moral law, the law of Moses. As long as we have that as our goal, and as long as we do that, we have attained unto righteousness and we have satisfied God.' So here they are running down the road, as it were, trying to arrive at the goal of righteousness. But, says the Apostle, they have not reached it, they have fallen short of it.

Of course, he is saying nothing new here. The first four chapters of Romans were devoted to an absolute proof of that. But here, for the sake of this particular argument, to show why the Jews are outside, he puts it in that summary manner once more. So they have not arrived at this 'law' and the fulfilment of this law. And the fact that the words 'of righteousness' are not in the best manuscripts, does not matter. It is implied and that is, of course, what the Apostle has in his mind.

Now the Apostle, especially in chapter 2, has demonstrated this very plainly and very clearly.[2] He says, in effect, 'You have been relying on the fact that you were possessors of the law and that you had a kind of knowledge of the law. You have thought that because God gave the law to you that that automatically puts you right. But', he says, 'it is not he that knows the law who is just with God, it is the man who does it.' He begins that chapter, you remember, with 'Therefore thou art inexcusable, O man' – and this is the Jew – 'whosoever thou art that judgest: for wherein thou judgest another, thou condemnest thyself; for thou that judgest doest the same things.' And his whole argument is that the mere possession of the law does not justify, it is the man who obeys it who is justified with God. And he works that out in great detail.

This, then, is the whole tragedy of the Jews; they had this great concern about righteousness, and they persuaded themselves that they had attained it; and they did that, you remember, in the way that our Lord exposes in the Sermon on the Mount, where He contrasts the righteousness as defined by the Pharisees with the true righteousness as it is defined in the law of Moses itself. They had been side-tracking the law of Moses; they had been drawing an artificial distinction between actually doing a thing in practice and having it in your mind, and so our Lord was able to convince them all of sin. They had missed the spiritual character of the law.

Indeed, the Apostle has put it all quite plainly to us in chapter 7, where he says in verse 9, 'I was alive without the law once' – that was when he was a typical Jew, a Pharisee, who had not realized the spiritual character of the law – 'I was alive without the law once: but when the commandment came' – when the Holy Spirit opened my eyes to the nature of the law – then 'sin revived, and I died' – and he was completely helpless and

[2]See *Romans: An Exposition of Chapters 2:1–3:20 The Righteous Judgment of God*, 1989.

hopeless. And what he says about himself in chapter 7 is also true, he now says, of all these people.

So we are confronted by this astonishing fact, that the people who never gave a single thought to God are right with God! Whereas the people to whom the biggest thing in life, in a sense, was religion and being right with God, are not right with Him. Now that is the statement of fact that he puts before us in verses 30 and 31, and, of course, he leads us into the secret at the same time. He, as it were, throws it in, there at the end of verse 30, 'even the righteousness which is of faith'. That is the key, and he was so concerned about it that he obviously could not restrain himself from putting it in, even in the statement of fact.

In other words, the reason why the Jews did not attain unto the law of righteousness, the goal of righteousness which they thought could be achieved by the observance of the Mosaic Law, was the point that is stated so clearly by the Apostle James in his Epistle: 'For whosoever shall keep the whole law, and yet offend in one point, he is guilty of all' [*James* 2 : 10]. That is the trouble with the law. It demands absolute perfection. It makes no allowance at all. To be 99.999 per cent correct is not enough. If there is any defect, one is totally condemned.

So that was why the Jews had never attained unto this goal of righteousness which was the big thing in their lives. They used to boast of it; they used to contrast themselves with the Gentiles, the 'dogs', the pagans, the outsiders. They were the people of God; they were right with God and these others were utterly hopeless. Yet the fact is, says the Apostle, that as we look at the Christian church, we see the outsider in and the people who ought to be in, outside. Now our Lord had said exactly the same thing. He had told the same people that the day would come when they would see Abraham and Isaac and Jacob and the Gentiles in the kingdom of God, and they themselves outside. It is one of the great themes of the New Testament.

So let us be careful, therefore, that we have Paul's great argument quite clearly in our minds. He has set out in this chapter to face this very position. The question is – Has the word of God failed to take effect? Verse 6: 'Not as though the word of God hath taken none effect.' It seemed to be that, did it not? And we have considered that. The Apostle's answer is: That is not so; the word of God *has* taken effect; but what the word of God has said is that, speaking generally, the Jews are going to be out and the Gentiles are going to be in. So he reminds them of the fact once more.

Then, having dealt with that, which is the simplest part of the matter before us, we now come to what many people have found to be extremely difficult. This is our general second division – namely, the explanation of this extraordinary fact which he puts before us in verses 32 and 33 and introduces with the word 'wherefore?' In other words, he is saying, Why is this the position? – and he proceeds to give his answer. 'Because', he says, 'they sought it not by faith, but as it were by the works of the law.' And then he gives his quotation to prove it – 'For they stumbled at that stumblingstone; as it is written . . .'

So a very important question arises here. Why is it that the Gentiles are in and the Jews are out? Or, still more particularly, Why is it that the Jews are out? Why is it that these people whose great business in life, in a sense, was righteousness and to be right with God, why are they not right with Him? Why are they outside the kingdom, fulfilling that prophecy of our Lord to the Jews: 'The kingdom of God shall be taken from you, and given to a nation bringing forth the fruits thereof'? – a prophecy which was verified and fulfilled in the Christian church. Here is the church, mainly Gentile with but a remnant of Jews; here is the kingdom of God. So the question is, Why is this? And then Paul gives the answer, 'Because they sought it not . . .'

Now, this is a great problem to people. Indeed many do not hesitate to say that here now the Apostle proceeds to contradict everything that he has been saying up until this point in the chapter. They say that from verse 6 to the end of verse 29 he has been arguing and showing from different angles that salvation is entirely dependent upon the sovereignty of God; and he has used that illustration of the clay and the potter in order to make it absolutely clear that man has nothing at all to do with it.

He has also told us that the difference between Jacob and Esau is something that was determined in the womb before they were born, before they could do either right or wrong; he has said that it is entirely of God: 'So then it is not of him that willeth, nor of him that runneth, but of God that sheweth mercy.' 'Therefore hath he mercy on whom he will have mercy, and whom he will he hardeneth' [*Romans* 9 : 16, 18]. Now that has been his great point, yet here, they say, he suddenly comes to us and says that what decides whether a man is in the kingdom of God or not is the way in which he seeks it; that what decides whether a man is saved or not is whether he has faith, whether he believes or not. So, after all, they say, it is a man's faith that saves him and not the sovereignty of God in His electing choice.

So is the Apostle contradicting himself here or not? There are two ways in which people have tried to solve this problem. The first is to say that though they do believe that God elects people unto salvation, yet, obviously, in the light of what the Apostle is saying here, His electing grace is conditioned by His foreknowledge. He only elects and saves those who in His foreknowledge He has seen are going to believe and exercise faith. They say that there is no other possible solution, because Paul says here, 'Why did they not attain?' 'Because they sought it not by faith, but as it were by the works of the law'; whereas we are told about the Gentiles that they 'have attained to righteousness, even the righteousness which is of faith'. The Gentiles exercised faith, they believed, therefore they are saved. The Jews did not believe, they did not exercise faith, they are outside. 'So', these people say, 'there is only one explanation; you can only reconcile all he has said from verse 6 to verse 29 with what he is saying here by the fact that obviously God's election is based upon His foreknowledge.'

But there is another way in which people try to solve the problem and this is the characteristic teaching of the Lutherans. Now you notice I say Lutherans and not Martin Luther, because Martin Luther himself did not teach it. The people who followed him, especially those who followed him by about a century, and modern Lutherans also, put it like this. They say that, yes, it is God alone who can and must do the saving; man cannot save himself; this idea, they say, that a man's faith saves him is wrong. God must do the saving but nevertheless man has the power, a negative power, by which he can resist or refuse to be saved. It is never man's faith that saves him, but man has the negative power and capacity of refusing to allow God to save him. There is not much difference, is there? And yet there is a difference between the two, as I think we shall see. The Lutheran view is a little nearer to what I suggest is the truth in this matter, but it is still grievously wrong.

Those, then, are the two ways in which men have attempted to resolve this problem; so that it comes to this: the question that is before us is the relationship between the sovereignty of God and man's responsibility; and really this is the first point at which the problem has been raised in this chapter. It should not have been raised by us before that. I have had to do so because I know the questions that some people raise, but actually, the Apostle does not put it before us until we come to this particular point. This is the logical point at which it really comes in, so we must face it.

So let us start by putting it like this. My first answer would be that we must not assume a contradiction in the teaching of the great Apostle. Now the two professors to whom I have referred on more than one occasion in dealing with this chapter – Professors C. H. Dodd and William Barclay – these men, of course, do not hesitate to say that. They have no trouble at all; the solution is quite simple, Paul contradicts himself! Their statement, more or less, is that, after all, Paul was human like the rest of us and everybody makes a mistake sometimes; he was in a real difficulty here and in such a difficulty he blunders out of it, as it were, by blankly contradicting himself in the course of one chapter.

Now why do I refuse to accept that as the way out of the problem? Well, firstly, to say that, of course, immediately means that you do not believe that the Apostle Paul was inspired by the Holy Spirit when he wrote these words. You cannot say that he contradicts himself and still believe in inspiration, because the Holy Spirit does not contradict Himself and He never makes a mistake. Now, of course, the two professors do not believe in inspiration; that is no trouble to them. But if you do say that you believe that this is the inspired word of God, and if you agree with the Apostle Peter that the writings of the Apostle Paul are to be put in the same category with 'the other Scriptures', then you simply cannot say that Paul was contradicting himself, because you immediately involve the Holy Spirit in the contradiction. That ought to be more than enough for us.

But, secondly, even if I did not believe that, I could not accept this idea of contradiction simply in terms of my feeling that it is a grave injustice to the mind of the great Apostle. I do not regard the Apostle Paul, even from the human standpoint, as one who is capable of contradicting himself so blatantly in the same context. With due respect to them I have a higher opinion of the Apostle than of his two modern critics! They are in a superior position; they understand all, and they just patronizingly feel a bit sorry for the Apostle blundering into a contradiction. But quite apart from inspiration, I find it inconceivable that a man of this ability and logical acumen could be capable of putting in at the end of a mighty logical argument something that contradicts the whole thing.

But, thirdly – and this to me is another very important argument – the proffered explanation is much too easy; it takes the mystery out of the Scriptures. Now that is a very good principle which we must always bear in mind. Never adopt an explanation of an apparent difficulty or impasse which makes it too easy. Let us always remember that the Scriptures are profound, that these matters are not simple; and this explanation is much too easy. There is no mystery left; you do not end by saying, 'Great is the mystery of godliness', or what the Apostle himself will tell us at the end of chapter 11. So I reject it for that reason also.

But further, my fourth reason for rejecting it is that really it does not solve the problem, it does not get me out of my difficulty. If the real explanation of the fact why the Jews are outside the church is that they did not believe the gospel when it was preached to them, that they trusted to justification by works instead of justification by faith – if that is the sole explanation, well, then, I ask in the name of conscience and of heaven, why did the Apostle write all he wrote from verse 6 to verse 29 – he must have been a fool! If this is the explanation, why say all that if it has nothing to do with it and if it is wrong? This is such a simple explanation and all he needed to say is this: 'Well, unfortunately I am experiencing this great heaviness and continual sorrow of heart over the fact that my kinsmen are outside; I would myself almost be accursed from Christ for my brethren, my kinsmen according to the flesh. But this is a tragedy, they are outside simply because they have been trying to justify themselves by works instead of believing the gospel by faith.' And that is all he would have had to say; it is enough. But he made all those other statements with the involved argument.

So it seems to me that, if you take that approach to this problem, you do not so much say that the Apostle is contradicting himself as that he is a lunatic; that he has brought in this tremendous passage from verse 6 to verse 29, which is completely irrelevant and has nothing to do with the question at all. He is creating a difficulty for himself, and then has to go on and contradict himself. But common sense dictates that a man like the Apostle Paul would never do that; he would never put in something that is unnecessary and then land himself in trouble and have to contradict himself to get out of it. The obvious thing to do is to say the one thing that needs to be said and no more. But we are confronted by verses 6 to 29, so I am not helped; they do not get me out of the difficulty at all. We must reject, therefore, this idea that the answer is a contradiction.

My second general heading, therefore, is the blunt assertion that there is no contradiction here. So what do we do about the statements? And my answer is that the doctrine of the sovereignty of God and the doctrine of human responsibility are both true and that the Apostle is stating the two doctrines here in Romans 9. Indeed he has already stated the doctrine of human responsibility in chapter 1 verse 20 where he says, 'For the invisible things of him from the creation of the world are clearly seen, being understood by the things that are made, even his eternal power and Godhead; so that they are without excuse.' That is enough.

He has stated it again more than once in the second chapter. He says that the Jews and the Gentiles are both without excuse. He says of the Gentiles in verse 15: 'Which shew the work of the law written in their hearts, their conscience also bearing witness, and their thoughts the mean while accusing or else excusing one another'. We have already expounded it in detail;[3] we cannot go over it again. But that is what it means. And the Jew, of course, is also responsible to the very hilt.

Now it is because these two things are true that the gospel of Jesus Christ is to be offered to all. You remember how the Apostle, preaching in Athens, says, 'The times of this ignorance God winked at; but now commandeth all men every where to repent' [*Acts* 17 : 30]. God commands it! That is

[3]See *Romans: An Exposition of Chapters 2:1–3:20: The Righteous Judgment of God*, 1989.

an assertion of human responsibility. The gospel is to be offered to all. That is where what is called 'hyper-Calvinism' is so terribly wrong and unscriptural. The gospel is to be offered to all. It is to be preached to all. And the apostles did so. Human responsibility is something that is asserted everywhere in the Scripture, and it is asserted side by side with the doctrine of the absolute free sovereignty of God, and that salvation is entirely the result of His election.

So this is what the Bible teaches. Election alone accounts for the saved, but non-election does not account for the lost. That is worth repeating! Election alone accounts for the saved, but non-election does not account for the lost. Let me explain. No man would be saved were it not that God in a sovereign manner has chosen him, as we have seen abundantly from verse 6 to verse 29. It is God's action alone that saves a man. So why is anybody lost? Is it because they are not elected? No! What accounts for the lost is their rejection of the gospel, and before that, of course, the fact that they are in Adam, that they belong to this mass of perdition. We have all sinned in Adam. And it is here that human responsibility comes in. We are responsible for our rejection of the gospel, but we are not responsible for our acceptance of it. That is the result of the electing grace of God.

So what the Apostle is doing here is this: in verses 6 to 29 he explains why anybody is saved; it is the sovereign election of God. In these verses he is showing us why anybody is lost, and the explanation of that is their own responsibility. In other words, the Jews, by their rejection of the gospel, are in a way, justifying God for punishing them. It is very much the same thing as we have seen happening in the case of Pharaoh. God did not make Pharaoh evil, or a sinner, he was already that in Adam. What God did was to harden his heart in sin, in order to bring it out, to show it.

You remember how we saw that so clearly; by His longsuffering He did this. The thing became more evident than it was before. That is his whole argument. You remember how it is stated in verse 17: 'For the scripture saith unto Pharaoh, Even for this same purpose have I raised thee up, that I might shew my power in thee, and that my name might be declared throughout the earth.' And the case of the Jews is exactly the same. They were lost in Adam like everybody else. They had confirmed that by rejecting the gospel and justifying, therefore, God's action in pouring His wrath upon them and in sending them to final destruction.

In conclusion, let me make clear the point at which we have arrived. The Apostle, you see, always has a method and he knows that these two things must be considered – divine sovereignty in election and human responsibility, and he states both. He taught both, he believed both. And so must we. There is no contradiction at all. But it depends upon how you look at these things. If you ask, How is any man saved? there is only one answer: It is because God has chosen him. Why is a man lost? A man is lost because he is a wilful and a deliberate sinner, and a proud and boastful sinner, who rejects the offer of salvation. That is the other side. There is human responsibility. So we must be careful how we handle this doctrine of election. If you have ever thought that the doctrine of election means that man is not responsible you have been entirely wrong. Man is responsible. But the fact that he is responsible does not mean that he can save himself. That is what the Apostle is telling us.

We shall go on to consider the justification for this teaching in the next exposition. But, meditate upon this, and meditate upon it in the spirit in which we have looked at this great argument from the very beginning until this point. Look at these two big things and avoid all these easy ways of getting out of the difficulty. This is profound truth! It is the truth of God! It is a great mystery! But it is here, and it is the teaching of the great Apostle at this particular point.

Twenty-three

*

What shall we say then? That the Gentiles, which followed not after righteousness, have attained to righteousness, even the righteousness which is of faith. But Israel, which followed after the law of righteousness, hath not attained to the law of righteousness. Wherefore? Because they sought it not by faith, but as it were by the works of the law. For they stumbled at that stumblingstone; as it is written, Behold I lay in Sion a stumblingstone and rock of offence: and whosoever believeth on him shall not be ashamed.

Romans 9 : 30–33

We have seen that if it is our belief and faith and acceptance that, after all, determines our salvation, then, in the first place, the Apostle is specifically contradicting himself, and going back on what he has said in the whole of the previous part of the chapter. But more, he is not only going back on what he has said here, he is going back on what he has said in chapter 8 verses 28 to 30, where we read, 'We know that all things work together for good to them that love God, to them who are the called according to his purpose. For whom he did foreknow, he also did predestinate to be conformed to the image of his Son, that he might be the firstborn among many brethren. Moreover whom he did predestinate, them he also called: and whom he called, them he also justified: and whom he justified, them he also glorified.'[1] The very fact that we are told that we are already glorified is a guarantee that salvation is all the result of God's purpose and God's action. So we cannot fall out of it; we cannot finally be

[1]For a detailed discussion of these verses see *Romans: An Exposition of Chapters 8:17–39: The Final Perseverance of the Saints,* 1975.

[287]

lost if we have ever been regenerate: '. . . whom he justified, them he also glorified.' We are already glorified in Christ. So to hold that other interpretation goes back on all that and makes the Apostle contradict what is his basic and central teaching.

But this teaching is not confined to Romans; you find exactly the same thing in the Epistle to the Ephesians – it is the essence of his teaching in chapter 2: 'You hath he quickened,' he writes, 'who were dead in trespasses and sins'; and he keeps on repeating it: 'But God, who is rich in mercy, for his great love wherewith he loved us, even when we were dead in sins, hath quickened us together with Christ, (by grace ye are saved).' And then he says it yet again in that same portion: 'For by grace are ye saved through faith; and that not of yourselves: it is the gift of God: not of works, lest any man should boast. For we are his workmanship, created in Christ Jesus unto good works, which God hath before ordained that we should walk in them.' Now you notice that the Apostle, in order to make it abundantly clear, not only puts it positively but also negatively – 'Not of works, lest any man should boast.' And so, you see, if you say that it is our belief and faith that save us, then you have turned believing into a work and a man is entitled to glory and to boast in that; so it means that the Apostle is contradicting that which is his basic teaching everywhere.

But let us go beyond that. Look at it like this. The position, says Paul, by which we are confronted is that the Gentiles who did not seek after righteousness are in the church, they are saved; but the Jews who did seek after righteousness are outside. Here is the same gospel preached to the Jew and to the Gentile; the Jews reject it, the Gentiles receive it. The only conclusion that you can draw, if you say that it is a man himself who decides it, is that the Gentiles were better people than the Jews and that they had greater spiritual understanding. It involves you, of necessity, in that position.

And yet when you remember what we are told about these Gentiles, for instance in Ephesians 4 and other places, the thing becomes plainly ridiculous. And in any case we are told about them that they were 'dead in trespasses and sins', and that that was their state and condition. You see, if you say that it is people's belief and reception that saves them, then you automatically have to say that the Gentiles had a greater understanding – the Jews refuse this, the Gentiles receive it.

This leads me to the third point, which is that if that is so, then the giving of the law of God through Moses to the children of Israel was a bad thing; it was a hindrance to them rather than a help. In that case the law must not be described, as Paul describes it to the Galatians, as 'a schoolmaster to bring us unto Christ' [*Galatians* 3 : 24]. It is the thing that keeps them out, and the Gentiles were very fortunate that they had never had the law at all. Because if you are given the law, there is this danger of your misusing it and misunderstanding it and thereby shutting yourself out of the kingdom. Better, by far, never to have had it!

But the Apostle will never receive such a suggestion; he glories in the fact that he is a Jew. 'What advantage then hath the Jew?' he says in chapter 3, 'or what profit is there of circumcision? Much every way: chiefly, because that unto them were committed the oracles of God.' He is proud of the fact that he belonged to the Jews. They were in a greatly superior position; they had the law and the Scriptures and the oracles of God. It is his argument in all the first chapters, and indeed he has reminded us of all that in this very chapter, Romans 9 : 4: 'Who are Israelites; to whom pertaineth the adoption, and the glory, and the covenants, and the giving of the law, and the service of God, and the promises; whose are the fathers . . .'

But, if you say that it is a man's faith that saves him and that the Gentiles are saved and the Jews are not, and that the Jews are not because of their misunderstanding of the law, then there is only one conclusion to draw, that the Gentiles were in that advantageous position because they had never had the law. It is an inevitable deduction, but it is one, of course, that one simply cannot accept for a moment, because it contradicts the teaching of the whole Bible.

Or let me put it like this; take it in our modern situation. If the trouble with the Jews was their knowledge of the law, while the Gentiles, who had not got that, were of virgin mind and soil, so that when they heard the gospel they believed it – if that is so, then the conclusion to draw from this is that it is a bad thing to teach children the Bible. It is a bad thing to bring them up in a religious manner; it is a bad thing to give people religious or moral teaching or anything that encourages them to seek after

God and after righteousness. It is the only conclusion you can draw; it is an advantage to be ignorant like the Gentiles and to know nothing at all about it.

Or let us put it in yet another way. Look at the position which is described by the Apostle in 1 Corinthians 1 – he really is making exactly the same point: 'For after that in the wisdom of God the world by wisdom knew not God, it pleased God by the foolishness of preaching to save them that believe. For the Jews require a sign, and the Greeks seek after wisdom: but we preach Christ crucified, unto the Jews a stumblingblock, and unto the Greeks foolishness; but unto them which are called' – there is the term, *called* – 'both Jews and Greeks, Christ the power of God, and the wisdom of God. Because', he continues, 'the foolishness of God is wiser than men; and the weakness of God is stronger than men.' Then he goes on, and notice it carefully, 'For ye see your calling, brethren' – you see the position that obtains in the church – 'how that not many wise men after the flesh, not many mighty, not many noble, are called: but God hath chosen the foolish things of the world to confound the wise; and God hath chosen the weak things of the world to confound the things which are mighty; and base things of the world, and things which are despised, hath God chosen, yea, and things which are not, to bring to nought things that are' [*1 Corinthians* 1 : 21–28].

So what do we deduce from all that? Well, if you say that it is a man himself who is responsible for his salvation, there is a further deduction that we must draw, and that is, that it is a very serious disadvantage to be born with a good brain, to be born with intelligence, or with what he calls there in Corinthians, 'wisdom'. You look at the Christian church, says Paul, and what do you find? Well, he says, you actually find that the majority of people in the church are not the gifted people, nor the intelligent, the able and the wise, but rather the people who are not very gifted and who are not learned, who certainly know nothing about learning and philosophy – the ignorant people, 'the things which are not'. What conclusion do you draw? I say there is only one conclusion to draw on that supposition and that is, that it is a very serious handicap to be born intelligent, or to have a good brain. The man who has the advantage in the matter of salvation is the man who is the least intelligent of all!

'Ah, but', says somebody, 'you are not being quite fair. What the Apostle is saying is not so much that it was their possession of brains that kept them out, but the fact that they were proud of their brains.' That is perfectly right! But it does not change the argument, because if you have not got much brain you have nothing to be proud of. So if the cause of the trouble is pride of intellect, then the man who has not got it is still in an advantageous position.

Now this is very important, is it not? All these things follow, you see, if it is a man's belief and faith that determine the fact that he is in the kingdom. The Gentile – with all that that connotes – is in an advantageous position over and against the Jew.

So we must go on in the fourth place to put it like this: to say that it is our belief, and so on, that saves us is completely to misunderstand what the Apostle is saying not only here but also in 1 Corinthians 1. He is not saying there that it is an advantageous thing not to be wise, not to be mighty, not to be noble. What he is saying is that God has called that kind of person for a specific object and purpose, which is a very different thing. What the Apostle is saying in 1 Corinthians 1 is that from the standpoint of salvation it does not matter whether you are wise or foolish; it does not matter whether you are mighty or weak, it does not matter what you are, because that is never what saves a man.

The moment you say that this salvation is something that is determined by man, then what is true of the man is the important thing. But according to the Apostle that is never the important thing at all. What saves is always the calling of God. 'Not many wise men after the flesh, not many mighty, not many noble, are called: but God hath chosen the foolish things of the world to confound the wise' – that is why He has done it – 'and God hath chosen the weak things of the world to confound the things which are mighty; and base things of the world, and things which are despised, hath God chosen, yea, and things which are not, to bring to nought things that are.' Why? For this reason: 'That no flesh should glory in his presence.' The wise man must not glory in the presence of God, neither must the foolish man; the strong man must not glory in the presence of God, neither must the weak man. Nobody must! By which he is saying that nothing in man matters at all. It is the choosing and the calling of God that alone matters.

Surely this ought to be perfectly clear and quite inevitable. And actually what God does, as he tells us, is to choose people of all types and all kinds. He does call some Jews as well as Gentiles; He does call some wise. What the Apostle says is not that there are no wise men in the church, but 'not many'! But do not turn that into saying that there are none and that you put a premium on ignorance and on an absence of ability and intellect and power. That is equally wrong. God does not need your brains, but He does not need your lack of brains either. He does not need your understanding; He does not need your lack of understanding. There is no advantage on either side at all.

Nothing, therefore, in us determines whether we are saved or whether we are not. Indeed the Bible makes it very plain and clear to us that there is only one explanation as to how the Gentiles ever got into the Christian church. It was not their ignorance, as we have seen. God forbid that we should ever put ourselves into the terrible position of saying that. Look at the condition of these Gentiles. The Apostle has given us a terrifying description of them in the first chapter from verse 21 to the end. Read those verses again and, also, 1 Corinthians 6 verses 9 and following and Ephesians 2 verses 1–3. Read also what he says in Ephesians 4 : 18 and following: 'Having the understanding darkened, being alienated from the life of God through the ignorance that is in them, because of the blindness of their heart: who being past feeling have given themselves over unto lasciviousness, to work all uncleanness with greediness' – sunken in iniquity and vileness and evil and sin.

So the question must be: How did such people ever believe the gospel? How is it that they ever came into the Christian church? 'Ah', you say, 'it is because when they heard the gospel they believed it, they accepted it and they gave themselves to it. They had the spiritual understanding to do so, they were sufficiently enlightened, whereas the Jews were not.' Can you say that about such people? They were 'without God' – 'in the world'. They were absolutely blinded and darkened in their minds. And yet you are asking me to believe that they had the ability and the capacity to recognize the truth and to believe it and thereby to save themselves! The thing is a sheer and an utter impossibility, and indeed it is a blank denial of the Scriptures.

This is what we are told in Acts 13. Here is Paul preaching at Antioch in Pisidia and he preaches first of all to a mixed company of Jews and Gentiles. We read in verses 44–48, 'And the next sabbath day came almost the whole city together to hear the word of God. But when the Jews saw the multitudes, they were filled with envy, and spake against those things which were spoken by Paul, contradicting and blaspheming. Then Paul and Barnabas waxed bold, and said, It was necessary that the word of God should first have been spoken to you: but seeing ye put it from you, and judge yourselves unworthy of everlasting life, lo, we turn to the Gentiles. For so hath the Lord commanded us, saying, I have set thee to be a light of the Gentiles, that thou shouldest be for salvation unto the ends of the earth. And when the Gentiles heard this, they were glad, and glorified the word of the Lord: and as many as were ordained to eternal life believed.'

And that is the one and the only explanation. You cannot postulate a spiritual understanding in these people who were dead in trespasses and sins, and sunk to the very depths of iniquity with darkened, blinded minds. It is impossible. There is only one explanation: 'as many as were ordained to eternal life believed.' And they were the only ones who believed. Nobody else believed at all. 'By grace are ye saved through faith; and that not of yourselves: it is the gift of God. Not of works, lest any man should boast. For we are his workmanship . . .' Obviously! – because we were dead and it is God's ordination of us to eternal life that leads us and enables us to believe.

There, then, it seems to me, the position is plain. It is obvious what the Apostle is saying. That is how the Gentiles have come in. But what keeps one out we have also seen in that same passage in Acts 13 : 46: 'seeing', says the Apostle, 'that ye put it from you, and judge yourselves unworthy of everlasting life, lo, we turn to the Gentiles.' It is the ordination of God that brings anybody in; it is a man's deliberate refusal and rejection that keeps him out.

Furthermore, as we saw with Pharaoh, though God spared him and withheld His wrath, far from melting Pharaoh or improving him or making him more ready to listen, it had the opposite effect; he became harder and harder. The grace of God hardened Pharaoh and thereby revealed his essential sinfulness. He deliberately opposed God, he deliberately disobeyed, he deliberately rejected. Very well, says Paul, that is precisely the position with the Jews. They have been disobeying God and rejecting Him for centuries. The Old Testament gives us the story and the account.

But God still spared them. And then 'when the fulness of the time was come, God sent forth his Son, made of a woman, made under the law' [*Galatians* 4 : 4]. The everlasting God gave this great honour to Israel, as the Apostle has reminded us in verse 5: 'of whom as concerning the flesh Christ came, who is over all, God blessed for ever'. When God sent His only begotten Son from heaven into this world He did not send Him to the Gentiles, He sent Him amongst the Jews. As a man our Lord was a Jew. Verse 3 of chapter 1 has already told us that: 'of the seed of David according to the flesh'. What greater honour could ever have been paid to a nation? So God sent His own Son and made Him a Jew, and He lived amongst them and taught amongst them, was subject to their own law, the law of Moses, in which they gloried so much.

Not only that, He preached grace to them, He told them that He had come to die, to save. All His preaching, all His life, all His teaching, His death upon the cross; yet what effect did it have upon the Jews? Did it soften them, did it melt them, did it fill them with joy and with thanksgiving and with praise? Well, the four Gospels answer that question. It hardened them! No one ever infuriated the Jews as our Lord did. They never showed such hatred and malice and bitterness against anyone as they did against the Son of God who had come amongst them. You see what it means: the grace of God in His Son, even His death upon the cross, hardened them, and revealed their essential lost, damned condition. They deliberately refused Him, they deliberately rejected Him and they are responsible for their own damnation. Exactly as Pharaoh was. Now that is all the Apostle is saying here. In these last two verses he is not dealing with what saves a man, he is dealing with what condemns a man; and he says that it is a man's own responsibility, a man's own action, a man's own refusal and rejection of the preaching of the grace of God in Jesus Christ.

What any man who is a true Christian says, therefore, is this: 'There but for the grace of God go I! I am what I am by the grace of God! I am a Christian not because I have believed, not because I have got some understanding that that other person has not got. No, I am a Christian; I am what I am, because God in His inscrutable purpose has ordained that I should have eternal life. And there is no other reason.'

The only alternative to that is to take credit to yourself for salvation. The only alternative is to say – 'It was my belief that did it. I am saved and the other man is not, because I exercised faith.' That means that you have saved yourself. There is something in you that is not in the other man. You have believed, he has not. Is that what saves you?

So let me ask the question that I have asked once before. If you believe that, then what is it that makes you believe and the other man not believe? 'Well,' you say, 'I understood the gospel and the other man did not.' But why was that? What is it about you that made you or enabled you to understand and not he? There must be something better in you than there is in him – a better brain perhaps, or you are more spiritually minded. But, how are you like that and why are you different? 'Well,' you say, 'I don't know, I just am.' Exactly! You do not determine it, do you? You were born like that.

So in the end it comes back to this: you either believe in accident and chance, or else you believe in the election of God. You have either got to say, 'Well, it is my natural condition; I was just born like this, and I find myself believing while the other man does not.' Or else you say that it is 'the purpose of God according to election'. And that is what the Bible teaches: 'as many as were ordained to eternal life believed.'

My dear friends, I am not saying these things because I understand all this. I do not! Do not ask me why God ordains some and not others, I do not know. I am not told in the Bible, and I know nothing except what I am told there. I will go further: I do not want to know. It is a mystery. It is a great mystery. That is the inscrutable mind of God. There is a hymn in which Charles Wesley puts this, it seems to me, so perfectly:

> *And can it be, that I should gain*
> *An interest in the Saviour's blood?*

And then, notice this!

> 'Tis mystery all! The imortal dies!
> who can explore His strange design?
> In vain the first-born seraph tries
> To sound the depths of love divine:
> 'Tis mercy all! let earth adore,
> Let angel-minds inquire no more.

Now that is the simple literal truth:

> In vain the first-born seraph tries
> To sound the depths of love divine.

And yet you are trying to do it, are you not? You want to understand? You say, 'I want to know this, I cannot understand that.' But the brightest seraph in heaven does not understand it! It is too deep a mystery. We are here looking into the mind of the eternal God and we are not meant to understand.

And that is exactly what the Apostle is saying in 1 Corinthians 1. It is because some of us are so clever and want to understand even the mind of God, and say, 'I am not going to believe until I understand', that 'God hath chosen the foolish things of the world to confound the wise'. It is not that your wisdom is a disadvantage but it does mean that you must realize that your wisdom is just nothing when it tries to pit itself against the mind and the wisdom of God. And it is in order to humble us that God has chosen those who are the foolish rather than the wise, and the weak rather than the strong. He has done it to let us all see together that we can do nothing, that 'no flesh should glory in his presence'.

Nobody must glory in the presence of God. Whether you are wise or foolish, it does not matter at all; whether you are a Jew or a Gentile. Whatever your nationality, whatever your gifts and propensities, it makes not the slightest difference. I will add to that. Whether you are a moral person or the most immoral, thank God it does not make any difference when you come to this question of salvation. Not the slightest difference. If you are glorying in anything, even in your belief or your faith, you are trying to justify yourself by works and you are not saved. 'Thou must save, and Thou alone.' 'But of him are ye in Christ Jesus, who of God is made unto us wisdom, and righteousness, and sanctification, and redemption: that, according as it is written, He that glorieth, let him glory in the Lord' [*I Corinthians* I : 30]. Exclusively! Only!

It is He alone who does save. 'As many as were ordained to eternal life believed.' Your believing is a proof of the fact that you have been ordained. Your believing is the first sign of the new mind that is in you. To the natural man these things are foolishness; he cannot receive them. The fact that you receive them means that you are not a 'natural man', you have become a 'spiritual man', you are a 'new man'. 'By grace are ye saved through faith; and that not of yourselves: it is the gift of God.'

Twenty-four

*

Wherefore? Because they sought it not by faith, but as it were by the works of the law. For they stumbled at that stumblingstone; as it is written, Behold, I lay in Sion a stumblingstone and rock of offence: and whosoever believeth on him shall not be ashamed.

Romans 9 : 32–33

We come back to this statement once more because here the Apostle is giving us the final explanation of the whole tragedy of the Jewish nation. He is dealing here not with individual Jews, but with the Jews as a nation, and the fact that they are outside the church, whereas the Gentiles as nations and as peoples have come in. Thank God – as he says in verse 24 – there are some Jews who are in, but they are a very small remnant. As a nation they are outside and the question he asks here is – Why?

This is, he says, for two reasons. The first, the positive reason – is that they had sought to be righteous and right with God by means of the works of the law, a 'works' righteousness, instead of the righteousness that is by faith alone. Then negatively he gives us a second reason, and that is that they had 'stumbled' at God's way of salvation, the way that God Himself had provided. He says 'they stumbled at that stumblingstone', and that stumbling-stone is none other than the Lord Jesus Christ Himself and His work on our behalf.

So now we must look in particular at this second reason, and at this extraordinary statement. It is a statement which is important not only from the standpoint of enabling us to understand the actual history of what happened to our Lord, and the old position of the church as it obtained at the time of the

Apostle; it is a crucial statement for all times and in all ages and in all places. In other words, we are looking here at what we may rightly describe as the very heart and centre of the Christian gospel.

Now the Apostle, you notice, again reminds us, as he has been doing all along, that all this had been prophesied and predicted. That is, of course, the standing enigma, the question as to how it was that these people, the Jews, with the Scriptures open before them could have been so blind. All this which is true of the church, he says, is something that had been foreseen. It had been given by God to the prophets to see it, and they had actually put it in writing. We have noticed that each time Paul makes a statement, he develops an argument; then he proves it and substantiates and underlines it by giving a quotation from the prophets.

So he does that now with regard to this last statement, exactly as he has done it with respect to the others, and this, in many ways, is of the very essence of the tragedy of the Jews. They are condemned, as it were, out of their own mouths. They gloried in their Scriptures, the oracles of God; they were proud of the prophets and the writings of the prophets. And it is those very writings that condemn them above everything else. 'As it is written', he keeps on saying, and what has been written is that they are going to be afflicted by this 'blindness' that leads them to stumble at their own Messiah, and at the salvation that God has gloriously provided in and through Him.

But now this prophetic reminder is again a matter of very great interest, and especially with regard to the death of our Lord upon the cross. His quotation from Isaiah here, his reminder that all this had been predicted and prophesied, refutes completely and finally the teaching which is so common – that our Lord's death came as a surprise to Him, and that He had never anticipated it. Some even go so far as to say that He died in utter disappointment and with a metaphorical broken heart.

Now that is finally refuted by this one statement without adducing any others. Our Lord knew the prophets; He was prepared; He knew what was coming. He had come to die. He was not taken by surprise. It also refutes the idea that our Lord's death need never have taken place at all, and might never have happened. There are many who teach that; that unfortunately it happened because of the blindness of these people, because our Lord, like many another prophet and great man, was ahead of His time and was therefore not appreciated; and that it might very well not have happened. But this statement gives the lie directly to that teaching also.

But also, it seems to me to be a final refutation of a very popular dispensational teaching which tells us that our Lord came into the world primarily to offer the kingdom to the Jews, and that it was only after the Jews had refused to believe and to receive the teaching about the kingdom, and as the result of that, that the gospel of grace by the death of Christ had to be introduced and brought in. It was, they maintain, an after-thought. If only the Jews had accepted the teaching about the kingdom this would never have happened; there would never have been any need for the doctrine of the grace of God. And then they go on to say that this doctrine of the gospel of the grace of God is only a temporary one, and that a day will yet come when the gospel of the kingdom will once more be preached, and people will either be saved by believing or lost by rejecting that offer of the kingdom.

But now it seems to me that this one statement alone is enough to refute that teaching. The cross was something that had been planned before the foundation of the world. There was no change in God's programme as the result of what happened to our Lord when He was here in the days of His flesh. This notion that the 'prophetic clock' was stopped then, and that the whole plan had to be rearranged because of the rejection of the Jews, seems to me to be a sheer denial of what we read here and in so many other places – how the cross is prophesied and predicted right the way through the Old Testament. All the types and shadows, the paschal lamb, the burnt offering, the sacrifices, all of them are proclaiming the absolute necessity of the Son of God's incarnation and sacrifice.

And here we are reminded that the treatment which was meted out to Him by the Jews was something that had long ago been prophesied by the prophet Isaiah. So this is an extraordinary refutation of any such teaching which suggests – the suggestion itself is monstrous! – that God's eternal plan had to be modified because the Jews rejected the gospel of the kingdom. No! As the author of the Epistle to the Hebrews tells us, He 'was made a little lower than the angels for the suffering of death' [*Hebrews* 2 : 9]. All this happened to Him that He might 'taste death for every man'. He came into the world primarily to die, and that is why this had been prophesied and predicted so long before, in the writings of the various prophets, and in the whole of the Levitical ceremonial and ritual.

But leaving that aside, let us now look directly at this momentous statement. What is its teaching? Well, I think we can put it in the form of three main principles. First, our relationship to God is determined solely and entirely by our attitude to the Lord Jesus Christ. He is the 'stone'. He is the test. It all comes to this. Why are the Jews outside? Because they stumbled at this Person. He determines everything. Nothing else finally matters. The Lord Jesus Christ is the acid test of the value of any supposed belief in God.

Now this is why this is such a crucial and momentous statement. I assert that He, and He alone, matters. That people say they believe in God is of no value whatsoever unless they believe in the Lord Jesus Christ; that people may have very exalted views about life and living does not matter at all unless they believe on the Lord Jesus Christ; that people do not believe in war, or that they do believe in doing good, does not make the slightest difference if they do not believe in the Lord Jesus Christ. The fact that people may make great sacrifices for the sake of others and, as they believe, in order to praise God, is utterly useless unless they believe on our Lord and Saviour Jesus Christ.

That is what the Apostle is saying here. What he does is to give us two quotations from the book of the prophet Isaiah and he does it in a way that we have already seen. He takes two quotations and conflates them into one. The first is Isaiah 8 : 13 and 14. The prophet is writing here to the children of Israel when they were in trouble, and this is his message to them: 'Sanctify the Lord of hosts himself; and let him be your fear, and let him be your dread. And he shall be for a sanctuary; but for a stone of stumbling and for a rock of offence to both the houses of Israel, for a gin and for a snare to the inhabitants of Jerusalem.' Then, Isaiah 28 : 16: 'Therefore thus saith the Lord God, Behold, I lay in Zion for a foundation a stone, a tried stone, a precious corner stone, a sure foundation: he that believeth shall not make haste.' The Apostle takes those two statements, merges them into one, and gives us this statement here: 'Behold, I lay in Sion a stumblingstone and rock of offence, and whosoever believeth on him shall not be ashamed.'

Now we have already had occasion to point out that the interesting way in which the Apostle handles these Old Testament quotations is the final proof of his own inspiration. No man, especially a man like this, who had been brought up and trained as a Pharisee, no man who had the respect that this man had for the word of God, the oracles of God, would dream of doing what he does here unless he was led and inspired of the Holy Ghost to do so. He is concerned to bring out one aspect of the matter, so he says, 'I lay in Sion a stumblingstone.' Isaiah did not actually say this, but when you take the two together it comes to that; as he is only interested here in the failure of the Jews to believe, this is the thing he wants to emphasize. And so led and inspired by the Holy Ghost he puts it in this particular form.

Another hint at the same truth is in Psalm 118 verse 22: 'The stone which the builders refused is become the head stone of the corner.' It is the same idea exactly. Our Lord Himself refers to it and makes use of it when He is finally condemning the Pharisees at the end of His ministry, and indeed condemning the whole of the Jewish nation! 'Jesus saith unto them, Did ye never read in the scriptures, The stone which the builders rejected, the same is become the head of the corner: this is the Lord's doing, and it is marvellous in our eyes?' And it leads to the next statement so germane to our matter here, 'Therefore say I unto you, The kingdom of God shall be taken from you, and given to a nation bringing forth the fruits thereof'. In other words, the church is taken from the Jews and given to the Gentiles. And then he goes on, 'Whosoever shall fall on this stone shall be broken: but on whomsoever it shall fall, it will grind him to powder' [*Matthew* 21:42–44].

Peter also uses the same quotation when he and John are arraigned before the tribunal: 'This is the stone which was set at nought of you builders, which is become the head of the corner. Neither is there salvation in any other: for there is none other name under heaven given among men, whereby we must be saved' [*Acts* 4 : 11–12]. And of course, the Apostle Paul uses it when he says, 'The Jews require a sign, and the Greeks seek after wisdom: but we preach Christ crucified, unto the Jews a stumblingblock, and unto the Greeks foolishness' [*1 Corinthians* 1 : 22–23].

But Paul is not content with that, so in the same letter he says, 'According to the grace of God which is given unto me, as a wise masterbuilder, I have laid the foundation, and another man buildeth thereon. But let every man take heed how he buildeth thereupon. For other foundation can no man lay than that is laid, which is Jesus Christ' [*1 Corinthians* 3 : 10–11]. The only One! And, finally, we read in 1 Peter 2 verse 8: 'a stone of stumbling, and a rock of offence, even to them which stumble at the word, being disobedient: whereunto also they were appointed'.

That, then, is what the Apostle is saying here. It means that the Lord Jesus Christ Himself, His life, His teaching, but especially His death upon the cross and His resurrection and ascension, are the foundation, the only foundation, whereon a man can be right with God, and righteous in His sight. This is the message of the Christian proclamation, that 'there is none other name under heaven given among men, whereby we must be saved'. Or what our Lord Himself had said, 'I am the way, the truth, and the life: no man cometh unto the Father, but by me.' The only foundation! Jesus Christ – in all the glory and the wonder of His person, and in all the glory and the wonder of His work – He is the stone, the foundation stone, the only one.

And, therefore, the Apostle rightly points out to us that because of that there are only two possible attitudes towards Him, and he tells us in this one statement what they both are. 'Whosoever believeth on him shall not be ashamed'; that is one reaction, that confronted by Him you believe in Him, you trust yourself utterly, absolutely to Him, you rest on Him, and on Him alone. Nothing in yourself but only in Him. You find Him to be a sanctuary, a place of deliverance, a place of rest and assurance, where there is no longer any fear and possible shame. That is one – 'Whosoever believeth on Him shall not be ashamed.' The other possible reaction and attitude to Him is that we stumble at Him, that He becomes to us 'a stumbling-stone, and a rock of offence', and that leads ultimately to shame, and to being ashamed and confounded.

Here then is the Apostle's first great fundamental statement.

[303]

Our relationship to God, he says, is determined solely and exclusively by our attitude to the Lord Jesus Christ and to what He has done. The Jews are lost, they are outside, they are reprobate. Why? Because they stumbled at Him. The Gentiles are in. Why? Because they believed in Him.

Then the Apostle is particularly concerned here about this tragic stumbling of the Jews, so we must take this as our second principle: why the Lord Jesus Christ is a stumbling-stone to some. He was a stumbling-stone and a rock of offence to the Jews, and to many of the Greeks also. He has continued throughout the running centuries to be a stumbling-stone to many people. Indeed, He is still a stumbling-stone and a rock of offence to the vast majority of people in the world. Why?

The New Testament gives us many answers to that question. His very person has been a stumbling-stone. It was to the Jews. The very way in which He came was an offence to them – the character of His birth. They were waiting and looking for the Messiah but they did not expect the Messiah to be born in a stable, in abject poverty, in a lowly humble condition. They were offended at that; they stumbled at it from the very beginning. They had notions of grandeur and of glory. That was their whole picture of the coming Messiah. He was to be a great king, a great military and political personage, and He was going to come with great magnificence – the very antithesis of what actually happened. And they stumbled at that.

Then there was His lowliness as He went on. As we read the Gospels we find that His entire lack of training was a stumbling-stone and a rock of offence to the Pharisees and to all the religious leaders. 'How knoweth this man letters, having never learned?' 'Who is this fellow? Who is this man setting himself up as a teacher, what does he know?' They stumbled at that – His appearance, His whole upbringing and His manner of teaching. He did not belong to the élite – the Pharisees or the Sadducees. As far as the Greeks were concerned also, He was not a philosopher; He had not been to the schools and the porches and the academies; and this has still continued throughout the centuries to be one of the grounds why people stumble at Him and take offence at Him. The thing seems monstrous and ridiculous – that one who claims to be the Saviour of the world should have come in that manner. And, of course, men stumble at the virgin birth and its miraculous character – we cannot consider that now but it is all a part of the same thing.

Then the Jews stumbled, likewise, at His claims for Himself. He kept on saying that He had come from God. He claimed equality with God. He claimed to speak with authority. He said, 'Ye have heard it said . . . but I say unto you.' And this was something that infuriated the Pharisees. He was arrogating unto Himself, as they thought, this authoritative teaching. On what grounds? – and especially these statements which He made with regard to His relationship to God the Father.

And then another thing, of course, at which they stumbled most grievously, was what He did not do. He did not set Himself up as king in Jerusalem. He did not gather an army together. He did not announce war against the Roman conquerors, and lead His army to liberate the Jews and lift them up to the supreme position amongst all the nations. That is what they wanted and He did not do it. Even John the Baptist stumbled at that particular point. Once, when they had been impressed by His feeding of the five thousand they tried to take Him by force and to make Him a king. But He would not! That was a grievous source of stumbling. Why did He not 'declare Himself'? His own brethren, you remember, chided Him with it later on.

But, of course, the thing that finally offended them and caused them to stumble was His death upon the cross. There He is – arrested, apparently unable to defend Himself; condemned by the court. He does not seem to say a word, but lets them do what they like with Him. He who claimed to be the Messiah, who could heal the sick, make the lame walk, give sight to the blind, raise the dead, calm the raging of the sea . . . 'Thou who savest others,' they say to Him as He is on the cross, 'come down, save thyself. If Thou be the Christ of God, come down'. Ridiculous – this display of weakness; utter failure and shame. To them this was enough to prove how ridiculous His claims were – that He was the Son of God, that He was the Saviour! 'Hail, thou Son of God', they said, with their sarcasm and scorn and derision. They put a crown of thorns upon His head, and they mocked at Him and they jeered at Him. Oh, His death was a terrible source of stumbling and rock of offence!

But there was something even worse than that. It was the teaching that came through His death, the implication of His death. This was what infuriated them above everything else. The Apostle Paul says, 'The preaching of the cross is to them that perish foolishness.' The preaching of the cross is a stumbling-block to the Jews, and it is foolishness to the Greeks. Why? Ah, it is because of the implication and the message of that cross! And this is the thing that really got them on the raw and made them finally hate Him and dismiss Him.

What is the message? Oh, the message is this – that the cross is the only way of salvation! In other words, as Paul goes on to say in the next chapter, 'Christ is the end of the law for righteousness to every one that believeth.' Here are the Jews trying to save themselves by keeping and observing the law. The cross proclaims that there is only one who can keep the law. And He has done it! That is the thing that finally infuriated them, that He and He alone can satisfy God's law; and thus all the efforts and the striving of the Jews, the Pharisees, the Sadducees, the scribes, the very best of them, are all useless! Paul has already told us: 'Israel, which followed after the law of righteousness, hath not attained to the law of righteousness.' And here comes this proclamation – You never can! You never will! Christ has come into the world because they have failed. He would never have come if they could have done it. But they cannot, and no one can. 'The Son of man came not to be ministered unto, but to minister, and to give his life a ransom for many.'

That is what finally causes them to stumble. That is the rock of offence – that He is the atonement; that He is the Lamb of God that taketh away the sins of the world; that He is the offering to which all the types have pointed forward, the great, the glorious antitype itself! It was the teaching and the message of the cross that caused them to stumble above all. And it still does. That is why the blood of Christ is ridiculed in the Christian church today. People hate it and they are repeating what was done by the Jews.

In other words, the ultimate cause of the stumbling and of the rock of offence is that by all His teaching, and supremely by His death upon the cross, He exposes all man's self-confidence, pride and self-righteousness. The cross tells me that nothing

[306]

that I can ever do will ever put me right with God, and that all my belief in myself and in my good works, in my righteousness, in my good deeds, in my beautiful thoughts, is 'filthy rags', dung and refuse. That is the whole trouble with them, says Paul: 'They being ignorant of God's righteousness, and going about to establish their own righteousness, have not submitted themselves unto the righteousness of God' [*Romans* 10 : 3]. Man, and the Jew in particular, is out to establish his own righteousness, but Christ in all His person and in all His works says, It cannot be done. I have come because it cannot be done. 'There is none righteous, no, not one' — that is the mighty argumentation of the third chapter of this glorious Epistle to the Romans. And Paul is summing it all up here in a phrase.

Those are some of the reasons, then, why the Lord Jesus Christ is a stumbling-stone and a rock of offence to many. He hits them at their most sensitive point – pride: pride of intellect, pride of morality, pride of good works, pride of achievement, pride of understanding. It does not matter what your pride is; any pride at all or any confidence or reliance upon anything you are or anything you can do, or anything you can ever make yourself, is damned and condemned once and for ever by the death upon the cross. And every natural man hates it, he abominates it, he stumbles at it, it is an offence to him. He wants to glory in himself, and the cross proclaims, 'He that glorieth, let him glory in the Lord', and in Him alone.

Then in the third place therefore, notice the tragedy of such stumbling, of such rejecting of the Son of God and His great salvation! The Apostle began the chapter with: 'I say the truth in Christ, I lie not, my conscience also bearing me witness in the Holy Ghost, that I have great heaviness and continual sorrow in my heart, for I could wish that myself were accursed from Christ for my brethren, my kinsmen according to the flesh.' He will say it again in the next chapter: 'Brethren, my heart's desire and prayer to God for Israel is, that they might be saved.' But they are not. The tragedy of it all!

This is the greatest tragedy in the world, and it is seen at its height, of course, in the case of these very Jews. But it is not confined to them. It is true of all who reject the Lord Jesus Christ, or to whom He becomes a stone of stumbling and a rock of offence. But one can see it with particular clarity in the case of the Jewish nation. Listen to the Apostle as he puts it: 'Behold, I lay in Sion' – in Sion! – 'a stumblingstone and rock of offence.' Do you see what that means? When the Messiah came, when the Son of God came into the world, where did He come? Not among the nations, but to Palestine! Amongst the Jews! He came unto His own! In Sion – their own glorious city of which they were so proud!

This is the tragedy, that they of all people should have rejected Him and stumbled at Him – for they were the people who were looking forward to the coming of the Messiah. They were a religious people, a people who were seeking after righteousness, as we have already been reminded by Paul. They were the people who had 'the oracles of God' – the Scriptures. Not the nations, the 'dogs'. They were God's people, and they had these precious things. And they read them and they studied them and, on the basis of that, they were waiting and longing for the coming of the Messiah. And He came to them, to His own people, 'and his own received him not'. That is the tragedy! The people who had had all the advantages that he enumerates in verses 4 and 5 of this chapter – that they of everybody should have stumbled at Him and should have found in Him a rock of offence!

We cannot go into this in detail at this point – we shall return to it in our next study – but you know we are witnessing a repetition of this very thing at the present time. Where is it that so often He is most patently a stone of stumbling and a rock of offence? Is it out in the world? No, it is in His own church, it is amongst those who claim His name. Only recently a church leader rejoiced in the fact that 'this new approach is not coming from the outside, but actually from within the church'; he is glorying in the stumbling! It is but a re-enactment of what happened nearly two thousand years ago – 'I lay in Sion'. But it is the people of Sion – of all people – who stumble at Him; whereas those Gentiles that are right outside have believed in Him and have come into the kingdom. There is no greater tragedy than this – that He came unto his own, and His own received Him not.

But even further, let us see what else is involved in the tragedy. 'Behold, I lay in Sion . . .' Who is speaking? The almighty and everlasting God! If you do not believe in the Lord Jesus Christ utterly and absolutely as your Saviour, what you are really doing is pitting yourself against God and flinging His own actions back into His face! '*I lay in Sion!*' This is God's way of salvation, prepared before the foundation of the world, intimated prophetically, as we have seen, right the way through the Old Testament. It is the plain message, the central message of the whole of the Bible. This is what men are rejecting – what God has revealed so plainly and so clearly. It is a rejection of God's own plan and God's own provision.

Let me quote the Apostle again: 'They being ignorant of God's [way of] righteousness' – the thing that he has gloried in at the very beginning. 'I am not ashamed of the gospel of Christ', he said in chapter 1. Why? Because 'it is the power of God unto salvation to every one that believeth; to the Jew first, and also to the Greek. For therein is the righteousness of God revealed . . .' [*Romans* 1 : 16–17] – God's way of righteousness! Paul has been repeating it; we have seen it in chapter 3 verse 21: 'But now the righteousness of God without the law is manifested.' That is his great theme. But this is what these people are rejecting. The Jews who claimed that they alone believed in God, unlike these pagan Gentiles who were worshipping dumb idols and vanities, they, the believers in God, are rejecting God's own way of salvation!

But the tragedy is still worse. They are not only rejecting God's purpose and plan and God's way of salvation; they are rejecting God's most glorious act, the most wonderful thing that God has ever done. It is a terrible thing to reject anything that God has done, but when you reject the most wonderful thing of all, what can be said concerning it? Let me quote again, 'Therefore thus saith the Lord God, Behold, I lay in Sion for a foundation a stone, a tried stone, a precious corner stone, a sure foundation: he that believeth shall not make haste'.

What does he mean by this 'tried stone', this 'precious corner stone', this 'sure foundation'? Oh, that is just a pictorial way of saying this: 'God so loved the world, that he gave his only begotten Son' [*John* 3 : 16]. Precious! His only begotten beloved Son! 'When the fulness of the time was come, God sent forth his Son' [*Galatians* 4 : 4]. He could not send more! He sends His own Son in all the perfection and the glory of His everlasting deity – He is the one whom God sends. Not a great man, not a prophet. His own Son! Yes, and one who is not only capable of standing all the tests, but has stood them all. 'A tried stone'! 'Tempted in all points like as we are, yet without sin.' The devil attacks Him, and brings out all his reserves. He stands! The mighty conqueror! He gave a life of perfect obedience to the law of God. Tried and tested by the law. He was 'made of a woman, made under the law'. Yes, and He obeyed it with absolute perfection.

Not only that. In order to save us He was told that He would have to be made a sin-offering for us. He would have to take our sins and our guilt upon Him and bear their punishment, and that would involve separation from His Father. Here is the test! Here is the trial! Can He stand this test? There He is facing it in the garden of Gethsemane, sweating drops of blood, and He says – 'Father, if it be possible . . . Nevertheless not my will but Thine be done.' He stood the test! 'I will go,' He says, 'I will drink and I will drain the cup to the last dregs.' And He did! He went as a lamb to the slaughter. Not only that; He rendered a perfect active obedience to the law; He rendered an equally perfect passive obedience to the law and its every demand. And there He is on Calvary's cross in an agony with the vials of the wrath of God poured out upon Him.

'He that spared not' – we have already considered this in chapter 8 : 32[1] – 'He that spared not his own Son, but delivered him up for us all . . .' – spared Him nothing of the horror of the punishment of sin. He took it all! He bore it all! A tried stone! A tested stone! A precious corner stone! 'But He died', you say. I know. But it is not the end. He rose again! 'It is finished', He cried on the cross. And He proved it had finished by rising on the morning of the third day, by manifesting Himself, by ascending, and by taking His seat at the right hand of God. But to these Jews, all that was an offence. That was a stumbling-stone, a rock of offence. This most marvellous, glorious thing that Father, Son and Holy Ghost have ever done! The marvel of eternity, rejected, dismissed with ignominy, ignominy and scorn!

But the tragedy does not even end there, because in doing all this they are rejecting such a glorious salvation. What are they rejecting? Free grace! They are rejecting something which tells

[1]See *Romans: An Exposition of Chapters 8:17–29: The Final Perseverance of the Saints*, 1975.

them, Just as you are, 'without one plea', you can be forgiven if you will believe in Him. Justification by faith only! Nothing to do but to believe! 'Come ye . . . come, buy . . . without money and without price; come to the waters.' 'By grace are ye saved through faith; and that not of yourselves: it is the gift of God.' They are rejecting the free gift! The gift of what? The gift of perfect forgiveness, your sins all blotted out, entirely forgotten and cast into the sea of God's forgetfulness. Not only that; you are regarded as if you had fulfilled the law perfectly, the righteousness of Christ is imputed to you. You have completed the law, you have kept it, you have finished with it, you have become dead to it. 'No condemnation' any more, for ever 'to them which are in Christ Jesus'.

But all that is refused. New life, a new nature, strength and help to fight the battle while we are left in this world; a hope of glory, being made children of God, and 'if children, then heirs; heirs of God, and joint-heirs with Christ', and the certainty of being with Him in the everlasting glory. It is all refused, though it is all offered for nothing! And all because of the pride of man, all because he thinks he can fit himself for God and heaven and glory. All because he is too proud to admit that he is a pauper and that he is helpless and hopeless and has nothing. He rejects it all. That is the tragedy.

But the end of the tragedy is this: 'Whosoever believeth on him shall not be ashamed'; but whoever finds Him a stumbling-stone and a rock of offence, shall be ashamed. Whoever does not believe in the Son of God as the only Saviour and the only way of being reconciled to God, will never find satisfaction in this life, never! He will always be striving and seeking, never arriving. He will know of no sanctuary in his hour of trial and of crisis and of need. 'I lay in Sion . . . a tried corner stone, a sanctuary', said God through the prophet Isaiah; a place into which you can rush and be safe. A sanctuary! But the man who rejects Him has no sanctuary. When his health goes, when illness comes, when death visits the family, when he is tried and tested, he has nothing. Nothing to fall back on, nothing to lean on, nothing to sustain him.

And when he comes to the hour of his own death and has his first glimpse of the law of God and the glory of God and the glory of Christ and all the spirits of just men made perfect, he will see his own vileness and he will be horrified; as he tries to stand before God he will not be able to stand. He will not be able to stand in the congregation of the righteous; he is like the chaff that is swept and blown away. He will realize that he has 'not attained to the law of righteousness', that all he had boasted of and put his confidence in is nothing but vile refuse in the presence of God, and he will see it for himself. But it will be too late; at long last he will realize his folly, the folly of a pride that prefers to go on with a vain useless endeavour, and rejects the free offer of salvation; he will realize it, but it is too late. And he will go on to spend his eternity in a state of useless and endless remorse.

That is the tragedy of the Jew! That is why the Apostle said, 'I could wish that myself were accursed from Christ for my brethren, my kinsmen according to the flesh.' That is why his 'heart's desire and prayer to God . . . is, that they might be saved' – that they may be delivered out of all this. The tragedy! The stumbling – finding nothing but 'a rock of offence'! In God's plan! God's Son! God's free grace! All the blessing of salvation in this life and the endless blessing of the life of glory in eternity!

Let us be clear about this. The Lord Jesus Christ is one of these two things to every one of us. You either believe in Him and rest your faith in Him alone, or else He is to you a stumbling-stone and a rock of offence. May the terrible lesson of the Jewish nation awaken anybody who may have been doubtful. May God open your eyes and show you the folly, the tragedy, the enormity in regarding God's own Son and His perfect glorious work, as a stone of stumbling and a rock of offence. May God have mercy! But may He open all eyes – including those who believe in Him. We do not believe enough, my friends! We do not glory as we should in Him! We say it; we take it for granted, but do we realize what has happened? God has laid this stone, and it is His own Son. It involved smiting Him that we might be delivered, forgiven and restored, that we might become God's children, and 'joint-heirs with Christ', and eventually enter into possession of the glory!

Oh, let us humbly beseech God to look down upon us all with mercy and compassion. We feel that our hearts are so cold. Let us ask Him by the Spirit to open the eyes of our understanding that we may see these things with such a clarity that we shall be moved in the very depth and vitals of our being, and be filled with a sense of wonder, love and praise. May God grant that henceforth when we sing the hymn of Isaac Watts we shall really mean it.

> *When I survey the wondrous cross,*
> *On which the Prince of glory died,*
> *My richest gain I count but loss,*
> *And pour contempt on all my pride.*
>
> *Were the whole realm of nature mine,*
> *That were an offering far too small;*
> *Love so amazing, so divine,*
> *Demands my soul, my life, my all.*

And may our prayer be, 'Take them, O Lord God. Thou hast already purchased them. We give them back to Thee.'

Twenty-five

*

We do not have any particular verse in Romans 9 as a text for this study because I am anxious to draw certain general lessons and deductions from the entire chapter. It is by any reckoning a vital and crucial chapter, not only in the argument of the whole Epistle to the Romans, but also from the standpoint of Christian doctrine and an understanding of the Christian truth. And I think that as we have been working our way through it we have all come to see that and perhaps to recognize it – at least I trust we have – in a deeper manner than we have ever done before.

Now while the Apostle, of course, was primarily dealing with the situation as it obtained in the Christian church actually in his own day and generation, with the tragic position of the Jews as a nation, he is at the same time laying down principles which are of universal application and which have, from time to time in the long history of the Christian church, emerged with particular clarity. And it is because of this that I am calling your attention to some of these general lessons which, it seems to me, stand out on the very surface of this teaching. And as I do so, I want to emphasize that our study of the Scriptures must always have this practical intent and object.

There is nothing which is so fatal – that is why I keep on repeating this – as to come to the Scriptures with a purely theoretical or intellectual or academic interest. That is one of the greatest dangers of all, a very real snare. It is a danger into which many have fallen. They approach the Bible in this purely detached intellectual manner, as if it were just a subject like any other subject, and they have never realized its practical relevance to themselves. So it is in order to show that this Scripture that we have been looking at is so full of practical lessons for us that we shall spend the whole of this study in drawing them out.

Now the first great lesson which I find here is the value of the Old Testament. We must start with that because it is so obvious in the whole of the chapter that, to Paul, the Old Testament is absolutely essential to his position and to his whole argument. And this is something which is equally true now as it was then. You may say, 'Ah, but there, of course, he was dealing with the Jewish problem and only with Jews; therefore he of necessity uses the Old Testament. But we are now Christians and because we are Christians and members of the Christian church, what has the Old Testament got to give to us?' Now there are many people, it seems to me, who think that as they now are in this new position, the Old Testament is quite useless and irrelevant to them and has nothing to give them.

Well, even if we had nothing but this ninth chapter of Romans, it surely ought to be enough to correct any such tendency in us. The Apostle uses the Old Testament constantly, and he does so not only here, but in all his other Epistles also. Indeed there is nothing that is so characteristic of the whole of the New Testament as the way in which it draws on, and quotes the Old Testament Scriptures in order to elucidate or to explain some point, or in order to establish some particular argument; and therefore I would draw these particular lessons with regard to the value of the Old Testament.

First, one sees the wisdom that was given to the early church in this respect. Remember it was mainly a Gentile church and it received some of its most bitter persecution from the Jews. What would have been more natural and instinctive than for them to reject the Old Testament, to say that they had nothing at all to do with the Jews, and that this was something entirely new? But they did not do that; they were led of the Holy Spirit. And they were led, therefore, when they developed their new literature, to incorporate it with the old literature and to form the book which we now call the Bible. There we see the wisdom of God given to the early church, a wisdom that has safeguarded the church throughout the centuries from many grievous errors and dangers.

The second point about the value of the Old Testament – and we must have noticed this as we have been working through this chapter – is what a great buttress it is to our faith. The Apostle, later on in this Epistle, talks about the 'patience and comfort of the scriptures', and how true that is! For instance, when you confront the problem which is dealt with in this chapter, that the Jews are outside the church while the Gentiles are in, it is a very great problem, and we have one like it. People whom you would expect to find as Christians very often are not, and vice versa. And it is very difficult to understand these things. But the answer is so often to be found in the Old Testament, and that is why we must never cease to thank God that He has given us the comfort and the consolation of the Old Testament Scriptures as well as the New. What a comfort it must have been to the Apostle as he was working out his argument that he could say, 'As Hosea said', or 'As Isaiah said', or some other quotation which he uses from the Old Testament.

Then a third lesson is that God's purpose is one. His purpose in the Old Testament and in the New is always the same. It is very wrong to make too great a difference between the New and Old Testaments. Many people do that; they say, 'We are not under law now, we are under grace.' All right, the Apostle has said that, but he does not mean that in the wrong way. He does not mean it in the sense that you can dismiss the Old. The purpose of God starts in the Old Testament and it works on and on and on till you come to the New, and it goes on. And it is still going on but it is the original purpose that was announced in Genesis 3 : 15. Surely this chapter has been putting that before us all along. We have been taken back to Abraham, to the very beginning of the Jewish nation, and Paul has led us right the way through to the prophets. Thus we see that the purpose of God is one, and it is still the same purpose.

Then, fourthly, we have seen that not only is God's purpose the same always, but God's method also is always the same. The method that He employed, for instance, with Isaac and Ishmael, is exactly the same method as He employed with Jacob and Esau. It is the same right through the times of the prophets; and it is the same now, says the Apostle – it is always the same method. In other words, as God's plan and purpose are one, so is His method. A principle of grace is as obvious in the Old

Testament as it is in the New. Now many people have never seen that. They think that in the Old Testament you have nothing but law. But that is quite wrong! The Apostle has been showing us the operation of grace; not only of grace but of election in the Old as well as in the New – and it is still continuing. This is a very wonderful thing to me. It means that we are in the centre of God's purpose and that He is working out that purpose even today as He has always done in past ages.

And the last lesson that I draw is that when you are confronted by some problem in the realm of belief or of doctrine, the thing to do always is to face it in the light of the teaching of the Scriptures. That is what the Apostle does. He reasons and he argues, but he has always got the Scriptures as his background: here is his final proof. So we have found him quoting the Scriptures in such a free and a liberal manner in order to establish his case; and that is to be our method. We must never face these problems in a kind of abstract manner as so many people are doing today. We must avoid that, and we must face them in the light of the teaching of the Scriptures.

Furthermore, it is astounding to notice the number of problems that can be solved merely with the Old Testament. Of course, it is really not surprising because, as I say, God's method is one, and therefore you will see, perhaps, in some historical illustration in the Old Testament, the dealing of God with some person or with the whole nation. You will find there teaching which is applicable to you personally and individually today, or with regard to some problem that is perplexing your mind. You see, here the Apostle really answers this great question of 'the purpose of God according to election' and he deals with it by means of a series of Old Testament quotations. He says, 'Do you not see that that is what God has always been doing? Do not be surprised, therefore, at what He is doing now.' And that argument is as valid today as it was when the Apostle used it nineteen hundred years ago.

So there are some general lessons that one can learn with regard to the use and the value of the Old Testament. Let us never forget it. This is the way to deal with a problem. Think! Think Scripture! Bring to bear upon your problem that which

God has so clearly taught and revealed in the Scriptures. We have the New Testament now as well as the Old, but that does not mean that we discard the Old.

But let me come to a second group of lessons, the personal lessons, which it seems to me we must learn from the argument of this chapter. When I say personal lessons we must, surely, all of us have seen more clearly than ever before, if we have been following this argument, that there are certain things which we must never rely upon in connection with our relationship to God. Now we might think that these things need no longer be said; we think we know them; but we do not! I think one of the greatest dangers in the Christian life is always to be falling back upon works in some shape or form. Like the Galatians we tend to start in the Spirit but we end in the flesh. We start by faith, we end with works. It is always trying to insinuate itself. If there is one chapter in the Bible more than another that ought to warn us against that danger it is this ninth chapter of the Epistle to the Romans.

What things does it exclude? Here are some of them. It puts out natural birth. Are we all clear about that? The fact that our parents, grandparents or forebears were great Christians does not mean that we are Christians. That was the whole tragedy of the Jews, as we have seen. Put next to birth, family, nation – none of these things matter at all. But oh, how much they have mattered throughout the centuries; how much they still matter! There are still people who think of this country as a Christian country. What utter nonsense! There is no such thing. There never has been a Christian country, and there cannot be in the light of this teaching. Whether your government calls itself Christian or not does not make the slightest difference to this spiritual teaching. No, these things must never be relied upon. This chapter shouts that out at us more clearly, perhaps, than anything else.

But we must add to that. Never rely upon your religion. The fact that you are a religious person does not of necessity mean that you are a Christian. The Jews were highly religious. You can be religious without being Christian; the things are not synonymous. You can believe in God and still not be a Christian. That is the great lesson here. 'They stumbled at that stumblingstone.' What was it? Not belief in God, but belief in the Lord Jesus Christ. That was the stumbling-stone! And it still is. We must not rely upon religion, we must not rely upon a belief in God, we must not rely upon our good works. Though they are good works they are valueless in the sight of God. One thing alone puts us right with God; not our works. We have had that put before us so clearly: 'For the children being not yet born, neither having done any good or evil . . .' That puts out our works once and for ever. They must never come in. They must never be allowed to put in any sort of appearance in our relationship to God. That is not what determines salvation.

And lastly, we should have seen very clearly that we must not rely even upon our belief; even our belief in the Lord Jesus Christ. It is not my belief that saves me; it is not my faith that saves me. If I say that, I am turning my belief and my faith into works. I am taking credit to myself, and I must not do that. This is the chapter of all chapters in the Bible that takes from man any sort of credit whatsoever: 'For the children being not yet born, neither having done any good or evil, that the purpose of God according to election might stand, not of works, but of him that calleth.' The Apostle took thirty-three verses to bring out that point. It is essential. God grant that we all have learnt that lesson. We are what we are by the grace of God, and by that alone. And as that is true of us now, so it will be true of us on our deathbeds. We will have nothing that we can rely upon save the purpose of God, and that we are included in it by His grace.

The first personal lesson, then, was to show us what is excluded and the second is the obverse of that: our relationship to Jesus Christ and Him crucified is the one and only thing that matters. We are justified in Christ, and in Him alone. It is what He is and what He has done for us that saves us and nothing in ourselves. It is altogether and entirely in this one blessed Person. Here He is: He is either a stumbling-stone and rock of offence, or else He is to us the all and in all – everything! That is the great purpose of this chapter, and that is the tragedy of the Jews. They were right in so many other respects, but they went wrong on the one thing that matters. Nothing matters but this. The one and only question is, What think ye of Christ?

So our third point on this personal lesson – and surely this must have come home to us in almost a terrifying manner – is the need of constant self-examination. Why? It is because of the danger of presuming or of assuming that all is well with us. The

Jews had never suspected that there was anything wrong with them. They knew that they were 'Israelites; to whom pertaineth the adoption, and the glory, and the covenants, and the giving of the law, and the service of God, and the promises; Whose are the fathers . . .' and they had gone on presuming that all was well. Here again is a most terrifying lesson which comes out, perhaps, more clearly in this chapter again than anywhere else in the whole of the Scriptures. Here is the tragedy of the Jew once and for ever; the tragedy of taking it for granted that all is well with us when all is not well.

Of course, our Lord deals with the same thing. That is the point of the great parable of the Pharisee and the publican who went up to the temple together to pray. It is exactly the same point. 'I thank Thee,' says this poor Pharisee, 'I thank Thee, O God, that I am not as other men are.' Perfectly happy, and yet all wrong! That is the great lesson of the Jewish nation. Let us examine ourselves, let us 'prove our own selves', as the Apostle says to the Corinthians, let us make certain that we are 'in the faith' [2 *Corinthians* 13 : 5], or, as Peter says, let us 'make our calling and election sure' [2 *Peter* 1 : 10]. The New Testament is full of these warnings and here, in this tremendous picture of the case of the Jewish nation, we are driven to see the importance of constant self-examination.

And the last personal lesson that I would draw – and it is here on the very surface – is the danger of reading the Scriptures with a prejudiced mind. Now here, again, is something that is so obvious in the case of the Jews. Theirs were the Scriptures. The Apostle has reminded us of that way back in chapter 3: '. . . because that unto them were committed the oracles of God'. The Scriptures! They said, 'Those other people, those Gentiles are dogs; they have no revelation, they have no Scriptures, God has not spoken to them; they never had any prophets or patriarchs; but we have got the Scriptures!' And they delighted in it. Our Lord said to them, 'Search the scriptures' – or 'You do search the scriptures' – 'because you think that in them you have eternal life.' That was their proud boast, and they read their Scriptures, and were experts in them. And yet they are lost, they are outside the kingdom, they are reprobates. Why? Well, as we have seen so clearly as the Apostle quotes from the Scriptures, they were blinded by prejudice.

Now this is the most alarming thing that we can ever realize about ourselves. Every one of us is subject to prejudice. There is not one of us that is free from it; the devil sees to that. And the prejudices are almost endless in number. So that when we come to the Scriptures we come with a prejudiced eye and we see what we want to see. That is what the heretics have always done, is it not? They have always quoted Scripture. Some of the modern heretics quote a little Scripture, not much, but even they do try to quote a little. And, if you take the Scriptures with this prejudiced mind and understanding you can make them prove almost anything you like. So the Jews were perfectly happy about themselves, because it seemed to them that the Scriptures everywhere were saying that they alone were saved and that everybody else was lost; whereas the truth was that they were lost and others were saved.

We must always beware of prejudice. We must never read the Scriptures without praying. We should never approach them without asking the Holy Spirit to lead us and to guide us and to direct us. We should deliberately humble ourselves, we should talk to ourselves and say, Now why am I going to the Scriptures? Am I going there only to find arguments to support my case, or am I going there to be instructed, to be enlightened, to have my eyes opened to the truth of God? We should always try to come as little children and be ready to find that we are wrong. There is no disgrace in changing our minds or in saying, 'I was wrong.' Why, it is a most wonderful thing to say. There is a kind of consistency that is most reprehensible, it is small-minded. We should be big enough to confess that we were wrong. We should not come merely to substantiate what we have always said and thought. There is nothing more wonderful than for a man to say, 'Whereas I was once blind, now I see'!

I do trust that some of us have passed through that experience as we have been working through the ninth chapter of Romans. If you take up the position of saying 'I will never believe that!' then I doubt whether you are a Christian at all. You must never say that with respect to the truth of God. We must never say that with regard to any aspect of it. We must be ready to listen, ready to examine, to have an open mind, a mind that is ready for the illumination of the Spirit. Here, you see, are these people; they are a perpetual warning to us; with the Scriptures open before them and their delight in it, they are all wrong. Why? Prejudice! What a terrible thing it is. God deliver us all from it.

There, then, are some of what I have called the personal lessons which we find in this chapter. But now I want to go a step further to a third group of lessons with a wider scope. There are certain general lessons here, it seems to me, which are very relevant from the standpoint of the church as a whole, and especially for the Christian church as she is in her present position. Here, for instance, is one lesson. This chapter is a perpetual warning to us against regarding all people, who are members of the Christian church in a visible sense, as being Christians. Let me say that again. The essential error of these Jews was that they thought that the mere fact that they were Jews meant that of necessity they were God's children and that they were right with God. Their argument was, 'We have been born Jews, we belong to the Jewish nation, therefore of necessity we are the people of God and we are the heirs of the promises.' The whole point of the chapter is to say that that is not so; it is stated, explicitly, as we have seen, in verse 6: 'They are not all Israel, which are of Israel.' You can belong to the visible Israel and yet not really be a member of the true Israel.

Now that is one of those points that are so true today. It seems to me that the main argument for the so-called ecumenical movement is just this – that all people who call themselves Christians and who are members of the Christian church are therefore Christians and that we must regard them all as such. But that argument would appear to me to be contravening the main argument of Romans 9. Alas, it is possible to belong to the Christian church and still not be a Christian. You can have your name on a church roll, you can be regarded as a Christian and yet not be one. It is the whole argument of the entire chapter. As it was possible for Israel to make that mistake, it is possible for us also to make it. What corresponds to the visible Israel is the visible church, and what the Apostle is saying is, All who belong to the visible Israel are not 'of' Israel; so all who belong to the visible church are not all of the true church.

The Jews, of course, thought they belonged to the true Israel because they were circumcised. How many, I wonder, think today that they are Christians because they have been baptized? There are many who think they are Christians because they were baptized when they were children. There are others who think they are Christians because they were baptized when they were adults. But baptism never makes anybody a Christian, whether an infant or an adult. The Jews thought that circumcision did it, many think now that baptism does it, but both are wrong. You can have passed through the rite, or the rite may have been performed upon you, but that is not what changes your condition. So we must be wary about this argument that says, 'Look here, why don't you join us? You are criticizing your fellow Christians.' 'But', you say, 'are you sure they are Christians?' 'Now there you are,' they say, 'you think that you alone are a Christian. Surely they are Christians; they are members of the Christian church, so they must be.' But that is a denial of the argument of the Apostle in Romans 9.

Then the second lesson I find here is the difference between true and false continuity. The error of the Jews was really based on the fact that they had come down in a lineal descent from Abraham. Their great argument always was, 'Abraham is our father'. They brought it against our Lord when He said to them on one occasion, 'If ye continue in my word, then are ye my disciples indeed; and ye shall know the truth, and the truth shall make you free.' They turned to Him and said, 'We be Abraham's seed, and were never in bondage to any man: how sayest thou, Ye shall be made free?' [*John* 8 : 31–33]. Lineal descent! Physical continuity! They thought that that was what guaranteed their salvation and proved that they, and they alone, were the children of God. Now that is what I call 'false continuity'. It is the continuity of Ishmael, Esau and company. There is a continuity there, of course there is, a direct continuity from Abraham, Ishmael, Esau and so on, right the way through. It is a continuity, but according to this argument it is a false one. The real continuity, says Paul, is Abraham, Isaac, Jacob, David and so on.

'But what has that got to do with us?' asks somebody. Well, there is in the Christian church also a false and a true continuity; and it is because people do not realize this that they go astray in their doctrine. There are people who take up the position of saying that nothing else matters and that this is the final question of authority – apostolic succession, that great argument of the Roman Catholic Church, and of the Anglo-Catholics. 'You Nonconformists', they say, 'do not have a ministry at all; you have not been ordained by a bishop who comes down in direct lineal descent from the Apostle Peter who was the first. But we do. Here is a direct line, here is the continuity.'

But that, too, is dealt with in Romans 9 – had you realized that? It is most germane to the present position. To start with, we would question and query that continuity. But we need not waste our time with that. Even if we were to grant them the apostolic succession and continuity – which we do not; but even if we did – it would prove nothing at all, because the argument of Romans 9 is, that it may very well be the false continuity. The true continuity is what matters. The true apostolic succession is not that which comes down with a mechanical laying on of hands from one to the next, even as Ishmael and Esau came from Abraham and Isaac in that false way. No, the real continuity is the spiritual continuity. The man who is in the direct line from the apostles is the man who preaches the doctrine of the apostles, the man who has the spirit of the apostles in him.

This is the argument, you notice, that is used so often in the New Testament. In Ephesians 2 : 11, where Paul tells us about the attitude of the Jews towards the Gentiles, he says, 'Wherefore remember, that ye being in time past Gentiles in the flesh, who are called Uncircumcision by that which is called the Circumcision in the flesh made by hands.' That is the false continuity. The circumcision made by hands – that is the false, the external. The true is the circumcision of the heart. Indeed Paul has already referred to it in Romans 2 : 29 where he puts it like this: 'He is a Jew, which is one inwardly; and circumcision is that of the heart, in the spirit, and not in the letter; whose praise is not of men, but of God.'

So we apply all that to the present position like this. What matters in the realm of the church is not the visible; it is the invisible. Paul, let me remind you, has argued, 'They are not all Israel, which are of Israel: neither, because they are the seed of Abraham, are they all children: but, In Isaac shall thy seed be called. That is, They which are the children of the flesh, these are not the children of God: but the children of the promise are counted for the seed.' You see the distinction? The false, and the true. There is only one really continuous church, and that is this invisible spiritual continuity of those who are 'born again', of those who are 'led of the Spirit'. Nothing else is of any value.

The other, I know, is a kind of continuity; you can start back with the Apostles and you can come down through church history and you see a continuation in an institution. But it is of no value. It may even be of the devil. It may be the continuity that damned the nation of Israel and blinded them to the spiritual truth, as it is blinding Roman Catholicism even today. Nothing matters here but the spiritual. The true seed, the real continuity, is not a mechanical, external, physical one of laying on of hands or of anything else; it is the continuity of the work of the Spirit.

Let us go on to a third lesson which we draw in this way. We must never be surprised if the church is to be found in a state of apostasy. I find this most comforting; indeed, that is why I find this whole chapter a most comforting chapter. If the nation of Israel could be apostate, then it is possible for anybody to be apostate. The fact that the church is the church does not prove that she is always right. The visible people of God can go all wrong. It has happened many times, and I believe it is happening today. So we must not assume that because people say, 'We belong to the church', they are all right. Neither must the church assume that, because she is the church, she is all right. The church must always put herself under the judgment of the word of God.

You see, the nation of Israel was the church under the old dispensation. The nation and the church were one. So what is true of the nation in the old, is true of the church in the new. The nation became apostate, the church can become apostate. I believe that that happened before the Reformation. I fear it is happening again, even in the Reformed church, but we must not be surprised at that. Here is teaching that prepares us for it. So, far from saying that the church can never go wrong as a whole, we must be ready to believe that she can.

Then as we come to the next lesson, number four, here is real comfort and consolation. If this chapter has not taught us anything else, it should have taught us that we need never have any fear about the future of the Christian church; we need never be alarmed about the future of the people of God. Why not? We have the answer here: 'Esaias also crieth concerning

Israel, Though the number of the children of Israel be as the sand of the sea, a remnant shall be saved.' Only a remnant! He repeats it: 'As Esaias said before, Except the Lord of Sabaoth had left us a seed, we had been as Sodoma, and been made like unto Gomorrah.' It looked as if the whole nation had gone – Sodom and Gomorrah! The end! Final destruction!

No! God preserved a seed. So we need never have any fear about the future of the Christian church. Let the enemy do anything he likes; talk as much as you like about Communism and all the other enemies of the Christian faith . . . Do not be frightened, do not be worried about what will happen to the church; this kind of thing has happened so often before. It is God who preserves, and He will always preserve a seed. We need have no fear, and His purpose will certainly and surely be brought to pass. There have been so many times when the end seemed to have come – Sodom and Gomorrah! But God has kept it going, and He will keep it going until His purpose is finally complete.

The fifth deduction is the question of the significance of numbers in connection with the church and her function. And the answer is that numbers do not matter at all. God preserves a remnant, He preserves a seed. Only a handful perhaps, it does not matter; we need not be concerned about that. We must not be ashamed of being a remnant, weak and small; this is God's way. In a sense it can even become a privilege. We must cease to think in terms of numbers, we must think in terms of the purpose of God and the purity of the witness and the testimony. God will preserve this seed. He will carry it on in spite of everything, thank God, if we belong to the faithful remnant.

The next lesson, number six, is that we must always beware of the danger of becoming a 'closed corporation'. Israel had done that. She had no interest in the Gentiles. She was concerned about herself, proud of her own position, always looking at herself, with no interest in those who were outside. They were 'dogs', barbarians, not worthy of consideration. Many a time has the church fallen into that particular error, and I detect signs of that in certain friends at the present time. You are to be concerned about the purity of the church, but that does not mean that you erect barriers and shut out the outsider and almost make him feel that he has no right to come inside. That is the very negation of a Christian church. Israel had turned in upon herself, and had become self-centred, proud and prejudiced. God save us from such a terrible fate! A church which is not actively propagating the truth, witnessing to it and concerned about the lost, is unworthy of the name of the church of Jesus Christ. All that comes before us here.

But then let me come to lesson number seven – and oh, what comfort there is here again. Indeed there is not only comfort here; there is something to me very glorious in this next point. It is this: if we have learnt the lesson of Romans 9 we must have learnt to expect revival to come in the most unexpected places and from the most unexpected persons. Do you remember: 'What shall we say then? That the Gentiles, which followed not after righteousness, have attained to righteousness, even the righteousness which is of faith. But Israel, which followed after the law of righteousness, hath not attained to the law of righteousness.' That is the biggest surprise of the ages, but it is so characteristic of the sovereignty of God.

So we must never be surprised at anything that happens in this realm. God constantly springs surprises upon us. I do not think there has ever been a revival in the history of the church but that God has more or less repeated this very thing. Where do revivals generally start? Well, they generally start in some unknown little village or hamlet that you have never heard of. Whom does God use? Not some man that was prominent or regarded by the church as great but somebody quite unknown and unexpected. A young man like George Whitefield, brought up in the Bell Tavern in Gloucester – who would ever have thought of it? And it is so true in all ages and generations. This is how God does His work, always full of surprises and astonishment and amazement. So let us be ready for this.

And so I come to my very last point, which is a very solemn one. You and I would not be studying this chapter in this way unless we held to the true faith, unless we were orthodox, unless we were concerned about doctrine, and about true doctrine. That is as it should be. That is right. That is excellent. But on one condition – that we do not presume upon it. The moment we do, the moment we begin to feel self-satisfied, the moment the spirit of the Pharisee begins to come in and we say, 'We are the people, thank God we are not like those others', then we are putting ourselves into this terribly dangerous position, that when God comes to revive His work He may well bypass us and use one of these despised people that neither we nor anybody else ever thought of as being in the centre of God's will and purpose.

Here is the terrifying lesson: It is the Gentiles who are in, in the centre of the church, and through whom God is spreading the good news, and the Jews are outside, bypassed! God forbid that any of this spirit of prejudice that was in the Jew should ever possess us and lead us to this pathetic position where we see God again having to take hold of the things that are not, to bring to nought the things that are, 'that no flesh should glory in his presence'. We must be orthodox, but we must not be proud of it, we must not rely upon it – even that. Let us realize this great lesson, the sovereignty of God, His great and glorious purpose; that it is He who calls, and He calls whom He wills: He raises and He puts down.

The only conclusion, therefore, to draw as the result of all this is that we should walk with reverence and with godly fear, that we should walk humbly with our God. His purposes are sure, and our longing and our heart's desire should be that we be such people that God can use us, that He will never in any shape or form have to lay us aside, as it were, or bypass us, in order to do what He wants to do. God forbid that in our desire to safeguard against certain errors and excesses we should become guilty of quenching the Spirit. We can be so assured of ourselves, and so much in control of the position, that we are not giving the Spirit of God an opportunity.

Let us, then, learn these great lessons from this ninth chapter of Paul's Epistle to the Romans. They are there shouting at us on the very surface; they are up to date, you see, with regard to the church in general, to our particular position, and to the whole of our life and conduct. But, above all, let us humble ourselves under the mighty hand of God and He will exalt us. He who exalts himself the Lord abases, but he who abases himself shall be exalted. Let us therefore ascribe unto God always, all the praise and all the honour and all the glory, and let us rejoice in this one thing, 'the purpose of God according to election,' and its ultimate, absolute certainty.